Library of
Davidson College

Australian National University
Monographs on South Asia

No. 1
The Congress in Tamilnad
Nationalist politics in South India
1919–1937

David Arnold
ISBN 0 908070 00 1

No. 2
Political change in an
Indian State
Mysore 1917–1955

James Manor
ISBN 0 908070 01 2

No. 3
Businessmen and Politics
Rising nationalism and a
modernising economy in
Bombay, 1918–1933

A. D. D. Gordon
ISBN 0 908070 02 0

No. 4
From Sangha to Laity
Nationalist movements of Burma,
1920–1940

U Maung Maung
ISBN 0 908070 03 9

No. 5
Ethnic in conflict
A comparative study of four South
Indian textile centres, 1918–1939

Eamon Murphy
ISBN 0 908070 05 5

No. 6
Workers and Unions in
Bombay, 1918–1929
A study of organisation in the
cotton mills

Richard Newman
ISBN 0 908070 04 7

No. 7
Sri Lankan Fishermen
Rural capitalism and peasant
society

Paul Alexander
ISBN 0 908070 06 T

No. 8
Women in India and Nepal
Michael Allen & S. N. Mukherjee
(eds.)

ISBN 0 908070 07 1

No. 9
Peasant Movements in
Colonial India
North Bihar, 1917–1942

Stephen Henningham
ISBN 0 908070 08 X

No. 10
The Making of a Colonial
Mind
A quantitative study of the
Bhadralok in Calcutta, 1857–1885

John McGuire
ISBN 0 908070 09 8

Australian National University Monographs on South Asia

No 1
The Congress in Tamilnad
Nationalist politics in South India
1919-1937

David Arnold
ISBN 0 908070 00 4

No 2
Political change in an Indian State
Mysore 1917-1955

James Manor
ISBN 0 908070 01 2

No 3
Businessmen and Politics
Rising nationalism and a modernising economy in Bombay, 1918-1933

A D D Gordon
ISBN 0 908070 02 0

No 4
From Sangha to Laity
Nationalist movements of Burma, 1920-1940

U Maung Maung
ISBN 0 908070 03 9

No 5
Unions in conflict
A comparative study of four South Indian textile centres, 1918-1939

Eamon Murphy
ISBN 0 908070 05 5

No 6
Workers and Unions in Bombay, 1918-1929
A study of organisation in the cotton mills

Richard Newman
ISBN 0 908070 04 7

No 7
Sri Lankan Fishermen
Rural capitalism and peasant society

Paul Alexander
ISBN 0 908070 06 3

No 8
Women in India and Nepal
Michael Allen & S N Mukherjee (eds.)

ISBN 0 908070 07 1

No 9
Peasant Movements in Colonial India
North Bihar 1917-1942

Stephen Henningham
ISBN 0 908070 08 X

No 10
The Making of a Colonial Mind
A quantitative study of the bhadralok in Calcutta, 1857-1885

John McGuire
ISBN 0 908070 09 8

Peasant Movements in Colonial India

North Bihar 1917-1942

Australian National University
Monographs on South Asia No. 9

General Editors
Professor D.A. Low, Vice-Chancellor of the
Australian National University, Canberra

Professor Peter Reeves, Department of Modern History,
University of Western Australia

Dr Robin Jeffrey, Department of Politics,
La Trobe University, Victoria

Dr J.T.F. Jordens, Faculty of Asian Studies,
Australian National University, Canberra

Administrative Editor
Mrs Margaret Carron, South Asian History Section,
Australian National University, Canberra

Australian National University
Monographs on South Asia No. 9

Peasant Movements in Colonial India

North Bihar 1917-1942

Stephen Henningham

ANU

First Published 1982
Printed in Canberra by ANU Printing for the South Asian History
Section of The Australian National University

© Stephen Henningham

This book is copyright. Apart from any fair dealing for the purpose of
private study, research, criticism, or review, as permitted under the
Copyright Act, no part may be reproduced by any process without
written permission. Inquiries should be made to the publisher.

322.4
H517p

Henningham, Stephen, 1950-.
Peasant Movements in Colonial India: North Bihar 1917-1942.

Bibliography
Includes index
ISBN 0 908070 08 X

1. Peasant uprisings — India — Bihar. 2. Labor and laboring classes
— India — Bihar — Political activity. 3. Bihar (India) — History —
20th century. I. Australian National University. South Asian History
Section. II. Title. (Series: Australian National University monographs
on South Asia; no. 9). 82-9761

322.4'2'095412

To the Memory of

MERLE FLORENCE GREER, 1914-1979

ABBREVIATIONS

AAR	Annual Administrative Report
AICCP	All-India Congress Committee Papers
BSA	Bihar State Archives
C	Collection
f	file
F	Fasli
FMP	Freedom Movement Papers
FR	Fortnightly Report
FR(1)	Fortnightly Report for first half of month
FR(2)	Fortnightly Report for second half of month
G	General Department, Raj Darbhanga Archives
GGB	Government of Great Britain
GB	Government of Bihar
GBEN	Government of Bengal
GBO	Government of Bihar and Orissa
GOI	Government of India
HP	Home Political Department [of the Government of India]
IOL	India Office Library
JPNP	Jay Prakash Narayan Papers
KW	Keep With (a file)
L	Law Department, Raj Darbhanga Archives
LR	Land Revenue Proceedings
NAI	National Archives of India
NML	Nehru Memorial Library
PP	Rajendra Prasad Papers
PS	Political Special Department [of the Government of Bihar (and Orissa)]
RDA	Raj Darbhanga Archives
WBA	West Bengal Archives

CONTENTS

	Page
Abbreviations	viii
Acknowledgements	x
List of Diagrams and Tables	xii
Maps: 1. North Bihar: districts and subdivisions	xiv
2. North Bihar: towns and villages	xv
INTRODUCTION	1
1 EARLY TWENTIETH CENTURY NORTH BIHAR	3
2 ANTI-PLANTER PROTEST, 1917–1923	36
3 SWAMI VIDYANAND'S MOVEMENT, 1919–1920	70
4 THE NON-COOPERATION MOVEMENT, 1920–1923	90
5 THE CIVIL DISOBEDIENCE MOVEMENT, 1930–1934	109
6 THE *KISAN SABHA* MOVEMENT, 1936–1939	139
7 THE QUIT INDIA REVOLT, 1942	170
8 CONCLUSION	196
Appendix: The Darbhanga Raj archives	201
Notes	208
Bibliography	259
Glossary	273
Index	276

ACKNOWLEDGEMENTS

This book is a revised version of a doctoral thesis presented to the Australian National University in 1978. I accept full responsibility for its contents but admit readily that it could not have been written without the financial assistance of the Australian National University and the advice and help of many people. My thanks to my doctoral supervisor, D.A. Low, who improved my drafts by kindly, constructive criticism. I also owe much to Ravinder Kumar, who originally sparked my interest in Indian history and who suggested that I undertake research in the Darbhanga Raj archives. He has been a continuing source of stimulus and assistance. I am much indebted also to Chetkar Jha, who acted as my research guide in Bihar, arranged my initial access to the Darbhanga Raj archives, and, with his brother Buddhikar Jha, gave much practical assistance and supplied me with information and insights into the history and society of Bihar.

I also am glad to record my intellectual and practical debts to M.V. Harcourt; to Walter Hauser; and to G. McDonald, who originally suggested the possibility and value of examining popular turbulence in 20th century Bihar. I owe particular debts to Roger Stuart, who did much to shape my analysis and clarify my argument and to Margaret Carron and Robin Jeffrey, who assisted greatly at every stage of the preparation of the book. My thanks also go to Pam Millwood, who prepared the maps.

There are a number of others whom I can only mention: my appreciation is not less for being expressed briefly. My thanks to: Paul R. Brass; Meredith Borthwick; Dipesh Chakrabarty; R.L. Chandapuri; the Director and staff of the India Office Library; Hetukar Jha; V.C. Joshi and the staff of the Nehru Memorial Library; Brij V. Lal; Jageshwar Mishra and M.A. Raziq and the staff of the Darbhanga Raj archives; M. Mishra and his colleagues at the Darbhanga University; Ramnandan Misra; the Director and staff of the National Archives of India; P.D. Reeves; Sachchidananda and the fellows and staff of the A.N.

Sinha Institute; R.S.P. Singh and the staff of the S.L. Sinha Library; Taran Sharan Sinha and the staff of the Bihar State Archives; Brian J. Stoddart, and Anand A. Yang. My thanks also to Bev Goodall, Franca Goodwin and Margaret Hall, who typed with cheerful efficiency, and to Ros Hall, who said "this is boring" but typed anyway.

Earlier versions of parts of this book appeared in the *Indian Economic and Social History Review* and in *South Asia*. My thanks to the editors of these journals for permission to reprint this material here.

I also owe more than words can usefully express to friends and family. My thanks to my parents, all four of them. The book is dedicated to the memory of Merle Greer, in tribute to her affection and vision. My thanks to Rama Amritmahal-Laws, Terrence Patrick O'Mahony, Kathryn M. Cole, and Alfred W. Croucher. I shall always be indebted to R.K. Chopra who, in Patna, provided a stranger from a distant land with cold beer and warm friendship. And of course my greatest debt, for advice, encouragement and assistance, is to Jeanette Hoorn.

LIST OF TABLES

		Page
1.1	Community and Caste groups in north Bihar, circa 1900	9
1.2	Income and Expenditure (1927-28 Budgets) per 1,000 inhabitants of each province of British India	18
1.3	Expenditure (1927-28 Budgets) on administrative services per 1,000 inhabitants of each province of British India	21
1.4	Ratio of people to police and cost of police in provinces of British India, 1929	26
1.5	Population and population density of North Bihar, 1881-1951	29
2.1	Average indigo prices, 1894-96, 1897-99 and 1904	42
2.2	Area under indigo in Champaran 1895-96 to 1914-15	43
4.1	Occupations of Bihar delegates to the Allahabad Congress Session, 1910	93
4.2	Electoral turnout in 1920 Bihar Legislative Assembly Elections	96
6.1	Primary produce and commodity prices, 1928 and 1936	140
6.2	Rent Suits in Bihar, 1928-1940	142
6.3	Formula for the restoration of *bakast* lands, 1938	154
7.1	Official wholesale prices for rice and gram, 1941-45	172
7.2	Collective fines imposed and realised in north Bihar to end of November 1942 and February 1943 (amounts in Rupees)	186

LIST OF DIAGRAMS

                                                                              Page

1.1   Social structure in north Bihar,   11
       circa 1900

3.1   Administrative structure of the   147
       Darbhanga Raj

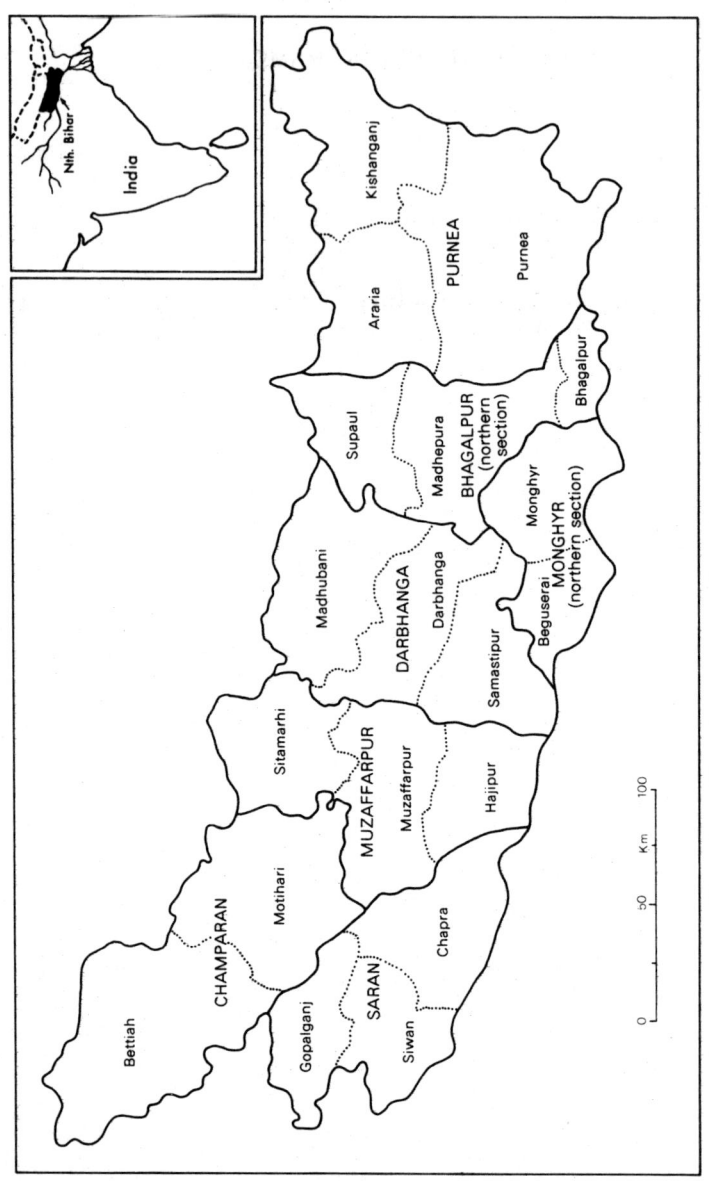

Map 1. North Bihar: Districts and Subdivisons

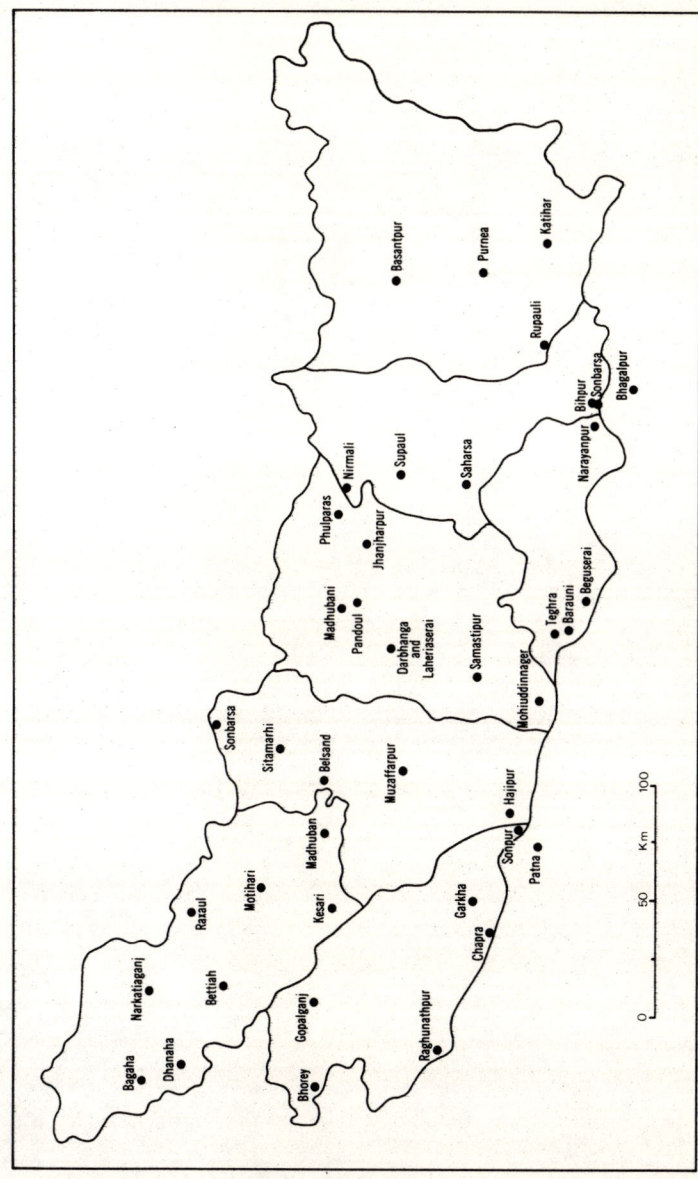

Map 2. North Bihar: Towns and Villages

INTRODUCTION

In August 1942 a revolt erupted throughout India, reaching its peak in the region of north Bihar. In north Bihar the rebels tore up railway lines, demolished bridges, and attacked the British and their allies. At Rupauli in Purnea district they burnt three policemen alive in their stationhouse; at Marhowrah in Muzaffarpur district they killed five British soldiers and an Anglo-Indian civilian. The north Bihar authorities found it necessary to concentrate their forces in the towns, and only regained control of the countryside through the deployment of substantial military force.

The 1942 revolt was the sixth major peasant movement to occur in north Bihar within the quarter-century beginning in 1917. The anti-planter movement of 1917-23 and Swami Vidyanand's campaign of 1919-20 were critical of aspects of the region's agrarian system. In contrast the non-cooperation movement of 1920-22 and the civil disobedience campaigns of 1930-34 challenged the framework of British rule rather than the structure of agrarian relations which provided its foundation. In 1936-39 the *kisan sabha* (peasant association) movement raised criticisms of the institution of zamindari landholding, which formed the core of the agrarian system.

In an impoverished and rigidly inegalitarian society the mobilisation of the peasantry offered an opportunity for the emergence of a radical challenge to the social order. This opportunity seemed particularly great in August 1942, with the temporary collapse of the law and order apparatus of the colonial state. Yet the peasants did not challenge the social order, neither in August 1942 nor during any of the five earlier movements. Why, in the 1917-42 period, did no radical challenge to the social order develop? Why did the peasants of north Bihar seek merely to reform existing social and political arrangements instead of attempting to transform the social structure to bring about a more equitable distribution of wealth and power?

This book seeks to answer these questions. After portraying the economy and society of north Bihar in the early twentieth century, it examines the peasant movements in detail. It explores their general context and particular setting, their leadership and following, their general characteristics and course of development, and their interactions with the colonial state and with the Bihar branch of the Indian National Congress.

Peasant unrest in north Bihar formed part of a general upheaval among the peasants of India during the final decades of British rule. Peasants comprise the majority of the Indian population, and their extensive mobilisation provided crucial impetus for the nationalist movement and made possible the partial expression of popular discontents and aspirations. This study draws on British and Congress records, on newspapers and private papers, and on the hitherto little used records of the Darbhanga Raj — the largest landed estate in Bihar — to supplement existing research on peasant unrest in modern India.[1] People other than peasants participated in the six movements. Nevertheless, the movements may be categorised as peasant phenomena because in the overwhelmingly agrarian society of north Bihar their development and character depended on the extensive participation of the peasantry.

In this study it is argued that the Bihar Congress and the colonial state combined to thwart the emergence of radical initiatives. The Congress wished to protect the interests of the small landlords and rich peasants who dominated the villages through their control over land and labour. Accordingly it directed mass turbulence against the British and helped contain potentially radical challenges. Meanwhile, British efforts to minimise social change reinforced the position of the small landlords and rich peasants, thus providing the Bihar Congress with a stable basis for its activities. Therefore the extensive mobilisation of the peasantry shook the framework of British rule but did not transform the social order.

CHAPTER 1

EARLY TWENTIETH CENTURY NORTH BIHAR

North Bihar covers 21,406 square miles in north-eastern India. The region comprises a vast, rectangular plain, stretching 250 miles from Uttar Pradesh (formerly the United Provinces) in the west to Bengal in the east and 80 miles from the Ganges on the south to the Nepal frontier on the north. The Nepal frontier runs parallel and adjacent to the foothills of the Himalayas. From the Himalayas the Gandak, the Bagmati, the Kosi and several lesser rivers flow south to the Ganges. Lethargic much of the year, these rivers become raging torrents once the monsoon arrives. They often flood, causing much damage but also leaving rich deposits of silt which enable the region to feed its teeming population.

At present north Bihar is incorporated with south Bihar and Chota Nagpur into the state of Bihar. A province of the Mughal Empire in the early eighteenth century, after the battle of Buxar in 1760 Bihar became part of the British administered Bengal Presidency. In 1911 the British separated Bihar from the Bengal Presidency and united it with Orissa to form the province of Bihar and Orissa. In 1936 the British separated Bihar and Orissa and established the province of Bihar. In 1947, Bihar became a state within the Indian Union.

In the beginning of the twentieth century north Bihar was a sleepy backwater of British India. Within its grossly unequal society, small landlords and rich peasants predominated. Social inequality created a potential for conflict, but the small landlords and rich peasants effectively controlled the social order, and open conflict only developed under their direction. The quiescence of north Bihar society provided a stable basis for the operation of a skeletal British administration which devoted itself primarily to the maintenance of public order and to the collection of land revenue. But the stability of this basis was threatened because the pressure of population growth on a sluggish agrarian economy was increasing the potential for the widespread occurrence of conflict. In this chapter the social structure in north Bihar is described, conflict and its control are discussed, the framework of British rule is examined, and the effects of population pressure on the region's under-developed economy are discussed.

I

In the early twentieth century, north Bihar had an overwhelmingly agrarian economy and society.[1] Less than 3 per cent of the region's inhabitants lived in towns, and four out of every five of them depended directly on agriculture for their livelihood. Land provided the chief resource, and an individual's standing depended upon his relationship to it. Within the 20,000 or so villages wherein the vast majority of north Biharis lived, pervasive inequality prevailed. Within the villages three social levels can be distinguished, albeit with imprecise boundaries. At the top were small landlords and rich peasants; beneath them were middle peasants; and at the bottom were poor peasants.[2]

The poor peasants were characteristically low caste, Harijan, or low status Muslim and comprised around 40 per cent of the population. The poor peasants may be defined by their possession of insufficient land on which to subsist, which meant that to survive they depended wholly or partially on the sale of their labour. They included sharecroppers, short-term tenants, petty occupancy tenants, and landless labourers. They also incorporated village artisans and fishermen, who characteristically combined their occupations with small scale cultivation and with agricultural labour.

The middle peasants generally came from middle and low castes and comprised some 40 per cent of the population. Their defining characteristic was control of sufficient land, generally as occupancy tenants but occasionally as petty zamindars, to provide subsistence through the use of family labour, thus freeing them from the necessity to sell their labour elsewhere. However they did not have enough land to be able to employ labour.[3]

Above the middle peasants stood the 'big men' in local society, namely the small landlords and rich peasants. These men may be described as the 'village elite'. They were generally high caste or else high status Muslim and comprised some 10 per cent of the population. Because they played a pivotal role in north Bihar society and politics they require careful attention.

The members of the village elite held substantial areas of land as zamindars or as occupancy tenants. They had this land cultivated by middle and poor peasants under a variety of tenurial arrangements. In villages in which the land was owned by a large absentee landlord, rich tenants comprised the elite. In the Madhubani subdivision of the Darbhanga district, for example, where the Maharaja of Darbhanga owned most of the land, Brahman occupancy tenants held sway over society. However wherever they themselves owned the land in a village, small resident landlords held sway. Muzaffarpur district, for example, was dominated by small landlords. Because zamindari landholdings were fragmented and dispersed, however, the ownership of the land in many villages was often divided between small resident, and large absentee landlords.[4] In this situation the village elite comprised both small landlords and rich peasants. Frequently, moreover, an individual had dual status '... both as a proprietor and a ryot ...',[5] For example circa 1910 Ram Sakhi Tewari, a Brahman of Dumari village in Darbhanga, held about fifty acres in the Dumari village and a larger area scattered through two neighbouring villages. He held some of this land as a zamindar, and rented the rest from the Maharaja of Darbhanga.[6]

Both conflict and collaboration occurred within the village elite.[7] Its members quarreled over the control of land and labour and were subject to inter-caste and intra-caste rivalry. Differences also arose out of conflicts of interest between zamindars and ryots. Nonetheless, as high caste men and as controllers of land and labour the members of the elite had common interests against those lower down in village society.

They also occupied a common position in relation to those who held power outside the world of the villages. The direct power of the members of the village elite was limited to their immediate locality. To exert influence beyond their village they needed to forge alliances with the elites of other villages and to interact with the great landlords and the urban professional and administrative elite.

Beyond the world of the villages, a small group of great landlords existed. These men were descendants of the ruling chiefs who had held sway under the Mughals. Their former princely status meant that, in contrast to developments in most of the zamindari estates in the region, their properties had been held together through primogeniture. The leading great landlord was Rameshwar Singh, Maharaja of the Darbhanga Raj, eighteenth in a line of landed magnates that had come to power in 1556, and head of the Maithil Brahman community, the elite religious community of Bihar. Rameshwar Singh's property covered some 2,400 square miles, which was about 11 per cent of the total area of north Bihar. Rameshwar Singh received, from land rents, an income of approximately Rs. 4,000,000.[8] He paid 10 per cent of this income as land revenue and cess to the provincial government, and spent another 10 to 15 per cent in the administrative costs of running holdings spread over a wide area. The remainder, supplemented by the proceeds from investments in industrial undertakings and real estate, formed a substantial sum, much of it spent in a manner befitting a Maharaja of ancient line.[9]

The Maharaja of Darbhanga owned much of the northern half of Darbhanga district, and had properties in the districts of Muzaffarpur, north Monghyr, north Bhagalpur and Purnea. Among the other great landlords, the Maharaja of Hatwa owned most of the northern half of Saran district, and between them the Maharani of Bettiah, the Maharaja of Ramnager and the zamindar of Madhuban owned almost all of the district of Champaran. The Maharajas of Darbhanga and Hatwa employed assistants to run their estates, whereas the other great landlords leased out, on a commission basis, the right to collect rents to *thikadars* (rent-farmers).[10] The *thikadars* generally came from among the small landlords and rich peasants, but in Champaran they also included European indigo planters.

Also outside the world of the villages were the towns of north Bihar. Less than 3 per cent of the population lived in the towns, which were sleepy backwaters rather than dynamic centres of growth. Patna, the nearest large urban centre and itself scarcely a thriving metropolis, lay south of the broad stream of the Ganges. The population of the towns consisted of professionals, government servants, bankers, merchants, shopkeepers, artisans and unskilled labourers. The professionals and government servants came from high caste backgrounds and had kinship and mutual interest ties with the landlords and the rich peasants. The bankers and larger merchants came from the Marwari and other Hindu trading communities, and underwrote the moneylending activities of small landlords and rich peasants. Muslims comprised the majority of the smaller shopkeepers and artisans, while the unskilled workers were generally low caste or Harijan. For a schematic representation of the structure of north Bihar society, please refer to Diagram 1.1 (page 8).

II

In north Bihar grave inequality in the distribution of property provided potential for the rise of tension and the emergence of conflict, but this inequality also created the relations of dependence which knit society together.[11] In the villages the small landlords and the rich peasants controlled most of the land. In consequence, they dominated the grain market, controlled the supply and distribution of credit, and decided the agrarian labourers' employment prospects and their wages and working conditions. Poor peasants were at the beck and call of rich peasants and small landlords. Through their possession of sufficient land on which to subsist, middle peasants had more independence, but they were generally entrapped within the credit and grain-dealing networks operated by those above them in the social scale.

These relations of dependence were articulated through the caste system. North Bihar had a predominantly Hindu population, and the caste hierarchy mirrored, reinforced and was reinforced by the differential distribution of economic and political power. The only substantial non-Hindu group consisted of Muslims, who made up 16.1 per

DIAGRAM 1.1

Social Structure in North Bihar, *circa* 1900

Agricultural Occupations	*Non-Agricultural Occupations*
The great landlords (high caste) European indigo planters	
The village elite: small landlords and rich peasants (high caste)	Lawyers, teachers, doctors and other professionals; money-lenders and big traders (high and middle caste)
Middle peasants: occupancy tenants and some petty zamindars (middle and low caste)	Artisans and small traders (middle and low caste)
Poor peasants: dwarf-holders, sharecroppers and labourers (low caste, Adivasi and Harijan)	Servants (low caste)
	Scavengers (Harijan)

cent of the population.[12] A small number of Muslims were notable as large zamindars, while the rest of the community were dispersed throughout village society.[13] For information on the size of the region's main caste and community groups, please refer to table 1.1.

TABLE 1.1

Caste and Community Groups in North Bihar, 1901

	Percentage of Population
a) *Hindu Groups*	
Higher Caste*	
Bhumihar	4.6
Brahman	4.7
Kayasth	1.4
Rajput	4.9
Total Higher Caste Groups:	15.6
Middle Caste	
Koeri	4.8
Kurmi	3.0
Yadav	12.0
Total Middle Caste Groups:	19.8
Lower Caste Groups (including *Harijan* groups)	
Chamar	4.1
Dhanuk	3.0
Dusadh	5.0
Hajjam	1.4
Kalwar	1.1
Kamar	1.3
Kandu	2.4
Kewat	1.2

Percentage of Population

Lower Caste Groups (Cont'd)	
Kumhar	1.1
Mallah	2.2
Musahar	2.6
Nuniya	1.8
Tanti	2.3
Teli	3.0
Other groups (all less than one per cent of the total population)	15.4
Total Lower Caste and Harijan Groups:	47.9
Total Hindus:	83.3

b) *Non-Hindu Groups*

Muslim	16.1
Miscellaneous (including Adivasis, Brahmos, Buddhists, Christians and others)	0.6
Total of all Groups:	100

Source: Census of India 1901, Provincial tables.

Figures adjusted to discount south gangetic portions of Monghyr and Bhagalpur districts.

* Hindu groups are designated as higher, middle or lower caste in terms of their economic wellbeing, political influence and social status. In most instances a high correlation existed between level of wealth, degree of influence, and social rank. The Kayasths form a partial exception, but they are listed here as a 'higher' caste because their wealth and power, based on land-holding and on their role as a literati, more than compensated for their relatively low ritual status.

The ideology of the caste system only sanctioned political initiatives among high caste groups. This ideology presented society as innately and unchangeably hierarchical, and insisted that the only legitimate course open to the individual was to accept without complaint his position in the social order and to fulfil the duties and obligations implied by that position. This ideology had been made concrete in an elaborate etiquette of day to day behaviour which, Barrington Moore Jr. comments, had decisive political results. 'Make a man feel humble by a thousand daily acts and he will act in a humble way.'[14]

The basic unit of the caste system, the *jati* or sub-caste, comprised an endogamous group whose members usually lived within a circumscribed geographical area. *Jatis* were internally differentiated economically. The poorer members of a *jati* generally gave allegiance to and received patronage from their more prosperous *jati* fellows. Through their character as 'social pyramids' *jatis* formed part of the prevailing patron/client pattern of politics, and encouraged the factionalisation, along vertical lines, of village society.[15]

In north Bihar, Brahmans, Rajputs and Bhumihars (also known as military Brahmans and Babhans) predominated. These groups all but monopolised land-owning and held first place among the tenantry. Brahmans, Rajputs and Bhumihars comprised only a small proportion of the population of the region. Particular high caste groups were concentrated within particular areas. In a village studied by Ramashray Roy, more than one-fifth of the population were Brahmans, while in the Beguserai area in north Monghyr around one-fifth of the population were Bhumihars. In Saran district, Rajputs comprised 10 per cent of the population.[16] In a context in which, with the exception of the Yadavs, the other groups in the social hierarchy were also small, local concentration of Brahmans, Rajputs and Bhumihars contributed to their social and political preeminence. Members of the Kayasth caste also had great influence. The Kayasths functioned as a literati. They monopolised the post of *patwari*, or village accountant, occupied many positions in the lower ranks of the bureaucracy, and dominated the legal profession.

The Yadavs (also known as Goalas and Ahirs), and the Koeris and Kurmis predominated in the middle range of the social hierarchy. The Kurmis and the Koeris had a reputation as skilful, hardworking cultivators, while the Yadavs, the most numerous caste group in north Bihar, combined their traditional occupation of cow-herding with tenancy cultivation.

Among the poor peasants low caste and Harijan groups predominated. Among the lower castes the Dusadhs and the Dhanuks formed the largest groups. Harijans comprised one-sixth of the north Bihar population. They were segregated into one of the three or four hamlets that made up the north Bihar village, and suffered discrimination in every aspect of their lives. The Chamars and the Musahars were the two largest Harijan groups. In 1909 one official patronisingly described the Musahars as 'field labourers, whose wages are paid in kind...They live in a kind of social thraldom, sometimes selling themselves, their wives, and children to lifelong servitude for paltry sums'.[17]

The inequalities which were integral to the relations of dependence in north Bihar contributed to social stagnation through their impact on the health and education of the mass of the people. The very conditions which provided reasons for tension curtailed its expression.

Among the mass of the population inadequate diet caused malnutrition, endangered the intellectual development of children, and made people easy targets for the impact of disease, an impact facilitated by the insanitary, overcrowded conditions in which most people lived.[18] Every year, cholera and typhoid took their toll. Recurrent intestinal infections and hookworm were widespread, and adversely affected people's vitality. Malaria was widely prevalent: a survey done in the 1920s on children under ten years of age revealed that 7 per cent of them had an enlarged spleen as a result of malarial infection.[19] Good health rarely existed among those who were worst fed and worst housed and most exploited. Those with the most reason to protest often had the least physical capacity to do so. One European planter, describing the workers employed in indigo concerns, condescendingly concluded that

> They are mostly of the very poorest class. Many of them are plainly half silly, or wholly idiotic; not a few are deaf and dumb; others are crippled or deformed, and numbers are leprous and scrofulous. Numbers of them are afflicted in some districts with goitre, caused probably by bad drinking water; all have a pinched, withered, wan look, that tells of hard work and insufficient fare.[20]

Moreover, inadequate education circumscribed the horizons of the people and thus helped limit the expression of conflict and tension. Only the landed could afford to educate their children. Illiteracy was all but universal; in 1921, less than 5 per cent of the population could read and write.[21] Though adept in the long established methods of winning a meagre living from the soil, villagers knew little of book-learning and of life and circumstances outside their immediate locality, and thus tended to accept existing circumstances as the only ones possible.

Poor communications limited the villager's mobility, and hence increased his parochialism and his dependence on the village elite. During the monsoon, movement became extremely difficult, and even during the dry seasons the railways were overburdened and the road system inadequate. Some villagers responded to oppression and economic pressure by migrating and others set out on long religious pilgrimages. But it seems that most lived their entire lives in close proximity to their place of birth.

Linguistic diversity strengthened parochialism. Most people spoke, as their first language, a distinctive village dialect current only in a limited area. In central and eastern north Bihar these dialects were part of the Maithili language, while in the west they formed the Bhojpuri language. Both languages were variants of Hindi, the lingua franca of the region. People from different areas could interact by means of Hindi, but their communication was imperfect.

In the early twentieth century the society of north Bihar was generally quiescent, but nonetheless open conflict did occur. Many riots erupted over agrarian disputes and numerous cases appeared before the courts. Characteristically, the open expression of conflict focussed within the 'landed interest', a term which can be used to incorporate great and small landlords, indigo planters and other *thikadars*, and rich peasants.[22]

Broadly speaking, two main kinds of conflict developed. One kind involved a struggle between the village elite and those who held power externally to the villages. In this kind of struggle the members of the village elite attempted to unite the people from their locality behind them. One leader in this kind of conflict was Babu Lal Chand of Dharampur in Purnea, a rich peasant who rented a large area of land from the Maharaja of Darbhanga. In March 1920 the local Darbhanga Raj manager described him as

> ...a reasonable man but never a friend of the [Darbhanga] Raj. He avoids open fight but covertly instigates tenants to challenge the Raj. His father Raja Chand (deceased) moved the whole Pergunnah [i.e. locality] against the Raj in the time of [the previous manager] Mr Mayer. He has great influence and cultivates Raj parta land [i.e. land lying fallow] without settlement [i.e. without paying rent].[23]

The second kind of conflict occurred within the village, between rivals for control over local affairs. In north Bihar, 'factionalism', in the sense of the crystallisation of two distinct groups whose leaders competed for local power, frequently developed within village society. Both factions would usually be led by high caste men, sometimes from the same caste group and on occasion from the same family group. Faction leaders relied for support on their kinsfolk and on their retainers and clients within village society. Inter-factional struggle perhaps performed a 'safety-valve' function, allowing the expression of tensions without threatening the stability of the social order.[24]

These two kinds of conflict can be isolated for analytical purposes, but in actuality they tended to overlap. Those involved in struggles against rivals within the villages tended to look outside for support. Meanwhile, external power-holders aligned against members of the village elite tended to try and undercut their opponents by linking up with their opponent's rivals for dominance within the village. Nonetheless, the boundary of the world of the village provided a threshold, and internal and external conflicts often proceeded independently.

The conflicts which developed concerned control over land and control over labour and hence were important to all members of village society. Yet because of the effectiveness of the control they exercised the leadership of conflict and the direction of dissidence remained in the hands of the members of the village elite. Middle and poor peasants seldom took independent initiatives in the development of conflict. They participated in conflict, but only as clients and retainers of the members of the village elite.[25]

In addition to conflict over land and labour, communal conflict also occurred. Like factional conflict, communal conflict involved vertical cleavages within society. Hindu-Muslim tension often manifested itself, and when on certain days of the year one or the other group engaged in the public espousal of its religion, violence frequently erupted. In part because the occasions for eruption could be predicted in advance, and in part because Hindus and Muslims directed violence against one another rather than against the village elite or the authorities, communal turbulence could be contained. Eruptions of communal turbulence also seem to have functioned as a 'safety-valve', allowing the dissipation of tensions deriving from economic, political and social inequalities. Communal conflict, like conflict over land and labour, generally operated under the direction of the village elite. In early twentieth century north Bihar the effective control exercised by this elite focussed on and contained the open expression of conflict, thus providing a stable basis for the continuation of British rule.

III

In the early twentieth century the administrative structure established by British rule overarched north Bihar. In each of the region's seven districts a Collector-Magistrate (also known as a District Officer) held responsibility, on behalf of the provincial government, for routine administration. The Collector-Magistrate, according to an official who served in the post, functioned as

> ...the pivot on which the whole administration turns; all those below him are under his orders and engaged in assisting him; all those above him depend upon him for information and are engaged in giving him orders and instructions.[26]

Junior officials known as Subdivisional Officers assisted the Collector-Magistrate and held responsibility for one of the two or three subdivisions of each district.

Above the level of the district the division, supervised by a Divisional Commissioner, comprised the next unit of organisation. The Tirhut division comprised the central and western districts of north Bihar – Darbhanga, Muzaffarpur, Saran and Champaran – and had its headquarters at Muzaffarpur town. The remainder of the region – comprising north Monghyr, north Bhagalpur, and Purnea – lay within the Bhagalpur division, which also included territory in south Bihar, and which had headquarters at Bhagalpur town on the southern bank of the Ganges. The Divisional Commissioners reported to the provincial government, which was stationed at Patna during most of the year and at Ranchi, in the hill country in southern Bihar, during the hot weather. The officials in charge of divisions, districts and subdivisions usually came of British stock and supervised a staff of Indian assistants and clerks.

District officials carried out the day-to-day work of administration. They held responsibility for the maintenance of law and order, for the collection of the land revenue, for the well-being of the population and for the successful completion of a variety of miscellaneous administrative duties. They sought to minimise social conflict by mediating between conflicting groups, using their authority to bring about a mutually acceptable settlement. District and Subdivisional Officers carried a heavy burden, working in large, thickly populated areas in which communications were very poor. Elizabeth Whitcombe comments that in the neighbouring United Provinces,

It was an easier matter for European officers in the later nineteenth century to leave a district for another or for a sanctioned spell abroad than it was for them to move about within one during the performance of their duties.[27]

Local officials in Bihar found it even harder to keep up with developments in their districts. The Bihar districts were twice as large as those in the United Provinces, and because of its financial weakness the Bihar and Orissa government spent less than any other provincial government on the maintenance of administration.[28]

As Table 1.2 illustrates, Bihar and Orissa was the poor relation among the provinces of British India. Each year the province, from land revenue and other sources, raised Rs.1,669 per thousand head of population, which was less than half the average amount (Rs.4,084) raised by the other provinces. Unlike most of the other provinces, Bihar and Orissa could not profit by increasing the amount levied in land revenue because, in common with the other areas in the former Bengal Presidency, the receipts of Bihar and Orissa from land revenue had been decided by the Permanent Settlement of 1793, and had only been subject to marginal increases since then.

The British had implemented the Permanent Settlement throughout the vast area incorporated within the former 'Bengal Presidency', which comprised the modern-day regions of Bangla Desh, West Bengal, Bihar, a substantial portion of Orissa and of parts of modern-day Uttar Pradesh. The British imposed the Permanent Settlement in an unstable, fluid context of land-holding in order to ensure economic and administrative stability by (a) vesting proprietary rights in the possession of established land-controlling families, and (b) declaring that the land revenue levied from those certified as zamindars (landlords) would not be increased.[29] The British administration exacted the land revenue demand according to a rigid timetable, irrespective of whether the harvest was good or bad, and in some parts of the Bengal Presidency social disruption occurred when established land-controllers, unable to meet their revenue payments, had to sell their land to urban-based speculators. In north Bihar, however, British revenue officials underestimated the productivity of the land and hence demanded only a moderate land revenue, which permitted most of the land-controlling families to retain their position.[30]

TABLE 1.2

Income and Expenditure (1927-28 Budgets) per 1,000 inhabitants of each province of British India

Jurisdiction	Revenue Rs.	Expenditure Rs.
Bihar and Orissa	1,669	1,766
Bengal	2,295	2,372
United Provinces	2,848	2,513
Assam	3,503	3,679
Madras	3,911	3,690
Central Provinces	4,036	4,229
Punjab	5,380	5,258
Burma	7,824	9,156
Bombay	8,003	8,227

Source: Adapted from table in Government of Great Britain, *Indian Statutory Commission* (12 vols., London 1930), XII, p.388.

The implementation of the Permanent Settlement established stability but had adverse effects on the finances of the British administration and on the economy of the region. By holding the land revenue demand constant the British ensured that any increase in the rental value of the land would benefit the zamindars. The British hoped that in order to be able to demand higher rents, the zamindars would improve agricultural methods and techniques so as to increase production. More generally, the British hoped that with the security of a clear title to the land the zamindars would display sufficient industry and initiative to bring prosperity to the region.[31] These hopes met with disappointment.

The zamindars were enmeshed within an economic, social and cultural context entirely different from that in which the British 'improving landlord' had emerged. To maintain and advance their local political position zamindars sought to increase the number of people under their control. They displayed little interest in new techniques and technologies which would enable them to employ less labour, and instead of re-investing their profits in capital improvement they used them to service extensive patronage and credit networks and to bolster their prestige by means of conspicuous consumption.[32] They could prosper without becoming improving landlords, not least because British policy inhibited the indigenous industrial development which might have galvanized the agrarian economy.

Steady population growth allowed zamindars to increase their profits without changing their style of land management. They profited as formerly uncultivated lands came under the plough, and the growing demand for land meant that rents could be raised without a commensurate increase in production. In addition an over-supply of labour kept their wage bill low. Most of the rising profits from land rent stayed with the zamindars. The designers of the Permanent Settlement intended that nine-tenths of the rent collected by the zamindars should be passed on to the government as land revenue. By the end of the nineteenth century this officially approved ratio had become reversed, and one-tenth of the rental income went to the government while the remainder stayed with the zamindars.[33]

In addition to their rental income, zamindars profited from the exaction of *abwabs*, which were illegal but customarily sanctioned dues. They also engaged in money-lending and grain-dealing. Through their various earnings they cornered much of the agrarian surplus, only to dissipate it in non-productive ways. The 'peasant was suffering many of the pains of primitive capitalist accumulation, while...society reaped none of the benefits'.[34]

The Bihar and Orissa government could not command more than a small portion of the agrarian surplus. Indeed, because of the original moderation of the zamindari settlement in the region, the government's share of the surplus was even smaller than that extracted as land revenue elsewhere in the Bengal Presidency. Because of the agrarian character of the provincial economy only limited funds could be raised from other sources, and the Government of India, itself subject to fiscal difficulties, was not willing to give Bihar and Orissa special financial aid.[35] The provincial government had extremely limited funds, yet had to provide administrative services to a numerous and rapidly increasing population. Before 1911, when Bihar and Orissa were still part of the Bengal Presidency,

> ...the standard of expenditure in Bengal was lower than in any other province in India; and in Bengal the standard in...Bihar and Orissa was little more than half of what it was in the rest of the province.[36]

This situation continued into the post 1911 period. (Table 1.3). In the administration of Bihar and Orissa, the provincial government commented in 1929, '...there has never been enough money in time past to provide anything like an adequate standard'.[37]

Because of financial stringency, the Bihar and Orissa administration could hold only a light rein over the people under its jurisdiction. In 1911, the management of affairs at the local level lay in the hands of less than 100 district officials, spread thinly throughout the twenty-one districts of the province. In north Bihar less than forty district officials held responsibility for the government of 21,406 square miles inhabited by more than 14 million people.[38] The provincial administration found itself fully occupied in the performance of its minimal tasks of collecting the land revenue and other taxes and of preserving public order. Because of the great disparity between the amount the zamindars collected in rent and *abwabs* and the amount they paid as land revenue, the collection of land revenue tended to look after itself. The collection of excise, stamp and other duties also proceeded smoothly. However the frequency of riots arising out of agrarian disputes and the high incidence of crime posed a challenge to the maintenance of public order. To uphold the law and to help preserve order, the administration looked to the judiciary and to the police and *chaukidars*.

The British boasted that they had brought the rule of law to India, but in north Bihar their laws were 'cobwebs for the rich and chains of steel for the poor'.[39] The courts

TABLE 1.3

Expenditure (1927-28 Budgets) on administrative services per 1,000 inhabitants of each province of British India

Jurisdiction	Education	Medical	Public Health	Agriculture	Industries
	Rs	Rs	Rs	Rs	Rs
Bihar & Orissa	256	88	44	45	26
Bengal	305	128	73	52	29
United Provinces	392	77	58	68	29
Assam	382	157	160	76	25
Madras	514	179	82	82	49
Central Provinces	407	114	28	127	21
Punjab	753	229	101	264	42
Burma	1,040	370	268	158	34
Bombay	1,073	260	128	150	5

Source: Adapted from table in GGB, *Statutory Commission*, XII, p.377.

handled a large number of disputes, but did not effectively redress grievances. Judicial processes moved at a snail's pace, the law was complex, vague and inconsistent, and the lower ranks of the legal profession were riddled with corruption. The rich and the influential exerted undue influence, and the tactic of harassing an enemy by 'getting up' a false case against him was much used. The enemy might, if all went well, be convicted, and at the very least, he would be put to the inconvenience of attending at court to defend himself.

In a traditional society in which few people had a modern-style sense of civic duty, individuals willingly perjured themselves for their kinsmen or patrons. And if such testimony proved inadequate, there were always professional witnesses hanging about the law courts, ready, for a small fee, to present whatever evidence was required.[40] In 1908 F.E. Lyall, the Bhagalpur District Officer, commented in his official annual report that

> No one who has not heard at first hand such tales as I have, can imagine the utter and cruel injustice now habitually worked in the name of justice through our Civil Courts, simply because all this tangled web of procedure has put the poorer man, the less educated, at the mercy of any unscrupulous man who chooses to ruin him by litigation.[41]

Yet it was because of its deficiencies that the judicial system operated as an effective bulwark of British rule. If the judicial system had operated more fairly, then it might have been employed by the disadvantaged in order to improve their position, thus upsetting the social order upon which British rule rested. Through their corruption, the courts reinforced and legitimised the dominance of the rich and the powerful. And through its indecisiveness and tardy pace, the judicial system operated as a 'safety-valve', providing a forum in which wealthy antagonists could let off their tensions and fight themselves to a financial standstill.

The police force operated in conjunction with the judicial system to preserve order. In north Bihar the core of the police force consisted of 3,000 trained career policemen. An auxiliary body of 26,000 *chaukidars*, or village watchmen, acted in support of the trained force.[42] The administration recruited an average of one *chaukidar* for each 500 members of the population, and stationed, in proportion to the number of its inhabitants, one or more *chaukidars* in each village. The *chaukidars* operated in their home villages. They were usually Dusadhs and generally inherited their posts from fathers or uncles. Their duties included guarding the villagers' crops, houses, and possessions against theft, reporting deaths, births, crimes and unusual events to the local police station, and assisting the police in the investigation of crime and the apprehension of criminals. In payment they received a miserly Rs.3 to Rs.5 a month, raised by a levy on the inhabitants of the village.[43]

An officially appointed committee drawn from among local zamindars, European indigo planters, and rich peasants, known as a *chaukidari panchayat* or union, held the responsibility of levying the *chaukidari* fee from the villagers and for recruiting, directing, and paying the *chaukidars*. Partly because of their low pay the *chaukidars* tended to be inefficient and corrupt. Not infrequently, they operated in collusion with local criminals. Their local residence and their employment by a committee made up of local notables greatly limited their independence. The *chaukidars*, Anand A. Yang comments, 'were never successfully incorporated into the official system'. Instead, they operated as the 'functionaries of the landholders' systems of control'.[44] The best that the author of the official 1921 Bihar and Orissa yearbook could find to say of them was that 'a large minority of *chaukidars* do their work with remarkable efficiency', and that 'no other class could perform these duties as cheaply'.[45]

The basic unit of police operations was the police station or *thana*. These two terms were used interchangeably, and denoted both the actual police station/*thana* building and the territory over which it had jurisdiction. Each district had some ten to twenty police stations, which meant that each station held jurisdiction over areas of tens of square miles populated by thousands of people. In Darbhanga in 1901, for example, there were twelve police stations and ten police outposts, manned by a total of 492 policemen. These policemen operated in an area of 3,348 square miles inhabited by 2,912,611 people. In

Darbhanga, there was one policeman to every 6.7 square miles and to every 5,919 members of the population.[46]

The staff of each *thana* consisted of a dozen or two constables under the direction of a 'Writer Head Constable', so called because of his literacy, and under the overall control of a Sub-Inspector. The constables were unarmed except for lathis, while the Sub-Inspector carried a revolver. Often, a couple of old shotguns lay about the *thana*, for use against bandits and rioters. The *thana* staff, with the assistance of the local *chaukidars*, handled the routine police business of the locality.

When a situation threatened to get out of control the local police could call for reinforcements from the Armed Reserve, a unit armed with muskets and made up of men seconded from the main police force for a two-year period of special training. In 1921 this unit consisted of 1,286 officers and men, of whom 400 were stationed in north Bihar. Help could also be requested from the Bihar and Orissa Military Police, an elite police unit of well-armed, highly-trained men divided into four companies, two of which were mounted. One company, the Gurkha Military Police Company, comprised 111 officers and men stationed at Muzaffarpur town; the other three companies were stationed south of the Ganges, delegated to protect the provincial capital, Patna, and the south Bihar coal fields. These units, recruited from among ex-army men, were under the command of the provincial Inspector General of Police. The military provided the last resort. From 1922 a company of British infantry was based at Muzaffarpur town; before then the nearest military help was south of the Ganges at Dinapur town, six miles west of Patna, the home base of a British infantry battalion.[47]

In north Bihar, a policeman's lot was not a happy one. It involved night duty, travel over difficult country, and physical danger. Because of its financial difficulties the provincial government kept the wages of the police to a minimum. Constables usually came from high caste but impoverished backgrounds and earned a wage, in 1921, of Rs.15 per month. Unskilled labourers earned about the same; rank and file railway and postal employees earned more. Most constables compensated themselves for their poor pay and hard working conditions by extorting money and by accepting bribes. Indeed the opportunity to profit by corrupt practices helped greatly to attract recruits to the police force.[48]

Nor was corruption limited to the lower ranks. Writer Head Constables earned twice as much as constables but had a better education, came from a higher social stratum, and were accustomed to a higher standard of living. A Writer Head Constable could not live on his pay and even if he wished 'to run straight' he found himself 'driven to dishonesty'. The Writer Head Constable, according to Inspector General R.J. Hirst, was 'the cancer of the force, spreading his evil influence above and below him'. The rank above the Writer Head Constable was that of the Sub-Inspector. In his secret report of 1929 Hirst commented revealingly that 'some of our Sub-Inspectors enter the service with the desire to earn an honest living and some of that number contrive to keep their honest purpose'.[49]

Among the more highly paid and predominantly British higher ranks, the Inspectors and District Superintendents of Police, corruption was less frequent, though here it also existed. In 1919 and 1920 the administration established that four Inspectors, along with four Sub-Inspectors and three Head Constables, had been drawn into the network of corruption which Police Superintendent Frank Lockwood Bussell had created in Darbhanga and adjoining districts. The official investigation also revealed the collusion of several other policemen.

The Bussell case posed a dilemma for the administration. Some of the suspected policemen refused to give any evidence to the investigation committee, while others provided ample information, thus establishing a strong case against themselves. Would it be fair to punish those who had given information, while those who had refused to co-operate escaped punishment because there was insufficient concrete evidence against them? Eventually, in a decision which reveals official acceptance that a certain level of corruption was unavoidable, the administration dismissed only Bussell and his closest accomplice, and merely subjected the other culprits to departmental disciplinary action.[50]

Many policemen supplemented dishonesty with brutality. The *Indian Police Commission* of 1902 revealed numerous instances in which policemen had beaten up convicts, suspects and witnesses and recorded some incidents of torture.[51] Because of their behaviour people feared and distrusted the police and did not assist them in the execution of their duties.[52] Their work also suffered because of their sparse numbers. As Table 1.4 illustrates, Bihar and Orissa spent the least on police per head of population and had the lowest proportion of police to population of any of the provinces of British India.

TABLE 1.4

Ratio of people to police and cost of police in provinces of British India, 1929

Jurisdiction	People to Each Policeman	Cost per 1,000 of Population
Bihar & Orissa	2,372	236
Bengal	1,853	314
Assam	1,772	303
United Provinces	1,343	328
Madras	1,526	370
Central Provinces	1,259	424
Punjab	1,053	481
Bombay	776	700
Burma	954	893

Source: Adapted from table in GGB, *Statutory Commission*, XII, p.389.

Policemen formed part of a garrison dotted across the countryside, rather than active participants in the day-to-day life of the people. Policemen depended on the information supplied by the *chaukidars*, and frequently only arrived on the scene well after serious trouble had begun. Sometimes, the police did not even get wind of serious disturbences. On 16 June 1923 a group of peasants clashed with servants of the Darbhanga Raj near the Bahora indigo concern in Purnea. The peasants, incensed by their grievances over the cultivation of indigo, assaulted several men, injuring one of them seriously. But the local Darbhanga Raj manager did not report the incident to the police because, he explained to his superiors, 'the Sub-Inspector of Pirpainti is exorbitant in his demands'.[53]

In north Bihar the British maintained only a skeletal apparatus of police/administrative control. District officials and regular policemen, the main representatives of the state in north Bihar, were so thin on the ground that in the early twentieth century peasants tended to perceive 'the State as a distant entity to which they attached both their hopes and fears'. The British administration operated, to use Ananad A. Yang's perceptive phrase, as a 'Limited Raj'.[54]

To keep their 'Limited Raj' running smoothly and cheaply the British depended upon collaborators drawn from the upper reaches of north Bihar society. These collaborators served in the *chaukidari panchayats* and participated in the organs of limited local government, namely the district and municipal boards. Some of the more prestigious of them also served in the Bihar and Orissa Legislative Council, a consultative committee which drew issues to the attention of the provincial administration. These collaborators came from among that privileged minority which dominated north Bihar Society. In the nineteenth century the effective control by this minority of a grossly unequal society provided a stable basis for the continuation of British rule. However by the first decades of the twentieth century the pressure of population on an under-developed agrarian economy was beginning to bring this basis under challenge.

IV

Throughout the nineteenth century the Bihar population had been increasing. In the eighteenth century famine, and the recurrent warfare during the final decades of Mughal rule, had kept the population down, but during the nineteenth century the Pax Britannica combined with effective famine relief measures to permit steady population growth. In 1800, vast tracts of north Bihar had been jungle or savannah, but by 1900 most of the previously uncultivated land had been brought under the plough. In 1881, the first year for which reliable census figures are available, north Bihar had a population of just over 13,000,000 and a population density of 615 per square mile. As Table 1.5 illustrates, population growth continued in the ensuing decades.

To judge from the figures of the decennial censes, the total size of the region's population remained relatively constant between 1881 and 1921. However it should be noted that famine in 1897-98 and scarcity and epidemic in 1918-19 made heavy inroads, which means that the 1901 and 1921 census figures do not indicate accurately the size of the population for most of the preceding decade.[55]

In the period from 1920, during which the administration brought infectious diseases more effectively under control, the population expanded rapidly. Population growth resulted in an especially high density of population in Saran, Muzaffarpur and Darbhanga. Already in 1907 one British official had remarked that

> Although exceeded by the figures for a few individual districts such as Howrah and Dacca, the portion of north Bihar which comprises the three districts of Saran, Muzaffarpur and Darbhanga has a more teeming population than any other tract of equal size in Bengal or Eastern Bengal.[56]

During the course of the twentieth century, political turbulence became particularly frequent in this part of north Bihar.

During the nineteenth century there had been sufficient untilled land in the region to absorb the rise in population.

TABLE 1.5

Population, Population Density and Decennial Change in north Bihar, 1881-1951

Year	Population	Population per Square Mile (Total Area = 21,406 Sq. Miles)	Decennial Change	Percentage Change
1881	13,169,378	615	–	–
1891	13,977,588	653	+ 808,210	+ 6.14
1901	13,995,889	654	+ 18,301	+ 0.13
1911	14,293,479	668	+ 297,590	+ 2.13
1921	14,186,246	663	– 107,233	– 0.75
1931	15,316,708	716	+1,130,462	+ 7.97
1941	16,899,665	789	+1,582,957	+10.34
1951	18,392,836	859	+1,493,171	+ 8.84

Source: *Censes of India 1881-1951.* Figures discount south gangetic sections of Monghyr and Bhagalpur.

In the first three-quarters of the century peasants had been able to take up the cultivation of lands previously held by zamindars as jungle or wasteland. At the start of the century Darbhanga, for example, included large tracts of uncultivated land. One official, writing in 1802, commented that 'For miles and miles are plains with only here and there a few bighas in cultivation, and the uncultivated land surrounding it apparently as well worth the trouble of agriculture as any part I have seen'.[57] Over the ensuing years the area under cultivation greatly expanded. By 1850, three-quarters of the total area of the district and by 1875 just under four-fifths of the total area was being cultivated. Of the land that had not been brought into cultivation, one quarter was devoted to mango groves and grazing, one quarter was unculturable waste, and half consisted of roads, rivers, house sites and tanks. In Darbhanga, the Settlement Officer concluded in 1903, 'there is very little room for the extension of cultivation'.[58]

By the beginning of the twentieth century only Purnea, north Bhagalpur and Champaran among the seven north Bihar districts had arable land not yet under cultivation. However the prevalence of malaria in Champaran helped check the extension of cultivation. As an endemic malaria and cholera area Purnea had a similarly bad reputation. 'Don't take poison,' the proverb ran, 'You have to die so go to Purnea'.[59] Moreover, the western portion of Purnea, and much of north Bhagalpur, suffered from the depredations of the torrential river Kosi, which changed its course frequently, ruining land by burying it in deposits of sand and endangering the lives and property of those who settled in its basin.[60]

The disappearance of surplus land boded ill for the future of the people of north Bihar. By the beginning of the twentieth century the region was entering a period of demographic crisis. In the ensuing decades population growth brought increased pressure on the land, and caused, because of the sluggishness of the economy, a decline in living standards.[61]

The sluggishness of the economy derived principally from the zamindari system, which encouraged inefficiency and ensured that much of the agrarian surplus was spent non-productively. Most of the actual work of cultivation

was done by poor peasants on small, scattered plots.
These poor peasants received a minimum return for their
labour, and any extra output they produced tended to be
skimmed off. Hence they had no incentive to increase
their productivity. Meanwhile, landlords and rich peasants
did not invest in technical innovation and organisational
modernisation because they could profit easily and substantially through renting out their holdings and by extending credit, at exorbitant interest rates, to the chronically indebted middle and poor peasants.[62]

Some development did occur within the north Bihar
economy, but it had only limited repercussions. From the
1880s the establishment of a railway network encouraged
the expansion of commercial agriculture through the growth
of internal trade in food-grains and in tobacco, indigo and
other cash crops. However only landlords and rich
peasants had the freedom from indebtedness and the
storage and local transport facilities necessary for the exploitation of the new opportunities. Moreover, even their
returns were limited by a marketing structure which siphoned off most of the profits into the pockets of European
entrepreneurs. Rather than re-investing them in the
agrarian economy, these entrepreneurs spent their gains
non-productively or else repatriated them overseas.[63]

Apart from encouraging, without notable success, the
lessening of population pressure through migration, the
British offered no solutions to north Bihar's agrarian problems. They spent only a token amount on research into
agricultural improvement and did nothing to arrest the
decline in the quality of the region's livestock resulting
from the shortage of pasture. Moreover, they ignored
the devastating ecological effects of deforestation, of the
cultivation of marginal lands and of the building of railway
embankments athwart natural lines of drainage.[64] The
British realised that the zamindars had failed to become
improving landlords and to galvanize rural society. However because of their respect for private property, and
because they relied on the zamindars for social and political support, they did nothing, (apart from some largely
ineffectual legal measures intended to limit the zamindars'
worst excesses)[65] to alter the land-holding structure so
as to promote greater efficiency and to encourage agricultural reinvestment. Indeed so crucial did the British re-

gard the stability of the zamindari system that they frequently, through the agency of the 'Court of Wards', protected zamindari estates from bankruptcy and disintegration.[66] The contradiction between economic rationality and political expediency could not have been more complete. Overall, the agrarian economy of north Bihar stagnated within the restrictive framework maintained by India's colonial rulers, but by virtue of its inclusion within an imperial system remained vulnerable to fluctuations in the world economy.[67]

Population increase pressed most heavily on the poor peasants. With growing numbers competing for the right to share-crop land and vying for employment as agrarian labourers, the bargaining position of the poor peasants became steadily worse. Some resorted to migration, either temporarily or permanently. For example, during the slack period in the agrarian cycle in densely populated Saran around 10 per cent of the population migrated to Bengal and elsewhere in search of work.[68]

When times were particularly hard, poor peasants also resorted to crime.[69] In 1919, 37 per cent of all convictions were for one month or less, and 64 per cent of all prisoners were serving sentences of three months or less. One British official concluded that 'A very large proportion of these short term convicts are...driven...by want of food to the commission of petty theft'.[70]

The pressure of population increase also threatened the position of the middle peasants. They had sufficient land to avoid having to sell their labour, but further subdivision of their land through inheritance threatened to cast them into the ranks of the poor peasants. They sought to acquire extra land in order to avert this development.

Population increase both benefited and disadvantaged the small landlords and rich peasants. It benefited them by increasing their leverage over those to whom they rented out their lands and over those whom they employed as labourers. Yet like the middle peasants, the break up of their holdings through inheritance threatened them with a decline in wealth, power and status.

By the beginning of the twentieth century inheritance
had greatly fragmented zamindari property. In many instances, formerly influential zamindar families had descended into the ranks of the middle peasantry. The history of
one Rajput family typified the fate of many. This family
had migrated into Saran in 1788 and had acquired control
of the villages of Gangapur and Bhagar. During the nineteenth century the property of the family became dissipated
'as successive generations of descendants inherited smaller
and smaller shares'.[71] Similarly, the challenge of fragmen-
tation threatened rich peasants, and therefore they and
small landlords continually attempted to increase the area
of land over which they had control.[72]

V

During the first half of this century, north Bihar's
population steadily increased but its economy continued to
stagnate. This circumstance underlay the political dissidence which characterised the region during the period
from 1917 to 1942. Its influence can be seen especially
clearly in the disputes and confrontations that developed
over the use and distribution of land. Its relationship
with nationalist agitation cannot be established so directly,
but it seems certain that the pressure of population growth
created a reservoir of tensions and antagonisms on which
the nationalist movement drew. And more directly,
nationalist propagandists blamed British mis-management
for the lack of economic development.

The first upsurge of mass unrest occurred in the period
between 1917 and 1923. This turbulence may be related to
the high prices and scarcity prevalent in these years.
War-induced economic dislocation increased the prices of
consumer goods and a succession of bad seasons resulted
in food grains being in scarce supply and highly priced.
Scarcity and high prices prevailed in 1915, 1919, and 1920
and high prices continued throughout the 1920s. Most
people had few reserves with which to tide themselves
over even one bad year, and suffered greatly from a re-
currence of bad times.

The poor peasants suffered most. The wages for labour
remained relatively steady, but from them labourers had

to pay higher prices for food. Fortunately, they customarily received part of their wages in kind. Sharecroppers, lacking storage facilities, had to sell much of their produce at harvest time, when prices were at a seasonal low, and then later in the year had to buy their food at a time when prices had risen.

The effect of scarcity and high prices on the middle peasantry was less well defined. The middle peasants devoted part of their holdings to cash crops, from the sale of which they earned enough to pay their rent and purchase consumer items while on the remainder of their land they grew food crops for family subsistence. Poor harvests could mean that a middle peasant produced both less to sell and less to consume. Higher prices might compensate for a lower outturn of cash crops. But since they often lacked storage facilities and because of pressing rent and debt obligations, middle peasants often had to sell cheap at harvest time and then contend with high prices in subsequent months. With the variables in the equation including higher prices, lower outturns, and a variety of rental and debt obligations it is impossible to generalise about the impact of scarcity and high prices on the middle peasants. The qualitative evidence in the provincial *Land Revenue Administration Reports* suggests that many suffered, but others may well have benefited.

In contrast to the poor peasants and many middle peasants, the members of the village elite benefited from high prices. Rich peasants found that higher food grain prices allowed them to pay their rents more easily. Small landlords earned more from the produce of the land over which they exercised direct control, and collected their rents more easily. Rich peasants and small landlords also profited as grain dealers, buying cheap at harvest time and selling dear later in the year. Yet despite these favourable economic circumstances members of the village elite took a leading part in popular protest.

Though it is clear that scarcity and high prices provided the background to much of the turbulence of the 1917 to 1923 period, the active part taken by members of the village elite indicates that the relationship between these conditions and dissidence can only be established in very general terms.

Partly this is a problem of sources. The statistics available are sketchy and unreliable and the qualitative evidence refers generally to developments within the province and its divisions rather than to the details of developments within the districts. Only a limited amount of detailed information is available about the particular situation at different stages of the agrarian cycle and about the variations in the incidence and impact of hard conditions in and between districts. Hence it is impossible to present a more fully detailed account of the chronologically and intra-regionally differential occurrence of scarcity and high prices.

But even if such an account existed it would only go part of the way in explaining the emergence and in defining the quality of popular dissidence in the 1917 to 1923 period. To understand this dissidence more fully, it is necessary to enquire in detail into the antecedents and course of particular protest campaigns. Accordingly the following three chapters deal in turn with anti-planter protest, with Swami Vidyanand's peasants' movement, and with the non-cooperation movement.

CHAPTER 2

ANTI-PLANTER PROTEST, 1917-1923

In north Bihar from 1917 to 1923 extensive protest developed against European indigo planters. In the first phase of protest, which ran from 1917 to 1919, anti-planter activity centred mostly in Champaran, the district in which indigo had become best established. Anti-planter activity in Champaran in 1917-19 marked the highpoint of a series of protests which had occurred intermittently during preceding decades under the leadership of members of the village elite. In 1917 these leaders brought in M.K. Gandhi to perform the roles of charismatic figurehead, organiser, and advocate. The strength of the Champaran agitation obliged the British administration to intervene and enact the Champaran Agrarian Act, a piece of legislation which, though not providing lasting solutions, resulted in a temporary quietening of protest.

The second phase of anti-planter protest ran from 1919 to 1923. During this phase protest continued in Champaran but also developed elsewhere throughout north Bihar. No single agency organised this protest; instead agitation proceeded under local direction and in a variety of ways. In this period anti-planter protest received considerable impetus from two other more centrally organised movements, namely the peasants' rights movement against the Darbhanga Raj led by Swami Vidyanand in 1919-20 and the non-cooperation movement led by the Bihar Congress in 1920-22.

This chapter portrays the context within which anti-planter protest developed, describes the course of the movement's two phases, and concludes with an assessment of the movement's impact and significance.

I

European planters moved into north Bihar in the first half of the nineteenth century. At this time, attracted by north Bihar's fertile earth, cheap labour and plentiful supply of water, they began the production of indigo.[1] In the second half of the century the indigo industry expanded greatly, partly because, in the wake of the 1857-59 rebellion, the administration encouraged its growth as a means of establishing pockets of European influence to bolster British rule.[2] Indigo production in north Bihar also increased because planter oppression in Bengal proper sparked off the 'Blue Mutiny' of 1859-61. In these years, assisted by the Calcutta intelligentsia and by liberal Englishmen the Bengali peasantry mounted a large-scale protest movement against the European indigo planters.[3] Peasant militance and administrative reforms made it commercially impossible for the indigo industry to continue in Bengal. Many planters transferred their activities to north Bihar, in the outer reaches of the Bengal Presidency, an area far away from Indian reformers, their British allies, and from the Calcutta base of the provincial government and the Government of India.[4]

The planters became established strongly in Champaran, the most remote of the districts of north Bihar. Here, by the late nineteenth century, Europeans held proprietary leases over nearly half of the land. In Muzaffarpur they held leases on 17.5 per cent of the land, while in the other districts they held only a few per cent of the total land area. By 1901, the planters of Champaran, with their families and European assistants, formed a tightly knit group of about 200. Another 200 to 300 members of the planter community were scattered across north Bihar.[5]

Even when they controlled only a small portion of a district's land, the planters exercised considerable influence because the administration favoured them. In Muzaffarpur they held one out of every four of the presidencies of the *chaukidari* unions.[6] Planters held seats out of all proportion to their numbers on the District Boards, had charge of cattle pounds, and held the contract for the upkeep of roads within an area.[7]

Officials and planters also mixed socially. They gathered for drinks at the club and set off together on hunting expeditions. Occasionally individual officials criticised the planters but generally planters and officials cooperated harmoniously. From the perspective of the north Bihar peasant, differences between planters and officials assumed far less importance than the cooperation between them and planters seemed to have the power and prestige of British officials.[8]

In north Bihar European planters began their operations by acquiring control over land. Sometimes they took land as ryots, and sometimes they purchased zamindari rights, but generally they assumed zamindari rights as lessees. The planters next established living quarters and a factory in a suitable position at the side of a river or lake, which would supply the large quantities of water necessary to the successful extraction of the dye from the indigo plant. Planters generally used the land in the immediate vicinity of the indigo factory as a homestead farm producing for home consumption – rice for the servants, for example, and oats for the horses. Almost all the indigo processed by the factory grew on the land held by the tenants. Sometimes ryots planted indigo on their own initiative, hoping to sell the harvested crop to a nearby indigo factory. More generally however the planter, helped greatly by his influence as the possessor of proprietary rights over the ryot's lands, arranged with each ryot for him to cultivate indigo on a certain portion of his land – usually on three *kathas* out of every twenty. This practice was known as *tinkathia*. When, after two or three crops, the land lost productivity, a planter would select another portion of the ryot's holding for indigo cultivation. The practice of *tinkathia* allowed a planter to ensure the use of the best land throughout the area under his control for the cultivation of indigo. Planters compensated the ryots for reserving their best land by providing an assured market for their indigo crop and by not increasing rents.[9]

To make a good profit by legitimate means a planter had to be active both as a landlord and as a supervisor of indigo production. As a landlord he had to ensure that all arable land was under cultivation, that the tenants paid their rents promptly and in full, and that his rights

in trees, hides, fishing and other miscellaneous items were
protected. The successful cultivation of indigo also demanded close attention. The planter had to ensure that
the ryots used their best lands for indigo, and that every
few years they compensated for soil exhaustion by employing a new area for the plant. The soil had to be carefully
prepared before the crop was sown and once sown had to
be frequently and carefully weeded. Members of the
colony of labourers attached to each indigo factory did
some of this work. However because the proprietory
rights that the planters leased applied to holdings scattered over a wide area, and because the need for labour
varied greatly throughout the year, the planters could
not afford to employ a full-time staff sufficiently large to
handle all the work associated with the cultivation of the
plant. Planters depended instead on their tenants, with
whom they arranged for the supply of labour, and also
for the provision of carts and bullocks for transportation.[10]

For managerial assistance the planters relied on Indian
amlas. The chief *amla*, the jemadar, functioned as 'a sort
of farm-bailiff or confidential land-steward'.[11] Assisted
by a staff of *amlas*, he supervised the work of labourers
and the cultivation of the crop. But the behaviour of the
amlas often caused tension. One planter commented that
if a jemadar was

> an honest, intelligent and loyal man, he takes half the
> care and work off your shoulders. Such men are how-
> ever rare, and if not very closely looked after, they
> are apt to abuse their position, and often harass the
> ryots needlessly, looking more to the feathering of
> their own nests than the advancement of your interests.[12]

Other factory staff similarly tended to abuse their positions
of authority.[13]

The close attention needed for the successful production
of indigo also created tension. The necessity of careful
preparation of the soil, repeated weeding, and quick efficient harvesting provided opportunities for disputes between ryot and planter. Also the indigo harvest coincided
with the harvest of the ryot's food grains. The planters
insisted on priority in the use of the villagers' carts and
in the employment of labour, both of which were in short
supply at the height of the harvest. And since the process of

growing indigo continued throughout the entire year the peasants could not use the good land set aside for indigo to grow other crops.[14]

The fundamental conflict, C.M. Fisher points out, lay between European entrepreneurs seeking to maximise returns from a single speculative crop grown on a large scale, and subsistence farmers operating on a small scale who sought to minimise risk rather than to maximise profit. Indigo, in contrast to rice grown for the market rather than for home consumption, could not be eaten if the market slumped. And indigo 'was very labour intensive, removed land from normal use and so involved a very high opportunity cost, and was very risky.'[15] Because of its unsuitability to small-scale production, peasants did not like cultivating indigo. Because of this reluctance, and because of the high costs involved in the production of the crop, free market relations could not ensure its cultivation. Hence the north Bihar planters employed extra-economic pressures, and particularly those they could exercise as lessees of proprietary rights, to oblige the peasants to grow indigo.[16] Rather than acting as a modern, galvanising force within the north Bihar agrarian economy, the planters accepted traditional forms and operated within established institutions. 'The indigo industry', Fisher concludes, 'created tensions for the peasant, subsistence economy but instituted no radical change.'[17] These tensions created a strong undercurrent of peasant antipathy to indigo cultivation.[18]

The character of the indigo planters intensified this antipathy. The planters were adventurers who had come to north Bihar to make their fortunes in what was, because of great fluctuations in yields and prices, a highly speculative industry.[19] One Collector-Magistrate described them as 'rough uneducated men, hard drinkers, loose livers and destitute of sympathy for the natives.' They attempted 'to get rid of as much as possible of the authority of the Magistrate, because it interfered with the despotic control which they considered it essential to exercise over the ryots.'[20]

Sometimes a planter was a benevolent despot who protected, as far as his own interests allowed, the welfare of the people within his realm of influence. A planter who acted fairly could gain the respect of the local people, who would then call upon him to arbitrate disputes which they did not wish to entrust to the lengthy, complicated and expensive processes of the official legal system.[21] But not all planters were cast in this image. Many were drunken ne'er-do-wells, who survived financially by extortion rather than by skilful management.[22] 'The factory influence', one planter testified in 1876, 'is generally represented by a peon with a stick... I do not think the factory influence extends beyond that. It is all due to coercion.'[23]

Despite their faults, the planters did bring some benefits to the people of north Bihar. They increased opportunities for labour, and sometimes paid their labourers better than Indian employers. They provided managerial employment for Indians, and assured ryots a steady income by providing a guaranteed market for indigo. They also gave loans to impoverished zamindars. The most striking example of their credit operations is the way a group of planters shored up the Bettiah Raj in Champaran by acting as security for a loan of £475,000, receiving in return rights as lessees over a large area.[24] Because of these benefits the administration viewed the planters favourably, though it sometimes expressed disquiet over the misbehaviour of individual planters. For the administration the planters provided a valuable buttress of imperial rule, not least because they were organised into the Bihar Light Horse, an auxiliary unit which had, in 1904, a membership of 141.[25]

But administrative support for the planters was not unconditional. The planters helped secure British rule, but this contribution would be nullified if, by mismanagement and oppression, they sparked off peasant protest and thus jeopardised the stability of administrative control.[26] Several times during the latter half of the nineteenth century the administration, in response to agitation, obliged the planters to make concessions, usually in the form of an increase in the amount paid for the indigo crop.[27] The administration also encouraged the formation, in 1877-78, of the Behar Planters' Association, an organisation intended both to protect the interests of the indigo industry and to ensure that the planters observed reasonable standards of behaviour.[28]

By the 1890s the north Bihar indigo industry had become well entrenched. Now and again, and especially at harvest time, small scale disputes arose between planters and peasants, but in these the planters kept the upper hand.[29] The planters enjoyed the sympathy of the administration and had strong links with important, Calcutta-based commercial enterprises.[30] Indigo generally provided good profits and the planters lived in a grand style.[31] Indeed, the industry offered such good returns that the Maharajas of Darbhanga and Hathwa both devoted part of their lands to indigo production, employing European managers to run their concerns.[32] But all at once the industry came under serious challenge. In the mid-1890s a German scientist invented a commercially competitive synthetic substitute for the indigo dye, and in the ensuing years the prices for indigo plummeted. (Table 2.1).

TABLE 2.1

Average indigo prices, 1894-96; 1897-99; and 1904

Period	Price per Maund
1894-96	Rs. 234
1897-99	152
1904	100

Source: Reid, 'Indigo in Bihar', p.257.

The price slump created a crisis for the indigo planters. Assuming that the industry would continue to prosper they had borrowed heavily to invest in their enterprises and to support their lavish life-style. They had found it necessary to borrow particularly heavily because each season the cultivation of indigo required a substantial initial investment which could not be recouped until many months later when the processed product finally reached the Calcutta market.[33] When the competition of the synthetic substitute for indigo began, their Calcutta financiers cut off the planters' supply of credit.[34] Some planters left the region when the slump began but others remained, partly because they were too financially committed to extricate themselves and partly because they hoped for an improvement in the industry's fortunes.

The planters who stayed on experimented with new techniques and with a different variety of indigo seed in an effort to improve production and increase the quality of their product. They also diversified their enterprises by lowering their indigo acreage (Table 2.2) and by beginning to cultivate sugar cane, mustard seed and other cash crops.[35]

In addition, the planters attempted to make the local population bear much of the burden arising from the slump in prices. They controlled their *amlas* more strictly so as to increase efficiency and to limit embezzlement of their concern's profits. (But sometimes this policy backfired,

TABLE 2.2

Area under indigo in Champaran, 1895-96 to 1914-15

Year	Acres
1895-96	54,000
1896-97	70,000
1897-98	86,000
1898-99	86,000
1899-1900	95,970
1900-01	86,000
1901-02	75,000
1902-03	84,000
1903-04	84,000
1904-05	84,000
1905-06	55,000
1906-07	38,600
1907-08	52,600
1908-09	47,400
1909-10	36,000
1910-11	46,200
1911-12	43,500
1912-13	36,200
1913-14	18,200
1914-15	8,100

Source: Mishra, *Agrarian Problems*, pp. 102-3.

and dismissed *amlas* led agitations against their former masters).[36] They also took advantage of the agreements that the peasants had entered into to grow indigo on a certain portion of land. The planters persuaded the ryots, often by dubious methods, that in return for being allowed to stop growing indigo in future, they should either agree to their rent being increased or else pay a lump sum as compensation to the factory.[37] The planters also increased the incidence of *abwabs* upon the villagers, dealt more stringently with their labour force, and took advantage of their rights in trees. Moreover, they exploited their rights as lessees to exact fees from those who provided goods and services to the villagers. For example they charged the Chamars a fee for permission to engage in their traditional occupation of skinning dead cattle and tanning their hides for sale. It seems probable that the planters had previously exercised such rights, but that with the slump in prices they exploited them more fully.[38]

By putting pressure on all those within their sphere of influence, the planters created discontent across a broad spectrum of the community.[39] Rich peasants, some of them former factory *amlas*, took the leading part in anti-planter protest. Because of the operation of patron-client networks and because of the widespread antagonism which had developed over the exactions of the planters, middle and poor peasants readily followed the lead of the rich peasants. Up until 1919, most of this anti-planter activity occurred in the district of Champaran.

II

In Champaran the first striking manifestation of increased tension occurred in 1907, when some ryots surrounded Bloomfield, the manager of an indigo concern in the north of the district, and beat him to death with lathis. The administration later explained that Bloomfield was attacked after an argument arising out of his refusal to sanction the transfer of some holdings, but according to a local inhabitant he was killed because he had been sexually exploiting the local women.[40]

In 1907-08 members of the Muslim *Sheik* community spearheaded protest against the Sathi indigo factory in the

Shikapur *thana* in the southwest of the district. Their grievance was the exaction of compensation money from tenants in return for their release from the obligation to grow indigo on part of their holdings. The tenants pointed out that since they had not entered any formal agreement to cultivate indigo on behalf of the factory, they were under no obligation to compensate the planter when he decided that he no longer required them to produce the crop. The disturbances continued for a year, only subsiding when the administration arranged a compromise under which tenants who stopped supplying indigo to the factory would pay a higher fee for the use of the irrigation works the factory had constructed.[41] In 1908-09 a wave of unrest spread throughout the Bettiah Subdivision, which comprised the western half of the district. To restore order the authorities brought in Military Police, instituted fifty-seven criminal cases, and convicted 226 people of acts of violence. They also arranged a compromise whereby the area under indigo cultivation was reduced from 3/20th to 1/10th of the tenant's holding and the price paid for indigo rose from Rs.12 to Rs.13 per acre.[42]

The next wave of protest in Champaran began in December 1911 with a large demonstration before the King-Emperor, George V, when he stopped at Narkatiaganj railway station on his way back from a hunting trip in Nepal.[43] Soon afterwards a press and petition campaign began which continued until October 1912.[44] In October 1913 the level of tension heightened with the commencement of survey and settlement revision operations, which involved the re-assessment and recording of all existing obligations and rights.[45] During 1914, activists sent a series of petitions protesting against the imposition of *abwabs*, and the administration responded with an investigation.[46]

In 1915-16 large scale unrest developed, similar to that of 1908-09, except that this time protest centred in the eastern half of the district in the Motihari Subdivision. The ryots contested the legality of the rent enhancements made in lieu of continued indigo cultivation, claiming that force had been used to procure their agreement. The ryots, 'throughout this period, manifested remarkable cohesion and persistence'. They, and especially the

Bhumihars of the Pipra and Turkalia areas, 'were inclined to be turbulent... and the settlement officers had a continuously unpleasant experience'.[47] Protest also continued outside the district, and members of the regional intelligentsia publicised the peasants' grievances in the Bihar and Orissa Legislative Council, at the annual meeting of the provincial Congress organisation at Chapra in 1915, and at the Indian National Congress session in Lucknow in 1916.[48]

Raj Kumar Shukul, a Brahman and a 'well-to-do middle class peasant and money-lender who also managed the farm of a landholder belonging to Allahabad'[49] led the agitation. In 1917 Shukul held more than 20 bighas of land, owned seventeen cattle and two houses and engaged in money-lending. The most notable of the other local leaders were Sant Raut, a prosperous peasant who had formerly worked as a planters' *amla*, and Khendar Prasad Rai, a peasant money-lender who held 125 bighas and whose money-lending business had a value of more than Rs.100,000.[50]

Raj Kumar Shukul, Sant Raut and Khendar Prasad Rai epitomised the group of rich peasants which assumed the leadership of anti-planter protest. Apart from the general grievances which all tenants shared against indigo and against the indigo planters, these rich peasants also conflicted with the planters over the control of labour and resented planter interference in their money-lending activities. The planters antagonised rich peasant money-lenders by giving cheap credit, by giving interest free cash advances to indigo-growing peasants and by using their zamindari rights to block the free transfer of the holdings of insolvent ryots.[51]

In April 1917, after repeated requests from Raj Kumar Shukul, M.K. Gandhi agreed to visit Champaran to enquire into the ryots' grievances.[52] This newcomer to the district was an unknown quantity in Indian politics. A Gujerati bania by birth, a lawyer by training, and a political activist cum religious philosopher by vocation, Gandhi was, at the time he came to Champaran, forty-eight years old. He had been inactive politically since his return to India two years before, after spending most of his adult life in southern Africa where he had achieved considerable fame and some success as a champion of the rights of immigrant Indians. He was adept both in conventional constitutional agitation and in his own distinctive brand of non-violent civil resistance, which he termed satyagraha.[53]

Gandhi arrived in Champaran during a period when primary produce prices had dropped sharply, affecting peasants 'who were accustomed to buying products imported into Champaran with the profit from the small surplus they grew over and above their own immediate needs'.[54] This economic pressure increased unrest and contributed to the interest inspired by his arrival.

Gandhi also attracted attention because of the maladroitness of the local British officials. When Gandhi arrived the Collector-Magistrate passed an order, on the grounds that his presence might cause a breach of the peace, forbidding him to engage in public affairs and requiring him to leave the district within a few days' time.[55] When informed the provincial government responded by instructing the local officials to drop the proceedings. As the Chief Secretary pointed out, the evidence concerning Gandhi's activities in Africa indicated that he would make the most of any opportunity offered to make a martyr of himself and attract attention to his cause.[56] Indeed by the time the countermanding instructions of the provincial government arrived Gandhi had already issued a statement declaring that, despite his general respect for the law and for legally constituted authority, he felt obliged, in this particular instance, to obey his conscience and to show his dedication to truth and justice by defying the order, even at the risk of being jailed.[57]

The matter did not come to the test: the administration took no action against him and without further hindrance he began making a detailed enquiry into the allegations and complaints of the ryots. Nonetheless, his willingness to stand up to the administration redounded greatly to his credit and confirmed in his support several professional men who were adherents of the Bihar Congress and who had been taking an interest in the dispute between the planters and the ryots. These men, who included two noted lawyers, namely Braj Kishore Prasad, from Darbhanga town, and Rajendra Prasad, from Chapra, the headquarters town of Saran district, assisted Gandhi by acting as scribes and interpreters.[58]

Gandhi involved members of the nationalist intelligentsia in his activities but did not bring the Bihar Congress into the campaign on an official basis. He wished to limit the scope of the campaign so as not to harass the British in time of war. In his view bringing in the Congress would widen the controversy without contributing to its solution. He may also have been unwilling to involve the Congress because at this stage of his career in India he was unsure about what his relationship with the Congress should be, because he did not want his place in the limelight stolen by established Congress leaders, and because at this time the Bihar Congress had only an embryonic agitational apparatus and thus could make only a limited contribution to the success of the campaign.[59]

Nor was the Congress enthusiastic to involve itself in the campaign. Rajendra Prasad and the other members of the nationalist intelligentsia only remained in Champaran during the period of Gandhi's presence. Nonetheless their intervention in the affairs of the district helped knit developments in Champaran into the wider fabric of provincial politics. They established local contacts and henceforth frequently referred to the situation in Champaran in their criticisms of the British.

Gandhi's activities in Champaran soon created a state of 'unparalleled excitement'.[60] His stand against the local officials, the aura of saintliness associated with his austerity and simplicity, his novelty as an outsider who had come from afar, his transparent sincerity and the enthusiastic help he received from his lawyer-scribes and from leading local peasants encouraged thousands of tenants to come forward and lay their stories before him.

The interest generated by Gandhi's unofficial enquiry inspired official fears that major turbulence was about to erupt.[61] With tension at a high level and with Gandhi producing strong evidence in support of the peasants' complaints the administration felt obliged to appoint a commission to enquire into the agrarian conditions in Champaran[62] and, to the dismay of the planters,[63] appointed Gandhi to it as the spokesman for the ryots. The committee conducted hearings from July to October 1917, and made recommendations which formed the basis of the Champaran Agrarian Act of 1918. This act outlawed the *tinkathia* system, reduced by either 20 or 26 per cent the rents which had been raised in lieu of indigo cultivation, and enforced the return to ryots of money taken in exchange for their release from the obligation to grow indigo.[64]

The compromise which Gandhi engineered in Champaran and which was enshrined in the Champaran Agrarian Act has been widely acclaimed as a verification, in India, of the value of the techniques of political agitation which he had developed during his years in southern Africa.[65] Many of those for whom he had acted did not share this view. According to J.A. Sweeney, the Settlement Officer, 'the more turbulent elements...frankly repudiated him and his agreement on their behalf, and raised all possible frivolous objections.' The Bhumihars, who held much land as rich and middle peasants, displayed particular dissatisfaction.[66]

The Champaran Agrarian Act quietened unrest by giving substantial concessions. Nonetheless dissidence continued because many planters responded to the legislation by seeking new means by which to extract extra income from their tenants. In doing so they took advantage of their status as long-term lessees of proprietary rights, which endowed them with a wide range of rights and privileges, some of which they had not previously bothered to implement fully. One of these hitherto relatively neglected rights derived from their proprietary control over much of the waste land which the tenants used for grazing purposes. From 1918 the planters began to take full advantage of their control of these lands by charging the ryots high grazing fees. In doing so, the planters were perfectly within their rights,[67] and since there were no effective legal or administrative provisions to control the situation, a heavy burden was placed upon the peasants. The planters also began taking greater advantage than hitherto of the rights they possessed as landlords to timber, hides, and extra rent payments for land on which houses had been built.[68] Indeed, they at times pushed their claims beyond their legal entitlements, but to prove this the peasants had to engage in lengthy and costly litigation. In addition, the planter could levy extra income by imposing *abwabs*, because when discussing the Champaran bill the legislature had 'rejected the clause...which was most of all designed to protect the raiyats' interest, that is the clause conferring on the Collector summary power to fine landlords for the exaction of abwab.'[69]

Moreover the new legislation only applied to Champaran, and did not affect abuses by planters in other parts of north Bihar.[70] Accordingly peasants continued to protest against planter oppression, both in Champaran and elsewhere in the region. Planter-peasant conflict also continued because during and immediately after World War One the industry temporarily revived because of the demand for dye for uniforms and because of the interruption of the supply from Germany of the synthetic dye.[71] This revival encouraged inefficient and oppressive planters to continue with the production of indigo.

Throughout 1918 and 1919 many Champaran tenants displayed dissatisfaction with the compromise that Gandhi had arranged. They delayed the payment of rents and refused to cooperate with the officials who were finalising the survey and settlement operations in the district.[72] They used Gandhi's name in efforts to rally support: in March 1919, in the Gobindganj *thana*, three activists who had returned recently from the Congress session in Delhi told the peasants that Gandhi had given instructions that rents were not to be paid and had promised to come to the area in the near future.[73] In the ensuing months anti-planter feeling continued to simmer in Champaran, and also expressed itself elsewhere in north Bihar.

III

From 1919 to 1923 anti-planter protest occurred in a number of places. The indigo concerns were scattered across north Bihar and no single agency directed anti-planter protest. Instead, protest proceeded under local leadership and in a variety of ways. One area of great turbulence lay in the vicinity of Sonbarsa village on the north bank of the Ganges in Bhagalpur.

The Sonbarsa villagers challenged the position of Mr Harry Grant, the principal owner of the Latipur and Narayanpur zamindari estates. Grant and his fellow owners had engaged in the cultivation and processing of indigo, but once indigo ceased to be profitable they concentrated on the production of other cash crops and on the efficient collection of rents.[74] The *diara* lands, which were situated on the bank of the river or as islands in the course of the river, provided a continuing source of profit. The word *diara* refers to land which is subject to flooding and which is not infrequently swept away during the monsoon season to be re-formed again somewhere else. Every year the *diara* lands received a rich coating of silt, which made them highly fertile. When left uncultivated they soon became covered with long grass, providing good grazing, and when cultivated they produced excellent crops. Consequently these lands were much in demand.

From around 1900 Grant repeatedly re-assessed *diara* lands, once they had re-emerged after the floods, at a higher rent than previously. Grant also usually levied a fee from each ryot before allowing him to commence cultivation on the newly-emerged land.[75] Grant justified these actions by pointing out that no rent was taken from the ryots for the period in which their *diara* lands were under water. For many years the ryots had accepted these practices, despite the fact that they were in contravention of a clause in the Bengal Tenancy Act which declared that no extra rent or fee was to be charged for newly emerged *diara* lands, because the rights of the tenant to these holdings continued even if the lands became submerged and/or relocated in a new position.[76]

From 1918, however, Grant's tenantry began to protest vigorously against the raising of rents on newly emerged *diara* lands. It is not clear what sparked off protest at this time. Perhaps the tenants decided that Grant was attempting to raise the *diara* rents one time too many, or perhaps they had been inspired by news of developments in Champaran. The large village of Sonbarsa, situated on the north bank of the Ganges about four miles from the Latipur station on the Bengal and North Western railway became the focal point of protest. Bhumihars, a group with the reputation of being 'a class of fighting tenants', made up much of the population of the village.[77]

This strong local concentration of Bhumihars meant that caste and kinship loyalties helped unite rich and middle peasants against Grant.

In 1918 600 *bighas* of *diara* land became fit for cultivation. Grant told the tenants that they would have to pay a rent of Rs.6 per *bigha* for the land. The tenants refused, insisting that they should only be obliged to pay rent at the prevailing village rate of Rs.3 per bigha. Grant then settled the holdings, at the rental of Rs.6, with a few local tenants whom he employed in his service and with a larger number of outsiders who previously had held no connection with the village *diara* lands. The Sonbarsa tenants responded by beginning judicial proceedings in an effort to have Grant's decision reversed.[78]

The villagers' resentment became intensified during subsequent months. In 1919 Grant called upon all his tenants to sign agreements to pay an increased rent, even though he had already, in 1902 and 1911, contravened the Bengal Tenancy Act by extorting similar agreements. The rent increase of 1911, moreover, had been forced upon the ryots on the legally dubious grounds that they should pay a higher rent in return for being released from the obligation to grow indigo for the landlord.[79]

Grant also put pressure on the ryots by attempting to restrict their access to grazing land. His men impounded some 500 cattle which they found grazing in some grass-covered *diara* land which belonged to Grant. The grassland concerned lay across the route the cattle took to the river to drink water. The ryots retaliated by rescuing their cattle and attacking Grant's *amlas*. When the case came to court the magistrate found that the ryots had an established right to graze their cattle in the grass-lands and found them not guilty of trespass, but fined them on the charge of committing assault. In a related case Grant attempted to prohibit all the cattle of Sonbarsa from entering into any part of the vast *diara* area even though the ryots had paid a grazing fee of half a rupee for each head of cattle. In the course of the hearing, however, Grant's lawyer 'curtailed his demand of restraining the raiyats from grazing their cattle on 2,000 bighas of diara to that of 400 bighas of cultivatable land only' and on this basis the plaint was accepted.[80]

Grant also used other means to harass the villagers. On 7 December 1918 three dacoities took place in the nearby village of Bisunpur. The first report of these crimes named no suspects, but subsequently Grant's *amlas* managed to throw suspicion on the leading ryots of Sonbarsa, who were then subjected to the inconvenience of being questioned and having their houses searched by the police. The confession of the accused in another dacoity case later exonerated the Sonbarsa ryots from involvement in the Bisunpur dacoities. Before this happened, however, Grant's men traded on the suspicion aroused by their allegations to lay criminal charges against several Sonbarsa tenants, including the prominent ryot Nathuni Kumar, who recently had attracted great attention by winning a rent suit against Grant. The case went to court but resulted in an acquittal for the accused. The trying magistrate later remarked that he had been 'surprised' by the blatant dishonesty 'of the prosecution witnesses most of whom were Mr Grant's men'.[81] Grant also tried to implicate the Sonbarsa tenants in a murder case. However the District Police Superintendent concluded after personal investigation that the most likely culprit was the complainant who had initiated the case 'on behalf of Mr Grant'.[82]

The Bhumihars of Sonbarsa reacted vigorously to their landlord's oppression. They refused to pay rent, initiated rent and tenancy cases, assaulted Grant's *amlas* and interfered with their work. Over the disputed *diara* lands they displayed such spirited opposition that on three occasions in 1919 and 1920 the authorities passed orders under the Criminal Procedure Code requiring them to abstain from breaching the peace.[83]

The tenants also sought the help of the political activist Swami Vidyanand, who visited the village in late 1919 and, according to a police report, 'began to preach his usual anti-landlord doctrines and queer ideas of the rights of tenants'. Under his guidance the tenants presented a petition listing seventeen grievances to the Collector-Magistrate. In this petition, in addition to the issues already mentioned, they complained about the *abwabs* levied by Grant's *amlas*, about restrictions on their right to cut bamboos and trees, and about the use by Grant of an undersized measuring pole in his assessment of the area of land held by tenants.[84] In subsequent months Vidyanand continued his interest in the Sonbarsa agitation, making it the focus of his activities in Bhagalpur.[85]

Grant responded to the campaign by asking the authorities to send extra police into the area to overawe the tenants. The authorities refused, explaining subsequently that they had not wished to take 'sides on behalf of the landlord in a contest between the landlord and the tenants'.[86] The decision reflected official dissatisfaction with the aggressive policy being pursued by Grant, which made the negotiation of a compromise difficult. The authorities also pointed out that Grant had supplied insufficient evidence to the local police about the bellicosity of the tenants. It seems that some of his *amlas* had failed him, and because of sympathy for the tenants had not presented evidence.[87] Official inaction at the local level may also have resulted from a reluctance on the part of the Sonbarsa police to do battle with the pugnacious Bhumihars.

In the absence of police help Grant hired some Gurkhas with whom to intimidate the ryots. The Gurkhas, who had previously been employed in a military labour corps, arrived at Narayanpur by rail from Lucknow on 30 January 1921. On 1 February thirty-seven of them set off, late at night and by a circuitous route, for the Sonbarsa *diara*. They arrived the following day at the bank of the Ganges from where, accompanied by some of Grant's *amlas* and some of his supporters among the tenants, they boarded two boats and crossed to the *diara* island.[88]

As they moved across the island towards the disputed land the Gurkhas came under attack from about 600 villagers armed with lathis, spears, swords, adzes and other weapons. Ten of the Gurkhas carried kukris, but the rest were unarmed. The Gurkhas fled to the shore of the island but found that Grant's *amlas* and supporters had taken refuge, in the two boats, in the middle of the river. The Gurkhas suffered severely. Few of them could swim and many of them were driven into the water where they drowned. Their final casualty list read: four unwounded, twelve wounded, seven dead from drowning and/or head injuries, and fourteen missing, presumed dead, probably from drowning. The villagers paid very little for their victory: there is no report of any of them being injured during the clash.[89]

The police did not learn of the massacre of the Gurkhas, which occurred around noon on 2 February, until the following morning. It seems reasonably certain that the delay was intentional. The events on the disputed *diara* land reflected badly on Grant and his assistants and they needed, in the words of a police report, time 'to concoct a plausible story'.[90]

Partly because of the delay in beginning the investigation but mostly because of the uncooperativeness of the Sonbarsa Bhumihars the police could not establish a satisfactory case against those responsible for the massacre. All but one of the accused won acquittal because they could not be satisfactorily identified. The authorities prosecuted Grant and his staff for taking initiatives likely to lead to a breach of the peace, but Grant was acquitted because his intention of using the Gurkhas as an offensive force was not proven, and in view of his acquittal the authorities dropped the charges against his subordinates.[91]

The Bihar branch of the European Association strongly criticised the way in which the administration had handled the disputes between Grant and his tenants.[92] The administration replied that it had acted properly because the rights of possession of the disputed lands could only be decided by judicial processes. The administration, moreover, publicly criticised the tactics adopted by Grant and emphasised his 'moral culpability with respect to the unfortunate Gurkhas.'[93] The attitude of the authorities and the self-confidence of the tenants after their overwhelming victory in the clash on the *diara* island obliged Grant to accept a compromise settlement. Grant agreed that in future he would not transgress the continuing rights of tenants to their *diara* lands and worked out a compromise with them over levels of rent.[94]

While the Sonbarsa campaign was under way, considerable anti-planter activity developed elsewhere in north Bihar. This agitation both received impetus from and gave impetus to the Congress Party's non-cooperation movement, which began in September 1920. In Champaran, Muzaffarpur and Purnea, where the struggle was against

European planter-landlords, the non-cooperation campaign provided considerable stimulus and support. Where, in contrast, the struggle was against the indigo concerns owned by the Darbhanga Raj, it drew strength from the tenants' rights movement which Swami Vidyanand led during 1919 and 1920.

In April 1920, the management of the Darbhanga Raj indigo concerns in Purnea reported to the Raj head office that the tenants refused to grow indigo and had returned the cash advances that had been given to them some months before as a consideration for their agreement to grow the crop. One of the ryots' complaints concerned the selection of land for indigo. Each year the ryots agreed, after consultation with the jemadar, to reserve a certain section of their fields for indigo. Then they would proceed elsewhere in their holdings to prepare the ground and sow the seed for other crops. According to one Raj official the jemadar would then arrive and tell them that some of the land they had just sowed with another crop would have to be reploughed for the sowing of indigo, because he had decided that the land earlier reserved was exhausted and could not be used. But after the ryots had bribed him he would leave them in peace.[95] Discontent also arose because the price paid for indigo was 'hardly sufficient to meet the costs of cultivation not to speak of the rent which the ryots have to pay for the land to the Raj.'[96] The local Raj management, moreover, impounded cattle if they wandered into a field sown with indigo, even if the field was part of the tenancy holding of the owner of the cattle.

The local officials of the Darbhanga Raj initially responded to protest with repression. In reprisal against the agitation in the Kabur indigo concern the house of one of the leading dissidents was burnt down, crops belonging to the ryots were trampled and their cattle were wrongfully impounded. The district authorities intervened, cautioning the *amlas* against continuing with coercion.[97] Subsequently more conciliatory measures were employed. The local Raj officials dismissed Singheshwar Prasad, an *amla* against whom there were many complaints, and as a result a number of tenants told an investigating police officer that they had no further complaint.[98] Another *amla*, M. Abdul Rahman Khan, who had recently been dismissed and who apparently had been playing a leading part among the dissident ryots, was told he would be reinstated if he could get the tenants to grow indigo.[99]

In the Debipur indigo concern, the other main centre of protest in Purnea, the tenants complained much of Ajodhiya Singh, a senior *amla* who had 'tried to bring them under his thumb.'[100] The local manager commented that Singh had served the Raj well and said that it would be inadvisable to dismiss him. Perhaps if he was 'persuaded to retire it would help matters'.[101] But the removal of Ajodhiya Singh could only be a partial solution to the problem: great interest had been created in the area by the presence of Jika Ram Sharma, a peasants' rights campaigner who had arrived in Purnea from Darbhanga.[102] The complaints of the tenants, one official of the Darbhanga Raj commented, were mostly justified, and this was particularly true of the charges against the factory *amlas*.[103] In order to keep the tenants under control, the local Raj administrators sought the help of the British administration. In August 1920, A.K. Khan, the newly appointed manager of the Gondwara circle, which included the Debipur concern, wrote confidentially to the Maharaja, claiming that the District Judge of Purnea district was an 'old friend' of his, and that he was known and liked by the other officials of the district.

> I have every reason to hope [he wrote] that I will receive great support from them in suppressing the agitation raised by Jika Ram...the ryots... are toned down because of my connection with the officials.[104]

Unfortunately little further information is available about the outcome of the campaign against the Debipur concern. Like the peasants' rights movement with which it was associated, in late 1920 the campaign faded away.

In April and May of 1921 tenant agitation in the indigo concern owned by the two Shillingford brothers in Purnea came to a head. The tenants were dissatisfied because of the terms under which they grew indigo and because the Shillingfords were, in the words of the Bhagalpur Commissioner, 'unsympathetic landlords who have been treating their tenants harshly'[105] Investigation by the District Magistrate revealed that the Shillingfords had exacted no less than nineteen different kinds of *abwab*. For example they had required a fee for permission to dig wells on ryoti land and had levied rent on dwelling houses built on ryoti lands. The *abwabs* mostly affected the rights of tenants, and thus particularly antagonised rich and middle peasants. However some of the *abwabs*, such as a tax on the sale of grain and a fee exacted at the time of marriage, had a wider application and thus affected every member of the local population.[106]

Because of their oppressiveness, the Shillingfords inspired peasant protest, whereas the other planters of the district, who acted less oppressively, inspired less antagonism. Protest against the two brothers came to a head when

> in the case of Mr Charles Shillingford a woman about whom there was some dispute in the village was found concealed at night in his factory and in the case of Mr Alec Shillingford when a respectable headman of a village whom he considered obnoxious was severely assaulted by his peons.[107]

The villagers arranged a complete boycott of the brothers' indigo concern. They stopped growing indigo and paying rent, and brought the factory market to a halt.[108] For a short time, even the Shillingfords' personal servants either had decided or had been compelled to stop working for them.[109]

The dispute ended in defeat for the Shillingfords. At a meeting with the District Magistrate present as a mediator, the Shillingfords had to accept all the villagers' demands concerning the cessation of indigo cultivation, the stopping of *abwabs*, and the fulfilment of rights to trees and to the unrestricted use of homestead lands. According to the Magistrate the villagers 'expressed their universal satisfaction' and agreed to end the boycott.[110]

While the disputes between the Shillingfords and their villagers were being resolved in Purnea, planter/peasant tension continued to prevail at the opposite end of the region in Champaran, where the issue of grazing rights provided a potent source of disagreement. In June 1921 tension erupted into violence at the Piprasi indigo concern in the Madhubani *thana*. The trouble began when a factory peon found 100 of the tenants' cattle grazing on an uncultivated tract that belonged to the factory. With the help of two other factory *amlas* he attempted to move the cattle off to the pound. They had succeeded in getting about half the cattle into the pound when about 100 villagers under the direction of Baiju Gur, the leader of the village, attacked them. The villagers beat the peon who had discovered the trespassing cattle with lathis and left him lying unconscious. The other *amlas* fled and the villagers released the cattle and burnt down the *amlas*' living quarters.[111]

Planter/peasant tension also manifested itself in Muzaffarpur. In August 1921 the Governor of Bihar and Orissa received a petition from the tenants of the Belsand factory, complaining that they were being forced to grow indigo, that they were being paid very low rates for carts and labour, that criminal cases had been instituted against those who had complained against the factory, and that deeds in which the tenants agreed to set aside a portion of their land for indigo cultivation had been taken under duress. The petitioners commented that in the Champaran Agrarian Act the *tinkathia* system and any other obligatory system of organising the growing of indigo had been declared illegal. The provisions of the Act had been restricted to Champaran, yet the petitioners pointed out that in Muzaffarpur the Belsand indigo concern alone had more than 1,000 *bighas* of land under the *tinkathia* system.[112]

Conflict and tension soon erupted into violence. According to the account of the District Magistrate, on 14 August 1921 a group of tenants assembled at Meyrick's Karnoul indigo concern and threatened to assault the factory *amlas*. Mr Meyrick intervened and 'laid out the local leader of NCO [non-cooperation] and another man', suffering as he did so 'no more injury than a broken topi.'[113] On 25 August a more serious incident occurred in the Motipur indigo concern at a village whose inhabitants were at odds with the factory. According to the Magistrate a local *mahant* (temple-priest)

> ... had been telling the villagers that Swaraj will soon be established and that then the zerait of the

> factory would be divided among the raiyats and
> they will only have to pay -/2/- a bigha rent.
> The raiyats are mostly low caste and uneducated
> and they appear to have believed the Mahant.[114]

These comments indicate both that the agitation against the Motipur concern had received impetus from the non-cooperation movement and that the villagers concerned, being 'low caste and uneducated', probably came from middle and poor peasant backgrounds. For some time the villagers had been refusing to pay rent. Two peons who went to the village to get the villagers to pay were waylaid and murdered. In the opinion of the Magistrate the *mahant* ultimately had been responsible for the death of the peons.[115]

The peasants of north Bihar also employed less bloodthirsty means of expressing their discontent. Many of the planters profited because regular *hats* or markets were held on land which they owned, which meant that they could levy fees from the merchants and vendors who offered goods for sale. In Champaran, anti-planter activists attacked this source of income by setting up a rival bazaar in an area of uncultivated land near to the planter's market place. The activists would 'induce the Banias who bring things for sale to leave the old site and take up their stands in the new'.[116] This tactic was first employed in the final months of 1921, and it seems likely that the notion of combining boycott with the establishment of an alternative institution was borrowed from the non-cooperation movement, which was reaching its peak at about this time.[117] Sometimes the merchants were attracted by the fact that they had to pay a lower or even no fee at the new bazaar; if this incentive was insufficient, they could generally be discouraged from attending the planter's bazaar 'by a slight show of force and shouting to intimidate them.'[118] As of 24 October 1921 some ten to fifteen bazaars belonging to European planters had been thus interfered with; however no bazaar belonging to an Indian zamindar had experienced any trouble.

According to the Police Superintendent the leaders of the boycott against the planters' bazaars generally had 'their own quarrel' with the particular factory concerned. For example in the Kesariya *thana*, Fazel Khan, a deportee

from Fiji who had been at odds with the factory for over
a year led the movement against the Karnoul factory.
Khan, with the help of some other 'locally influential residents' had managed to force the closure of three bazaars
owned by the Karnoul concern.[119]

Apart from the massacre of the Gurkhas at Sonbarsa,
the most dramatic of the events arising from planter-peasant tension occurred in the northwest of Champaran
in November 1921. At 7 a.m. on 1 November a crowd
gathered a few hundred yards away from the Chauterwa
factory. Shouting 'Gandhi *ki jai*' (i.e. 'Victory to Gandhi')
the crowd marched past the main buildings of the factory,
surrounded the houses of the factory *amlas*, set the houses
afire to force the *amlas* to come out into the open, and then
beat them up. Thirteen *amlas* were injured, seven of them
seriously.[120]

The crowd received little opposition. Broucke, the
manager of the concern, was absent at his other factory
on the other side of the Gandak river, and there was nobody staying at the bungalow. The original purpose of
the crowd seems to have been to assault Kali Singh, the
head *amla* of the factory, but Kali Singh had been out at
work when the *amlas'* quarters were surrounded. Unable
to find Singh the crowd looked for other targets.[121]

The crowd next set fire to a grain store room, to a
building used for processing sugar cane, and to the factory office buildings. Then they attacked the factory
bungalow. One of the house scavengers, a Musahar, indicated the location of the store of kerosene oil. The oil
'was immediately seized and poured all over the beds and
doors and furniture and set alight.'[122] The bungalow, a
large two-storey building, was completely gutted. The
firing of the bungalow and the other factory buildings
was also accompanied by some small scale looting of factory
property.[123]

According to a police report the events of 1 November
resulted from a situation which had

> been volcanic for the past two years being kept in
> a continual state of unrest by the truculent element
> among the ryots. This situation is really the after-

math of the Gandhi agitation. The N.C.O. agitation has given the final fillip to the unrest.[124]

Apart from the oppressiveness of Kali Singh and the other *amlas* one important cause of unrest concerned grazing rights. A few days before the attack on the factory tension had increased when Broucke appointed Magahiya Doms, members of a Harijan group noted for its alleged criminal propensities, as *chaukidars* to keep the villagers' cattle off lands belonging to the factory.[125] And according to the Bihar and Orissa Chief Secretary,

> The immediate cause of the outbreak is attributed to the institution earlier in the month of a case against some of the tenants who had beaten one of the factory guards when he tried to impound cattle grazing on land which the factory claims to be reserved.[126]

The background of unrest ensured substantial support for the attack on the factory. At first the crowd numbered only some 150 to 200 but in the course of the morning it grew to a size of about 5,000 and 'consisted of men of all the neighbouring villages within a radius of 4 miles to 5 miles of the factory.'[127] Detailed information about the social composition of the crowd is not available, but it is clear that poor peasants played a significant part in the riot. According to a police report 'low caste men of the Musahar and Nonia classes' were prominent within the crowd.[128]

In the period immediately after the burning of the Chauterwa factory great tension prevailed in the surrounding area. Armed police arrived to make patrols, rumours of impending attacks on other indigo concerns spread and at a couple of other factories there were minor cases of arson. Quiet only returned after additional police were posted in the area and the administration obliged the villagers to pay a massive collective fine to cover the Rs.98,000 bill for the upkeep of the extra police and to provide Broucke with Rs.82,500 as compensation.[129] The police attempted, with limited success because of lack of cooperation from the local people, to bring charges against the rioters.[130]

The excitement created by the Chauterwa arson case made it more difficult for the administration to avoid taking sides in disputes between planters and tenants. In December 1921 Mackinnon, a planter who operated in the Dhanaha area, asked for a police patrol to be sent out to intimidate his tenants, who were refusing to supply him with carts and labour. The police complied, and a force of mounted troopers, accompanied by Mackinnon and two of his *amlas*, marched through three villages. While the column was spread out in line of march some of the police, encouraged by the *amlas*, looted goods and money from the huts of the villagers. Soon afterwards a large crowd of villagers waylaid the column. They showered the police with clods of earth, jostled the factory *amlas*, and did not disperse until the police had returned the stolen goods.[131] The Champaran Police Superintendent later explained that

> The deputation of the Mounted Military Police on the trip in which they misbehaved was as usual quite a mistake simply due to the approach of the Christmas holidays and the general rush of the Prince's visit.[132]

This 'mistake' proved an embarrassment for the authorities because the nationalist press publicised the incident, thus heightening anti-British feeling.[133]

In January 1922, the non-cooperation movement reached its climax in north Bihar. In Muzaffarpur, a district in which the movement had had great impact, non-cooperation helped inspire demonstrations against and the boycotting of indigo concerns. In one incident 1,000 men demonstrated against the Mia Chapra indigo concern in the Patepur *thana*. Gray, the owner of the factory, took refuge inside the bungalow with his family while the crowd moved around outside, shouting 'Gandhi *ki jai*'. The crowd demonstrated for some time and then destroyed a considerable amount of the factory's sugar crop before dispersing. The police laid charges against the leaders of the demonstration and the villagers responded by boycotting the factory. But after the Police Superintendent instituted further charges they abandoned the boycott.[134]

Another boycotting incident occurred in the concern at Shahpur Maricha owned by Shyamnandan Sahay and managed by Captain Harvey. This boycott related closely to the non-cooperation movement: the villagers had not been paying their *chaukidari* taxes, and Sahay, as the president of the Chaukidari Union, issued warrants against them. In retaliation, the villagers boycotted the factory. They intimidated the factory *amlas* into not working, and attempted to stop the postman making his delivery to the factory. They stopped labourers working for the factory; according to a police report 'The factory labourers appear to be poor and willing to work, but dare not.' This boycott also broke down after police investigation and intervention.[135]

With the waning of non-cooperation during the course of 1922 the associated anti-indigo agitations ceased to occur. In the indigo concerns owned by the Darbhanga Raj, in contrast, renewed anti-indigo agitation developed. Anti-indigo protest in the Darbhanga Raj centred in the Bahora indigo concern in Purnea. In October 1922 the ryots of the concern petitioned the Maharaja. They said that hitherto they had willingly grown indigo on their lands because 'it was paying to us' and because 'the Raj used to show us great favours'. These favours included the waiving of rent on the land used for building purposes and the letting out to tenants at favourable rates of the Raj's *bakast* lands, i.e., those lands held under direct cultivating control by the Raj. But of late these concessions were not being given and the price paid for the indigo crop was too low to cover the rental cost of the land used to grow it, let alone the costs of cultivation. Furthermore, 'the high-handedness and the excessive extortions of the Raj amlas' were causing great suffering.[136] In another petition, sent to the Collector-Magistrate of Purnea, the ryots complained particularly of the behaviour of the Bahora factory jemadar, Ilialal Jha.[137]

The ryots also initiated a boycott of the factory. In early 1923 they refused to supply labour, carts, or boats. McDonald, the factory manager, set out to break the boycott. He had the crop sown by labour from outside the locality and by some of the local ryots who had refused to join the agitation. When harvest time came he brought in coolies and carts from outside and arranged for the hiring of boats in order to take the harvested crop over the river to Bahora factory. On 16 June, while the harvesting was under way under the direction of the jemadar, Hialal Jha, a group of 300 ryots attacked. They beat Hialal Jha, injuring him seriously, dispersed the rest of the harvesters, stole one of the factory carts and destroyed half of the crop that had been cut. The riot, McDonald wrote to his head office, 'was not reported to the police as the Sub-Inspector of Pirpainti is exorbitant in his demands'. McDonald also urged that strong measures be taken, lest the ryots be encouraged to pursue their protest even more vigorously.[138]

Unfortunately no further information exists on the outcome of the agitation in the Bahora indigo concern. Nonetheless it seems clear that before long efforts to get the ryots to grow indigo ceased. The wartime and immediate post-war revival in the industry came to an end, and the long-term trend towards low prices reasserted itself. In 1922, in the three concerns on which there is information, the Darbhanga Raj lost on indigo cultivation, and the following year prices fell even lower. By the mid-1920s the indigo industry, both in the Darbhanga Raj and elsewhere in north Bihar, had all but disappeared.[139]

With the disappearance of the indigo industry from north Bihar, many European planters left the region. Others devoted themselves to the production of sugar, tobacco and other cash crops. These crops were viable in a free market situation, and hence planters could produce them without having to put non-economic pressures on the peasantry. These planters remained in north Bihar until the 1940s when, realising that their future in the region was bleak, they took advantage of high prices to sell up and leave India.[140]

IV

Until the late nineteenth century, the indigo industry in north Bihar had flourished. Intermittent peasant protest against the planters had occurred, but the planters had been able to withstand these challenges. From the 1890s to the 1920s, in contrast, the indigo industry went through a period of crisis and decline. The planters pressed down much more heavily upon the peasantry, and the peasantry responded by engaging in extensive protest. Initially this protest was centred in Champaran, but by 1920 it had manifested itself across the region. The leaders of anti-planter activity usually came from rich peasant and small landlord backgrounds, but planter-peasant tension reflected more than just conflict within the landed interest. The planters had abused their zamindari rights to 'squeeze' all levels of society, and middle and poor peasants readily joined the village elite in anti-planter protest. The planters were vulnerable before the wave of protest. They comprised an alien elite, and hence could not depend on caste and kinship ties and on the prestige flowing from high ritual status to consolidate their position.

Protest occurred extensively in Champaran during 1917 and 1918. In Champaran the planters were established strongly and a long tradition of anti-planter protest existed. In 1917 local activists brought in Gandhi as a charismatic figurehead, as an advocate, and as a co-ordinator of protest. Gandhi mediated between the local activists and the administration, and effectively publicised the peasants' grievances. Nonetheless the compromise he engineered provided only a temporary solution.

In Champaran and elsewhere in north Bihar from 1919 to 1923 extensive protest developed, receiving impetus both from Swami Vidyanand's movement and from noncooperation. Partly because the indigo concerns were scattered across the region, and partly because the Bihar Congress declined the opportunity to supply organisational support, this phase of anti-planter protest lacked effective co-ordination. In many instances protest consisted more of spontaneous acts of retaliation against planters and their *amlas* than of a systematic attempt to bring pressure to bear.

Partly because of ineffective organisation, anti-planter protest failed to dislodge the planters from north Bihar. In addition, the planters maintained their position because the administration frequently intervened to arbitrate and to diminish dissidence through the initiation of concessions. Ultimately the planters gave up the production of indigo. But they did so not because protest had made their position untenable but because by the early 1920s indigo production had become commercially unfeasible.

The disappearance of the indigo industry from north Bihar eased the pressure on the British administration. The Bihar and Orissa administration had an ambivalent attitude towards the industry. Officials regarded the planters as a useful bulwark of British rule, and because they had similar ethnic backgrounds and mutual sporting and social interests strong ties often developed between planters and district level officials. But the administration also knew that the grievances of the peasants were genuine and that planters and officials were closely identified together in Indian eyes. Accordingly the administration reacted unfavourably when planters created dissidence among the peasantry and hence endangered the stability of British rule. But though the administration tended to be critical of the planters, it would not propose radical reform of the indigo industry. The administration realised that the influence of the planters depended on their possession, under long term leases, of zamindari rights, and that any attempt to restrict the exercise of these rights would be an attack on the foundation of British rule over north Bihar, namely the zamindari system established by the Permanent Settlement of 1793.

The British presented themselves as impartial arbiters standing over north Bihar society, and in consonance with this stance they sought to minimize and contain protest by acting as arbitrators, by encouraging the institution of limited concessions, and by dealing determinedly with protest when it involved violence and illegality. Sometimes, as in the Shillingford concern in Purnea, the administration successfully contained protest. But in other cases its efforts did not achieve lasting success. The Champaran Agrarian Act of 1918 did not deal effectively with all the peasants' grievances, and protest continued to simmer in Champaran. By failing to take a strong, unequivocal stand against an industry which for economic reasons would eventually collapse of its own accord, the British administration, in the event to no real purpose, made itself the target of extensive dissatisfaction.

The police also lost public sympathy as a result of anti-indigo protest. As the instrument of the administration the police were theoretically neutral in planter/peasant disputes, but they became identified as acting in the interests of the planters. In the involvement of mounted troopers in a looting expedition in the Dhanaha area in Champaran, they sided with planters and their *amlas* against villagers. And after the Sonbarsa and Chauterwa riots the police who came to investigate cast themselves as supporters of the planters.

Fortunately for the stability of British rule in the region, the Bihar Congress made only limited use of the potential for mass action inherent in anti-planter protest. The attitude of the Bihar Congress was shaped by its determination to preserve the social order and to unite landlords and peasants against British rule. The planters were an alien elite with few ties with the local population. They were predominantly European, were closely associated with the British, and were clearly visible as exploiters of the peasantry. Accordingly they provided an extremely useful target for propaganda designed to put pressure on the British administration.

Yet as possessors of zamindari rights, the planters were knit into the fabric of north Bihar society. The planters were also landlords, and a wholesale attack on them might develop into an attack on landlords in general. Rather than encourage such a possibility the Bihar Congress did not involve itself substantially in what remained essentially a series of local campaigns. Instead of supplying organisational support and providing access to the all-India level of institutional politics, the Bihar Congress was content merely to provide space in the nationalist media for criticism of the planters. This criticism focussed on the planters as Europeans and exploiters, rather than on the structure of land-holding within which their oppression of the peasantry occurred.

Because of the conservative influence of the Bihar Congress, because of the leading part taken by members of the village elite, and because of the absence of an alternative leadership and ideology the anti-indigo movement failed to develop a radical dimension. Eventually the possibility of anti-indigo planter protest having wider repercussions disappeared along with the cultivation of indigo. In later years the Bihar Congress found that the memory of indigo planter oppression and of anti-planter protest continued to provide useful propaganda. Indeed, once the wider possibilities inherent in the support of anti-planter protest no longer existed, the Congress was able to exaggerate the importance of what had been in fact its rather limited contribution to anti-planter activity.[141]

CHAPTER 3

SWAMI VIDYANAND'S MOVEMENT, 1919-1920

In 1919 and 1920 the agrarian activist Swami Vidyanand attracted extensive support for a movement which championed the interests of the peasants of north Bihar. The movement focussed on the misbehaviour of the Darbhanga Raj *amlas* and on the interference by the Darbhanga Raj with the rights of occupancy tenants to the use of land and to timber. Swami Vidyanand won sufficient support from rich peasants to win election, along with three fellow activists, to the legislature under the provisions of the Montagu-Chelmsford Reforms. However his movement also attracted considerable support from middle and poor peasants. The middle peasants and some poor peasants held occupancy rights, and oppression by *amlas* tended to bear down most heavily on those least able to resist it, namely the poor peasants.

Swami Vidyanand's movement aimed to bring the redress of grievances rather than to alter the agrarian and social structure, and the Darbhanga Raj managed to contain it through a combination of concessions, propaganda and coercion. Yet despite the movement's limited aims the Bihar Congress failed to come to its support. The Bihar Congress sought to unite all sections of society against the British, and opposed any initiative which heightened landlord-peasant tension. This chapter examines the context within which the movement emerged, describes its development, and concludes with an assessment of its significance and impact.

I

Swami Vidyanand's campaign emerged in a context of economic and demographic pressure. Post World War One economic dislocation increased the prices of consumer goods while a succession of bad seasons meant that in 1915, 1919 and 1920 food-grains were scarce and highly priced.[1] Rich peasants, who generally had a surplus of produce, benefited from these conditions, but many middle peasants and all poor peasants suffered from them. By the early twentieth century, moreover, north Bihar had reached the verge of demographic crisis. A scarcity of land, timber, and of grazing areas for cattle, had developed, and rights to resources had become increasingly contentious. Population pressure helped increase dissatisfaction with the highly inequitable zamindari system of land-holding. In 1793 the Permanent Settlement had clarified and guaranteed the landlords' rights, but it had done little to protect the rights and interests of their tenants.[2]

Legislation to protect the rights and interests of the tenants did not come until the passing of Act X of 1859 and the Bengal Tenancy Act of 1885. These Acts abolished the landlords' power to compel ryots to attend when summoned to their offices, protected the ryot from summary eviction, guaranteed the continued occupancy of ryots who could establish that they had rented land from a zamindar for a period of twelve successive years, and required zamindars who wished to raise rents to prove legally that their claim was reasonable.[3] But legislation alone could not secure the position of the tenantry. The key problem concerned the successful implementation of the laws: the tenants often knew little about their rights and often found that in legal contests the zamindars benefited from being at the centre of a wide circle of influence. Zamindars also usually commanded more resources, a crucial advantage when legal struggles frequently became tests of financial endurance.[4]

As an alternative to legal proceedings the tenant could engage in direct action against his landlord. He might be able to put up a good fight,[5] but in the long run the struggle was likely to go against him, not least because the police took the side of the zamindar. Until the early twentieth century flight provided another option to those under severe pressure. North of the border Nepal had vacant land for cultivation.[6] In the 1880s, large areas of Darbhanga became all but depopulated when ryots and their families responded to oppression by the rent collectors of the Darbhanga Raj by fleeing into Nepal.[7] The possibility that his ryots might decamp, thus depriving him of rental income, encouraged a zamindar to keep his behaviour within certain limits. Once they heard that conditions in north Bihar had improved, the ryots could return either to the area from which they had come or to some other place. Even relatively well off peasants generally had a minimum of material possessions, which facilitated changes of residence.[8]

By the turn of the century the relationship between ryots and zamindars had begun to change. From the last decades of the nineteenth century the administration became more concerned with the position of the peasantry. The survey and settlement operations conducted throughout north Bihar during the 1890s and the 1900s revealed numerous instances in which *abwabs* had been imposed and in which the rights and privileges of the tenantry had been ignored.[9] The administration strongly criticised the zamindars for this misconduct and scolded them for their abuse of the legal system. The survey and settlement operations also involved the detailed recording of patterns of landholding, of rental rates, and of occupancy rights, thus creating an authoritative documentary basis to which tenants could refer in legal disputes. Nor was the alternative of fleeing temporarily from an extortionate zamindar as feasible as it had been. There was still land, though less than previously, to be tilled in Nepal. But because of demographic pressure and land shortage in north Bihar, anyone who emigrated would have to leave permanently, since his landlord would jump at the chance to replace him with a sharecropper or a temporary tenant.

With greater protection from the law, and with temporary emigration a less attractive proposition, tenants were more likely to agitate to secure and advance their interests. Indeed, this response increasingly was forced upon the ryots since, because of demographic pressure, the zamindari system impinged upon them with ever greater force. The small zamindars, threatened with impoverishment, competed keenly with their tenants for control over land, collected their rents rigorously, and intensified their exaction of *abwabs*.[10] Even when not under the same financial pressure as small zamindars,[11] the large zamindars held indirect responsibility for much oppression. They employed as their *amlas* men from small landlord or rich peasant families.[12] Some of these *amlas* profited at the expense of those over whom they had authority, thus inspiring opposition. In the largest zamindari in the region — the Darbhanga Raj — protest developed on an extensive scale.

II

The Darbhanga Raj covered 2,400 square miles and consisted of holdings scattered across five of the seven districts of north Bihar. The proprietor of the Darbhanga Raj, Maharaja Rameshwar Singh, employed 3,000 people to administer his estates. The diagram below illustrates the structure of the Raj administration.

DIAGRAM 3.1

Administrative structure of the Darbhanga Raj

MAHARAJA OF DARBHANGA
|
CHIEF MANAGER, ASSISTED BY HEADQUARTERS STAFF
|
CIRCLE MANAGERS, ASSISTED BY CIRCLE OFFICE STAFF
|
ASSISTANT MANAGERS (TEHSILDARS)
|
JETH RYOTS, PATWARIS, PEONS AND BARAHILS

At the top stood the chief manager who ran the head office located in Darbhanga town and reported directly to the Maharaja. The chief manager directed the circle managers, each of whom administered one of the fourteen circles which formed the basic unit of the Darbhanga Raj. Each circle manager controlled four or five *tehsildars* (assistant managers), who each held responsibility for Raj activities within a subdivision of a circle. Beneath the *tehsildars* were the 'village servants' - a category which consisted of *jeth* ryots, *patwaris*, peons and *barahils*.[13]

The *jeth* ryots had charge of the collection of rents from the tenants within one or two villages, and received a commission of a few per cent, varying upwards in proportion to the percentage of the total rental demand which they managed to collect. The *patwaris* kept the rent and land records of the villages owned by the Darbhanga Raj. They and the *jeth* ryots got assistance from the peons and *barahils*, who acted as messengers, retainers, guards and stand-over men.[14] In theory a *jeth* ryot and *patwari* counter-balanced one another, checking each other's actions and ensuring that each did his job properly. In fact, they frequently acted in collusion to oppress the tenantry and to defraud the Darbhanga Raj.[15] The Raj found it difficult to deal with this situation. In order to collect rent from holdings dispersed over a wide area, the Raj had to employ locally influential peasants in the positions of jeth ryot and *patwari*, and such men generally put their own interests first.[16]

The demands of the Darbhanga Raj and the oppression of its *amlas* frequently inspired opposition from the villagers. Prior to 1919 this opposition expressed itself in a sporadic, small scale and localised manner.[17] However in 1919 and 1920 a movement developed which involved large numbers of people and covered a wide area. The rise of this movement owed much to the leadership and organisational skills of Bishu Bharan Prasad, a member of the Pachhima Kayasth *jati* who came from the village of Sughar in Saran. Bishu Bharan Prasad had been born into a well-established family: his father held 30 *bighas* of land as an occupancy tenant and sat on the local *chaukidari* panchayat.[18] He was educated to a reasonable standard and became a religious mendicant under the name of Swami Vidyanand (also spelt Bidyanand). Swami Vidyanand was associated with Madan Mohan Malaviya and admired M.K. Gandhi's saintly dedication to social work and political activism. His critics alleged that, when speaking to villagers, he claimed to be Gandhi's disciple; but he denied this charge.[19] Vidyanand may or may not have presented himself as Gandhi's *chela*, but he certainly had been impressed by Gandhi's impact on the people and politics of Champaran in 1917-18.[20] And like Gandhi, Vidyanand combined traditional religious appeal with an ability to publicise his cause and a capacity to organise political protest.

Vidyanand's campaign began in June 1919, when he participated in a meeting held at the village of Narar in Madhubani, the northernmost subdivision of Darbhanga, and talked about the rights of cultivators and the need for village schools. The meeting extended over four days from 26 June and provided opportunity for the airing of a number of grievances.[21]

Some weeks later, on 31 July the 'inhabitants of Narar' addressed a petition to the Lieutenant-Governor of Bihar and Orissa complaining that their landlord was denying them their customary rights to the fruits and timber of the trees on their holdings; that they were being required to pay a mutation fee when their holdings changed hands; that the landlord had unjustly resumed some of their lands; that they were being forced to supply, without remuneration, labourers, ploughs and carts for the cultivation of this land; that the 'well-to-do people of the village' who had refused to supply labour and utensils were being harassed by the institution of false criminal and civil cases; that customary grazing rights were being denied them because former grazing lands were being settled for cultivation; and that 'even in these days of fearful scarcity' the *amlas* obliged the vendors of oil and ghee to give them a free supply of these commodities.[22]

This petition began a long series. The petitions varied in detail, but usually featured complaints relating to the tenants' rights in trees, the disappearance of grazing lands, the levying of mutation fees, the interference by the landlord with occupancy rights, and the exactions and oppressions of *amlas*.[23] As the year progressed Vidyanand extended his field of operations. In mid-August he took part in the framing of a petition on behalf of the inhabitants of Narar and seventeen other villages in the Madhubani subdivision. Some six weeks later, on 2 October 1919, his associate, Anirudh Singh, presided over a meeting attended by about 5,000 'lower and suppressed class tentants', on whose behalf he sent a telegram to the Lieutenant-Governor, urging the establishment of a commission of enquiry.[24] The grievances of the tenants, one official of the Darbhanga Raj later commented, 'took shape when Bidyanand [sic] came on the scenes' and it was merely chance that he started his movement in the north of Darbhanga. If Vidyanand had 'gone elsewhere to commence with...the results would have been the same'.[25]

Throughout the final months of 1919 Vidyanand continued his activities in Darbhanga and also made forays out of the district. In November he went to Supaul subdivision in north Bhagalpur intending to address a meeting, but the officials of the Darbhanga Raj, in collusion with the local representatives of the British administration, deterred him from doing so.[26] In early December he travelled to Patna in a fruitless attempt to gain the support of the nationalist intelligentsia. Later in December he visited the Sonbarsa area, on the banks of the Ganges in north Bhagalpur, and enquired into the grievances of the local peasants.[27] Encouraged by the favourable reaction to his tours and meetings Vidyanand planned to institutionalise peasant activism through the creation of an extensive organisation with branches in every village. This project did not come to fruition, but he managed to establish an agitational machine which employed activists at the rate of eight annas a day to tour from village to village.[28]

Hoping to gain the support of the Indian National Congress Vidyanand journeyed, with 200 peasant delegates, to the annual Congress session held at Amritsar in December 1919. But the other participants showed little interest in his campaign and he returned to north Bihar.[29] He continued working in Madhubani but also visited other areas. In February he toured in the Supaul subdivision of Bhagalpur. On 5 February a meeting of between 15,000 and 20,000 people from the Supaul area demanded that in Permanent Settlement areas rents should be immune from increase; that common grazing lands be provided in all villages; that ryots should have an unrestricted right to all the trees standing in their holdings; and that ryots, without having to gain the permission of the zamindar, should be allowed to build houses and dig wells in their occupancy holdings.[30] During March Vidyanand initiated protest in Purnea and in Madhepura, the more southerly of the two subdivisions of north Bhagalpur.[31]

Vidyanand repeatedly made efforts to gain the support of the Bihar branch of the Indian National Congress. At first, aware that the grievances Vidyanand publicised were genuine and impressed by his ability to mobilise extensive support, Congressmen displayed some sympathy, but little active support, for Vidyanand's movement. Congressmen also sympathised with Vidyanand because the Maharaja of Darbhanga, Rameshwar Singh, was a leading opponent of the nationalist intelligentsia and a staunch supporter of the British.[32] But as popular support for Vidyanand grew Congressmen became less willing to be associated with him. At meetings held in August and December in 1919 Vidyanand received rebuffs when he tried to champion the cause of the Darbhanga Raj peasantry. At the Bihar Provincial Congress held in April 1920 Vidyanand moved a resolution calling on the British administration to form a committee of enquiry into the grievances of the Darbhanga Raj tenants. The leading Congressman Rajendra Prasad succeeded in having the motion shelved. In opposing the motion Prasad alleged that Vidyanand was untrustworthy, had falsely claimed to be Gandhi's *chela*, and was a charlatan out to make a career for himself by exploiting the discontents of the peasants.[33] In the following months Vidyanand and the Congress steadily moved apart. The final break came when Vidyanand reversed his adherence to the non-cooperation movement by running in the November 1920 elections. Subsequently Gandhi publicly disassociated himself from Vidyanand, and at least one of Vidyanand's meetings was broken up by non-cooperation workers.[34]

The opposition of Congress to Vidyanand resulted from the conservatism of the nationalist movement in Bihar. Vidyanand's activities in 1919 and 1920 sought to protect the rights and interests of the peasantry but involved no attack on the legitimacy of the zamindari system itself. The aims of the campaign were reformist rather than radical. Despite Vidyanand's moderation the Bihar Congress became greatly concerned. Many Congressmen came from small zamindari backgrounds and the Congress sought to unite all Indians against foreign rule. The Congress therefore disapproved of any movement which heightened landlord-peasant tension and which could possibly develop into an attack on the entire zamindari system.

Throughout 1920 Vidyanand continued his campaign in Darbhanga and Bhagalpur. He also led an agitation against E.C. Danby, the proprietor of the Dholi indigo concern in Muzaffarpur. The leading figure in the Dholi campaign was Saudagar Sau, a Teli and the son of Zahuri Sau, a substantial money-lender who held more than 100 bighas of land. Zahuri Sau was at odds with E.C. Danby over the control of land and because the Dholi factory lent money at less than half the interest which he demanded. This campaign subsequently broadened in a process which was 'all inter-connected through the relationship of the Telis in these villages'.[35] Vidyanand also visited the Gogri *thana* of Monghyr and spoke to the tenants about their grievances over the embankments which the government had built to protect the Bengal and North-Western railway and which obstructed drainage during the flood season.[36]

In his speeches Vidyanand struck a militant note. For example at a meeting in Samastipur town he argued that villagers had a right to use violence in self defence against the oppression of zamindars and their retainers.[37] Some peasants needed little encouragement to engage in direct action. Some violent incidents occurred, and on many occasions peasants cut down trees and used their wood in defiance of the claim of the landlord to exclusive or substantial rights in trees standing on land which he owned.[38] The authorities became concerned over the excitement that Vidyanand generated.[39] Some members of the administration cooperated covertly with the Darbhanga Raj in suppressing the agitations he inspired. Publicly, however, the authorities avoided taking sides in landlord-tenant disputes. They stayed aloof from Vidyanand's movement, and merely attempted to ensure that both parties stayed within the bounds of the law.

In late 1920 Vidyanand ran for election to the Bihar and Orissa Legislative Assembly. The electorate had been expanded under the Montagu-Chelmsford reforms to include the best-established among the occupancy tenants. His campaign succeeded; in electorates in northern Darbhanga and northern Bhagalpur he and three other tenants' representatives won victories.[40]

During 1919 and 1920 Vidyanand attracted extensive support. The petitions framed under his auspices and the meetings over which he presided concentrated on two categories of grievances which were of central importance to most of the rural population. One category of grievances concerned the behaviour of the *amlas* whose characteristic dishonesty and oppressiveness is amply documented.[41]

The other category of grievances concerned the interference, on the part of the management of the Darbhanga Raj, with what the tenants regarded as their rights both in the light of long established custom and under the provisions of the Bengal Tenancy Act of 1885. In the period 1896 to 1907, survey and settlement operations had helped create a new awareness among the tenants of their rights. Moreover, population pressure and the demand for land had multiplied and magnified disputes over the possession of holdings and tempted zamindars to rent out 'waste lands' that had formerly been used for grazing.[42] The demand for land created a market in land tenancies. Rich villagers acquired occupancy rights as an investment and then profited by sub-letting the holdings to sharecroppers and short-term tenants. Landlords benefited from the transfer of tenancies by levying mutation fees both on transfers by sale and transfers by inheritance.[43] The fees were widely resented both because they obstructed the taking over of land by the poor and because they interfered with the investment strategies of the better-off.[44] With the disappearance of large tracts of standing timber, destroyed for building and fuel, wood assumed an unprecedented scarcity value, and disputes over rights in timber multiplied. Cow dung provided an alternative fuel for domestic use, but wood was essential for building and for the proper fulfilment of Hindu funeral rites.[45]

Peasants displayed support for Vidyanand by coming in large numbers to his meetings. Vidyanand attracted 10,000 villagers to a meeting held in Darbhanga on 11 October 1919. Five months later some 15,000 to 20,000 people attended a meeting he presided over in the Supaul subdivision of Bhagalpur.[46] In a region in which communications were very poor, the ability to attract such numbers was impressive. Of course, an individual's ability to attract large numbers is in itself not decisive evidence that he has extensive support. Such is the tedium of life in rural India that large numbers of people will flock to any kind of public event. More convincing proof that

Vidyanand commanded considerable support is supplied by the Darbhanga Police Superintendent's report that at the 11 October meeting peasants donated Rs. 8,000 to help finance the campaign in defence of their rights. 'There is no doubt', commented the Superintendent, 'that this man is following the footsteps of Gandhi and inflaming the minds of the Ryots against the Darbhanga Raj as Gandhi did in Champaran against the planters'.[47] A few days later he reported that the movement was developing rapidly and that Vidyanand's influence over both Hindus and Muslims was 'increasing steadily'.[48]

Further evidence of the extent of the support which Vidyanand commanded may be found in the reports from the managers of the fourteen Darbhanga Raj circles. In March 1920 one account came from the manager of Rohika, a circle situated in Madhubani Subdivision in which well-established Brahman tenants predominated. 'At the end of the year', the manager reported,

> a peasant agitation was started in the circle by a charlatan calling himself Swami Bidyanand, [sic] he had meetings instigating ryots to rebel against landlords and defy their authority, he very soon got a large following as he promised them all their desires, though of course he could not fulfil any of his promises.[49]

In a report from the Padri circle in south-east Darbhanga the manager commented that the local population consisted of 'low caste men such as Gowalas, Koeris, Mussalmans etc. and they are most obstinates.[sic]' Some of these people had been cultivating holdings belonging to the Darbhanga Raj on a sharecropping basis. But 'this year', the manager reported in August 1920, under 'the instigation of a Swami ...who came out in this elake twice, they have changed their minds not to share the produce but to pay rents'. In demanding to pay a cash rental rather than give the landlord a half share of the crop the sharecroppers no doubt hoped to be able to take advantage of the unusually high food-grain prices. The demand also indicated an awareness that, if they continued tilling the land as cash rent payers, by collecting receipts they could establish occupancy rights to the land. Indeed they already claimed such rights, and contended that they had some documentary evidence to support their claims. The Padri manager stressed the 'need for orders as to how to handle this urgent business'.[50]

In addition to being extensive, support for Vidyanand came from a broad spectrum of the social hierarchy. In the Rohika circle, he won support from well-established Brahman tenants. In the petition from Narar village which initiated the movement the petitioners contended that they had 'to supply labourers' to their landlord, a complaint suggesting that the petitioners were rich peasants with tied labour at their command. The petitioners also complained that the 'well-to-do people of the village' who had refused to comply with the wishes of the Darbhanga Raj were being harassed by the institution of false cases. But the Narar petitioners also alleged that the Darbhanga Raj *amlas* insisted on a free supply of oil and ghee 'from those dealing in these commodities'.[51] The producers and suppliers of these commodities were from lower caste groups, namely Yadavs in the case of ghee and Telis in the case of oil. Members of these groups characteristically were middle and poor peasants. In the Dholi agitation, Vidyanand associated himself with a group of Telis whose leader came from a prosperous money-lending background. In the Padri area, Vidyanand drew support from low caste and Muslim sharecroppers.

Swami Vidyanand's campaign strongly challenged the lower level staff of the Darbhanga Raj. The allegations made against members of this group often rang true, and hence they initially had no sympathy for Vidyanand's activities. Nonetheless many of them became covert supporters of Vidyanand. 'The people we should be able to rely on to keep up Raj prestige and influence in the villages' one manager reported, 'have many inducements to sell Raj interests'.[52] The village level staff were paid at rates fixed around 1880, when the price of food was about a third of the price prevailing in 1920. Previously they had increased their income by extracting *abwabs* from the villagers but they could less easily do this now that Vidyanand's movement had encouraged the villagers to defy them. Because of the shaky morale of its lower level staff the Darbhanga Raj was faced at the beginning of 1920, 'with a crisis and a danger never known before'.[53]

The upper level staff of the Darbhanga Raj knew staff morale was poor and acknowledged that many of the complaints made against their subordinates had much justification.[54] Dissidence among the tenantry and discontent among the lower level staff interfered with the collection of rent and thus handicapped the running of extensive estates. Therefore the higher management of the Darbhanga Raj was willing to make concessions to keep both its staff and its tenants reasonably contented. In some instances compromise was essential because the law favoured the tenants. P.T. Onraet, the manager of the Rohika circle, urged the Raj to meet the tenants 'half way', because legally 'the Raj will not be able to back its demands on the grounds of ancient custom'.[55] The imminence of an election to the Legislative Assembly, due in November 1920, also affected the attitude of the Raj administration. This election would be held on an enlarged franchise which would include the best established ryots. In order for 'acceptable' candidates to win office, the head office and circle managers decided at a conference held in January 1920, it would be necessary 'to have the tenants in our hands'.[56] In the event, however, Vidyanand won the votes of the rich peasants.

To protect the interests of the Darbhanga Raj and gain the support of the peasantry the participants in the January conference took five initiatives. They agreed that the village level staff should be paid more, so that they would have less need to exact *abwabs*. They also decided that the mutation fee, currently being realised at the rate of 25 per cent of the purchase price, should be reduced to about 10 per cent; that the Raj should waive some of its claims concerning the use of timber; that tenants should be allowed to build houses on their holdings without having their rent increased; and that the rates being paid for the hiring of labour and of ploughs should be increased.[57] The managers also considered some of the special problems that had arisen in the Raj properties in Purnea and made appropriate concessions.[58]

The administrators of the Darbhanga Raj supplemented conciliation with counter-propaganda. Badrinath Upadhya, the manager of the Rajnager circle, compiled a 52-page pamphlet in which he replied to the charges laid and the grievances raised both in Rajnager circle and elsewhere.[59]

The circle managers sent retainers to keep a close watch on Vidyanand and his associates and to dissuade people from supporting them.[60] At the January conference one circle manager argued that

> We should keep the few influential men in our hands. The tenants are completely in their hands and simply by keeping these few men in our hands we shall practically have the whole tenantry in our hands.[61]

A *tehsildar* of the Alapur circle in northeast Madhubani acted in accordance with this suggestion. Early in 1920 Vidyanand contacted some influential men in the circle and arranged to give a lecture on 26 February. Before the meeting the *tehsildar* engaged in counter-propaganda among the leading members of the locally influential Yadav *jati*. Thanks to these efforts 'a partition was created. The better class of the leading Goalas [i.e. Yadavs] carefully avoided visiting him; and Vidyanand had for his audience only the insignificant low class people.'

The Swami, the *tehsildar* reported, left Alapur disappointed, having 'failed to achieve any success.'[62]

The administrators of the Darbhanga Raj also used a variety of coercive means to dissuade people from supporting Vidyanand. At one stage a full-scale programme of repression was planned for the Rohika and Rajnager circles. This programme does not seem to have been implemented, apparently because it conflicted with the conciliatory policy adopted at the January conference.[63] But both before and after the conference individual Raj officials employed coercive methods. In the Supaul division of north Bhagalpur the Raj *amlas*, 'being enraged at the stopping of perquisites', harassed the tenants by refusing to accept their rent payments when they were proffered.[64] By this means the *amlas* exposed the tenants to the danger of being sued for not having paid their rent, and subjected them to the inconvenience of having to keep their rent money on hand. In Purnea a local Raj official decided that two Raj *amlas* who had given evidence unfavourable to the Raj in a criminal case arising from the movement should be dismissed.[65] In the Naredigar circle of the Raj, in the northwest of Bhagalpur, the manager kept a close eye on peasant activists. Late in 1920 he described one of them, a Bengali tenant by the name of Suresh Chunder Laha, as 'a very dangerous person and...the instigator of much evil', and followed this comment with the cryptic phrase 'I am looking after him'.[66] The same official had urged in January 1920 that good tenants be rewarded with concessions, but insisted that

> absolutely no concessions should be made unless and until all other means of gaining over disaffected tenants, if there be such tenants, are exhausted. A good Manager will use his tact and judgement in winning over unruly, turbulent and disloyal men, and he should be allowed the fullest possible latitude in dealing with them in any manner which seems most expedient to himself. He will always be acting in the Raj interests, and he must be permitted to exercise his fullest discretion.[67]

Raj managers also directed coercion against the Swami himself. On 13 July 1919 Vidyanand was menaced by a group of ruffians while he was journeying from one village to another. In another incident a short time later he discovered that men were awaiting him along the roads and had to take to the fields to avoid them. While travelling to a meeting at Madhubani town in October 1919, he was menaced by a large armed mob, and was saved only by the intervention of the local *chaukidars*.[68] On 12 November Vidyanand attempted to hold a meeting at the village of Parsa Madho, near Nirmali town in northwest Bhagalpur. By noon on the day of the meeting some 15,000 tenants had gathered. About forty minutes later a Raj *amla* arrived accompanied by fifty *lathials*. Vidyanand asked the local Sub-Inspector of Police to request them to leave. The Sub-Inspector made this request but the *lathials* replied

> that if the meeting would be held at that spot they would be dismissed from their services and that it was the order of the Sub-Manager Bhaptiahi circle. Hence they would try their best to prevent the holding of the meeting.[69]

In view of the determination of the Raj servants to disrupt proceedings, Vidyanand, on the advice of the Police Sub-Inspector, suspended the meeting.[70]

In theory the police and the administration were committed to assume a neutral attitude to Vidyanand's movement and to administer the law impartially. In reality police and local officials tended to side with the Darbhanga Raj. The police did not effectively protect Vidyanand against harassment and, rather than protect Vidyanand's right to speak, were happy to see his meetings suspended when a breach of the peace appeared likely because of the interference of his opponents. The administration had sympathy for the peasants' grievances, but because of its support for the zamindari system, and particularly for the Maharaja of Darbhanga, the premier zamindar of north Bihar, it did little to express this sympathy.

With the covert assistance of policemen and officials the Darbhanga Raj contained Vidyanand's movement. The Darbhanga Police Superintendent remarked that 'In working against the Raj, the Swami was up against an unlimited purse and as the months passed the attendance at his various meetings became smaller and smaller'.[71] The movement also declined because in 1920 prices were lower and scarcity was less than in 1919, with the result that economic pressure on the poorer peasants decreased. Moreover, after a time the novelty value of Vidyanand's tours and meetings wore off, and people, finding that change did not come as completely or as quickly as at first they had hoped, lost their initial enthusiasm.[72] Vidyanand commanded sufficient support among that small minority of occupancy tenants which had gained the franchise to win election in November 1920. But this victory marked an end rather than a new beginning for his campaign. Vidyanand seems to have been satisfied, at least temporarily, with his electoral victory and to have become absorbed with legislative politics.[73] No doubt also the alternative attractions of the non-cooperation movement drew attention away from his activities.

III

In 1919 and 1920 Swami Vidyanand attracted support from a broad spectrum of the people of north Bihar. Vidyanand did not achieve the complete redress of the peasants' grievances, but he managed to bring them concessions. His movement also had longer-term repercussions.

For example on 20 March 1922, a petition arrived at the head office of the Darbhanga Raj from the Telis of the hamlet of Mohamedpur in the Maksuda *mauza*. The petitioners complained about the dishonesty of the local *amlas*, who, 'quite contrary to custom', had been exacting free supplies of oil from them, and said that though unwilling to supply free oil, they would agree to pay a cash rate, like the Teli ryots in neighbouring localities, for the right to extract oil from the seeds of the linseed and teli plants. They said that they had approached the circle manager with their complaint. In response the circle manager reprimanded them for having, on an earlier occasion, approached the head office of the Raj, demanded 'in insulting terms' that they supply the free oil, and refused to accept their rents, saying that he intended to realise the rents by litigation.[74]

According to the circle manager the Telis, every day 'since the time immemorial' had given small quantities of oil to the *patwari* and to the other village *amlas*, but had stopped doing so in November 1921. The circle manager justified the exaction of the oil by pointing out that the village *amlas* received 'very low pay'. He also commented that this issue had originally been raised in the area 'by the so called Swami Vidyanand and since then from time to time the agitation breaks out as in this instant'. He contended that the Telis should be made to supply the oil lest a

> precedent...be established and if so what is to prevent such attacks from being made on other such established customs. As it is we have before us the pernicious teachings of the Gandhi cult not to pay land revenue and also that the day of swaraj approaches when rents are no longer to be paid.

Though the issue of the oil was in itself only of minor importance, he concluded, the effect of the custom being successfully defied 'will be vast and far reaching for further mischief', and contended that the oil should be collected 'at any cost'.[75] The senior management of the Raj responded by commenting that since the exaction of the oil was an *abwab* the Raj had no legal redress against the Telis. 'Our remedy', one official decided, lies in finding out and stopping the privileges we might have been hitherto allowing them to enjoy as a matter of favour and in putting other tactful pressure forcing them to come to their senses and realise that they should not be recalcitrant and ungrateful to the landlord. [sic][76]

The Chief Manager of the Darbhanga Raj therefore requested the Pandoul manager to find ways of putting 'tactful pressure' on the Teli ryots.[77]

By means of 'tactful pressure', the exact nature of which remains obscure, it seems that the administration of the Darbhanga Raj defused the situation. The course of the Telis' campaign illustrates both that Vidyanand's movement had repercussions, and that the Darbhanga Raj had managed to weather the movement successfully, and still had effective means with which to bring dissident villagers into line. Vidyanand had drawn peasants into an extensive agitation, and had encouraged them to take a militant stance in defence of their interests. These successes helped pave the way for peasant protest in the 1930s. But Vidyanand's movement had been dominated by the more powerful peasants, and had had limited, reformist aims. The movement had achieved some successes, but had done nothing to alter the basic structure of the Darbhanga Raj and the distribution of power and wealth within it.

The most important reason for the ebbing away of Vidyanand's movement was the skilful strategy of the senior management of the Darbhanga Raj. The senior Raj managers set out to win the allegiance of 'the few influential men' who held a leading position among the peasantry.[78] These men and the rest of the peasantry were at odds with the Raj because of the misconduct of the Raj *amlas* and because demographic pressure had heightened tensions over the control and use of the means of agrarian production. The senior Raj managers enacted concessions which mollified the 'few influential men'. Because the rich peasants were profiting from the conditions of scarcity and high prices, it seems probable that they were satisfied with the concessions instituted. The less well established peasants, who were under great pressure, may have been less impressed by the concessions, but they depended on the rich peasants for leadership. In addition, the Darbhanga

Raj effectively supplemented concessions with propaganda and coercion.

In containing Vidyanand's campaign the Darbhanga Raj received the covert assistance of the British administration. By their response to Vidyanand officials revealed their partiality to the zamindars. The administration and its police tended to side with the Darbhanga Raj against the dissident peasantry. The administration had sympathy for the peasants, but was unwilling to do anything substantial to help them. But the administration adopted a public stance of impartiality so as to avoid directing popular discontent against itself.

In coping with Vidyanand's campaign the Darbhanga Raj also benefited from the policy of the Bihar Congress. At first Congress displayed some sympathy for Vidyanand but eventually it disassociated itself from him. Many congressmen came from zamindar backgrounds and had little sympathy for criticism of zamindars and their *amlas*. Moreover, the Congress looked particularly for support to the large numbers of small landlords in Bihar, and sought to unite landlords and peasants against the British.[79] Congress therefore adopted a 'neutral' stance on landlord-peasant disputes. Given the existing distribution of power this neutrality amounted to support of the landlords.

Vidyanand knitted together local discontents into a mass movement but failed to establish an enduring organisation to represent peasant interests. In 1919 and 1920 the organisational framework of the Bihar Congress was limited and insubstantial, but even so it could have been of valuable assistance to Vidyanand. Moreover the Bihar Congress controlled the nationalist media and provided the main means of access to the all-India level of institutional politics. Unlike the United Provinces Congress, which displayed some tolerance of militant peasant protest, the Bihar Congress took a consistently conservative line.

Only in exceptional circumstances did the Bihar Congress favour peasants against their landlords. Congress did display sympathy for the peasants in the anti-indigo planter campaigns which developed in north Bihar from 1917 to 1923. But these campaigns were mainly directed against a small group of European planter-landlords who were identified with the British administration and who, as an alien elite, lacked close ties with the local population. Otherwise, during Vidyanand's movement, and subsequently during the struggle for independence, Bihar congressmen discouraged anti-landlord protest. By doing so they helped protect their own privileged position in north Bihar society and helped maintain an alliance between peasants and small landlords against the colonial state.

CHAPTER 4

THE NON-COOPERATION MOVEMENT, 1920-23

In September 1920 the Indian National Congress launched a civil disobedience campaign against the British administration of India. Under the direction of M.K. Gandhi, the Congress denounced recent British constitutional concessions as inadequate, demanded that India be given swaraj or 'self rule', and undertook to force Britain to grant India freedom by mobilising Indians to refuse to cooperate with alien rule. British rule depended 'on the active collaboration of some Indians and the acquiescence of the rest',[1] and if Indian co-operation ceased then the Indian Empire would collapse like a house of cards.

The programme of non-cooperation was designed to ensure this collapse through the boycott of the forthcoming elections to the provincial legislature, the gradual boycott of government schools, colleges and courts, the abandonment of titles, the resignation of honorary offices, the giving up of government jobs, and the boycott of foreign goods. Later, the programme also called for the boycott of liquor producers and sellers, in order to reform society and to pressure provincial governments by reducing their income from the collection of excise. The movement would culminate in active civil disobedience: the refusal to pay cesses, taxes and revenue and complete non-cooperation with the authorities in order to bring about administrative paralysis.

In India in 1920-23 non-cooperation 'became a chameleon campaign, taking colour from its surroundings as it was shaped in each locality.'[2] In north Bihar nationalist agitation received impetus from the Khilafat movement, interacted with anti-indigo protest, and in addition provided a vehicle for the expression of a variety of discontents. Members of the village elite took the lead in protest, but middle and poor peasants and townsfolk also actively participated. Non-cooperation did not achieve its declared object of forcing the British to allow Indians to govern themselves, but in north Bihar it gave the apparatus of British rule a severe shaking. This chapter examines the development of the Bihar Congress and of the nationalist movement up until 1920, describes non-cooperation in north Bihar, and concludes with an assessment of the campaign.

I

In 1920, the Bihar branch of the Indian National Congress was a new actor on the political stage. Twenty years earlier the editor of the *Behar Times* had likened Bihar, in terms of the energy displayed in public life, to 'a pool of stagnant water.'[3] Yet even in 1900 new eddies were beginning to swirl in Bihar politics.

Throughout much of the nineteenth century the imperial state had been a distant, autocratic entity which played a limited part in the lives of most north Biharis.[4] But from the last decades of the century this sense of distance began to lessen. To improve the political and financial stability of their far-flung Empire the British made several constitutional concessions. Set in train in 1882, 1909 and 1919, these concessions progressively increased the opportunities for some members of Indian society to participate in institutions of representative government, particularly in the sphere of local government. Constitutional advance and devolution of government power directly affected only a small minority of the population, but had wider repercussions because this minority commanded considerable wealth and influence. Through the extension of representative institutions the state linked the politics of the locality and the region into a wider imperial structure and itself became a more obtrusive factor in local politics.[5]

The constitutional concessions were less rapid and less substantial than many had hoped, and thus their implementation created as much animosity as it won support. And because of the structure of imperial control in north Bihar, and particularly because of the zamindari system, government had few resources at its disposal after it had covered the costs of revenue collection and of seeing 'that the districts remained quiet'.[6] Hence it could spend little on social and administrative services which might have reaped a valuable harvest of support. Through intervention in local political arenas the imperial state created expectations which, because of its pattern of rule, it did not have the capacity to fulfil. More than they had in the nineteenth century, people came to look at the state as a resource and to blame it for many of their problems.

The development of a new political awareness in Bihar accelerated when in 1912, as part of a general re-organisation of the Bengal Presidency, Bihar and Orissa were formed into a new province, with the sprawling riverside town of Patna as its capital.[7] The formation of the province of Bihar and Orissa made little or no impact on the lives of the vast majority of its inhabitants, most of whom had no clear notion of the designation or extent of the administrative unit within which they now resided.[8] But for a tiny, high caste, middle class and educated elite the creation of the new province brought opportunities both for private professional advancement and for public social and political activity. Administrative separation meant that henceforth Biharis would suffer less from the competition of skilled and educated Bengalis, who for generations had been radiating from Calcutta in search of careers. And the sleepy town of Patna, by becoming the locale for a new hospital, a new university, a new high court, and a large and impressive secretariat to house the provincial administration, began to reverse the strong attraction that had previously drawn young, middle-class Biharis off to distant cities, and particularly Calcutta, in search of education, jobs and advancement.[9]

The Patna-based Bihar Provincial Congress had been inactive since its founding in 1907 but began a new lease of life in 1912. At this time most of its members were small zamindars and/or lawyers and landlords and lawyers dominated its leadership. (Table 4.1). In 1917 the Bihar and Orissa Chief Secretary commented disparagingly that 'The Congress here is a most hollow business. The whole thing is run by half a dozen wire-pullers and the audience consists chiefly of the junior bar.'[10]

But increasingly from around 1919 the membership of the organisation broadened. Merchants and businessmen,

TABLE 4.1

Occupations of Bihar delegates to the Allahabad Congress Session, 1910

Occupation(s)	Number of Delegates
Zamindar	12
Landholder*	3
Zamindar and Lawyer	6
Banker and Zamindar	2
Lawyer	14
Member, Servants of India Society¶	1
Not Known	1
Total number of delegates:	39

Source: Datta, *Freedom Movement in Bihar*, 1, Appendix VII.

* The term 'landholder' is generally used as a synonym for a **tenant** or to refer to a lessee of proprietory rights. In this instance it probably refers to lessees.

¶ The Servants of India Society was a charitable organisation whose members devoted their lives to good works.

---

and particularly those of the Marwari community, began to participate, in part because of the rise to prominence of that ascetic bania, M.K. Gandhi.[11] And of special importance in overwhelmingly rural north Bihar, rich peasants and a large number of small landlords gravitated towards the Congress. Members of the village elite wishing to expand upon their local influence found themselves in natural alliance with politically aspiring urban professionals. Their mutual opponents were the great landlords and the established, conservative professionals who, supported by the administration, dominated provincial-level social and political life and controlled the organs of local government, namely the municipalities and district boards.[12]

Because only members of the landed interest could afford to educate their sons to a professional level, caste and kinship ties knitted together the village elite and urban professional alliance. For example Rajendra Prasad, who graduated in law from Calcutta before returning to Bihar in 1912, was the son of a small landlord from Saran.[13] Mutual interest further strengthened the alliance, since urban professionals supplied the legal, educational and other services required by the village elite. The extent of mutual interest between urban professionals and members of the village elite was increased, moreover, by the Montagu-Chelmsford constitutional reforms. These reforms, which were announced in April 1918, extended the electorate to give the rural and urban middle classes substantial say in future elections and ensured them control over local government.[14]

Nationalist Biharis, responding to initiatives that originated in other provinces, supported the Indian Home Rule Movement between 1915 and 1918 and participated in the Rowlatt Satyagraha of 1919.[15] In Bihar before 1920 the nationalist movement received support from only a limited section of society, and this was reflected in the urban centred, small-scale, and peaceful character of Congress protest. But from 1920 agitation associated with the nationalist movement developed throughout the countryside, occurred on an unprecedented scale, and included many violent incidents. The transition point in the character of nationalist agitation in Bihar came in September 1920 when at the special session in Calcutta, the Indian National Congress decided, with the crucial vote being strongly supported by the Bihar delegates, to make non-cooperation its official policy. Already, the previous month, a meeting of the Bihar Congress at Bhagalpur town had passed a resolution in favour of Gandhi's suggested non-cooperation programme.[16]

The decision of the Indian National Congress and of its Bihar branch to embark on non-cooperation resulted partially from the impetus supplied by the Muslim-based Khilafat movement. After the victories of Britain and her allies in Western Asia during the final years of the First World War, many Indian Muslims joined the Khilafat campaign to protest against the unsympathetic British treatment of the Khalifah, the ruler of Turkey and the spiritual head of Islam. The leaders of the Khilafat campaign aligned themselves with the nationalist movement in order to challenge the British more effectively.[17] In north Bihar the Muslims comprised 16 per cent of the population, and because many of them were settled in urban areas, because of their sense of special identity, which existed despite the stratification of their community, and because of their custom of weekly congregational worship, they could be readily mobilised over issues of religious importance and thus were a potent political force.

The decision to support non-cooperation, and in particular the decision to boycott the elections to the reformed legislatures, also resulted from a realisation on the part of many Congressmen, many of whom were of the smaller fry in Bihar political life, that they did not stand a good chance in the elections against the great landowners and the established, influential, non-nationalist members of the intelligentsia.[18] Partly too, the decision reflected the new militance of the Bihar Congress because of the influx into its membership of rich peasants. Many peasant-Congressmen had been drawn into Congress activity via the *kisan sabhas* or peasant associations. These associations were Congress front organisations which had been established in 1919 in order to mediate in landlord-tenant disputes and to widen the basis of support for the Rowlatt Satyagraha.[19] Rajendra Prasad comments that the Congress meeting at Bhagalpur town in August 1920 was the first Bihar Congress conference 'where delegates...were drawn largely from outside the professional classes'.[20] The peasant delegates at the Bhagalpur Congress secured the passing of the non-cooperation resolution by voting as a block in its favour.

It may also be suggested that some Congress leaders favoured non-cooperation because it promised to provide an alternative attraction to Swami Vidyanand's movement, which conflicted with the efforts of the Bihar Congress to promote social harmony and a united landlord-peasant front against British rule. This consideration became particularly important when Vidyanand, after at first supporting non-cooperation, changed his mind and ran in the November 1920 elections. By calling for an electoral boycott in the name of the wider social and national interest the Bihar Congress could attempt to represent Vidyanand as an adventurer out for his own ends.

II

In Bihar non-cooperation began with efforts to dissuade voters from participation in the elections held in November under the terms of the Montagu-Chelmsford reforms. This campaign had considerable success though the low turnout may also have resulted from the novelty of the extended franchise.[21] (Table 4.2).

TABLE 4.2

Electoral Turnout in 1920 Bihar Legislative Assembly Elections

Classification of Voters	Percentage which voted
Electors of Tirhut Division	13
Urban Hindus	27.3
Rural Hindus	41.8
Urban Muslims	12.1
Rural Muslims	28.2

Source: Brown, *Gandhi's Rise to Power*, p.288.

The electorate in 1920 comprised less than 2 per cent of the adult male population.[22] Other than persuading a section of this tiny electorate not to vote, non-cooperation workers achieved little during the final months of 1920. In mid-December the provincial government told the Government of India that the main impact of the movement had been in urban areas, and particularly among students, and that the countryside had remained quiet. But during December the movement received new impetus. In the first half of the month Gandhi made a brief tour of Bihar, attracting substantial interest and helping to raise funds. Then in late December the Indian National Congress assembled in session at Nagpur in western India.[23]

The Nagpur Congress reaffirmed, more positively, the non-cooperation programme. And to make the Congress a more effective instrument of mass politics it established a Working Committee to provide continuing executive leadership, reorganised the constituent units of the Indian National Congress along linguistic lines, extended Congress organisation to the sub-district level, and lowered the membership subscription.[24]

Spurred on by Gandhi's tour and by the Nagpur Congress, non-cooperation achieved considerable success in north Bihar during 1921. In addition to gaining support in the towns, where professional people, students and the urban poor were suffering from high prices and scarcity, the movement rallied support among a broad spectrum of society in many parts of the countryside. Because the privileged minority eligible to protest by resignation lacked sympathy for mass protest and stood to lose materially, only a meagre response came to the call for the resignation of titles, honorary positions and posts as lawyers, teachers and government servants. But the boycott of foreign cloth received a stronger response, as did the call to withdraw from government schools, particularly once alternative 'national' institutions had been set up. Because of pervasive dissatisfaction with the legal system, moreover, the boycott of government courts achieved great success, and in less serious disputes many people accepted the jurisdiction of Congress-organised 'national' *panchayats*.[25] Sometimes these *panchayats*, one official reported, contained 'men of the lowest castes, such as Doms and Chamars.'[26]

Non-cooperation also exhibited 'the curious appearance of a temperance movement, not planned or anticipated by Gandhi or Congress, though both encouraged it once it had caught on.' The prohibition campaign attained social respectability because of the disdain with which Muslims and higher caste Hindus regarded the consumption of alcohol and drugs. In Bihar prohibition workers picketed liquor stores, preached against the consumption of alcohol and other drugs, and sometimes engaged in the intimidation and social ostracism of liquor vendors and customers. Because the provincial government placed substantial reliance on its income from excise duties the prohibition campaign put it under serious pressure. In the financial year 1921-22 in Bihar and Orissa the campaign succeeded in decreasing the government's excise income, which usually amounted to around Rs.13,000,000, by Rs.1,000,000.[27]

Non-cooperation also drew on the social tension and racial feeling that had crystallised during the anti-indigo movement. Because of the ethnic identity between European planters and British officials, and because they supported each other politically, popular antagonism to the planters spilled over into hostility to British district officials. In July 1921 the Tirhut Commissioner commented that 'the *izzat* (prestige) of Europeans is nothing like it was and is diminishing.'[28] The interest created by Vidyanand's campaign also contributed to non-cooperation — in the Madhubani subdivision in mid-1921 peasants who had previously engaged in protest against the Darbhanga Raj became enthusiastic supporters of the movement.[29]

Non-cooperation also provided an opportunity for the poor to express discontent with the price-supply situation. In January and February 1921 commodity and food-grain prices reached high levels and goods were in short supply. While this situation prevailed many incidents of market looting occurred. Four incidents occurred in both Purnea and north Bhagalpur, two in north Monghyr, six in Darbhanga and nineteen in Muzaffarpur. At Saraya in Muzaffarpur a man arrived at the bazaar on horseback and, proclaiming himself as Gandhi's disciple, demanded that prices be lowered. The merchants disagreed; they and members of the crowd quarrelled and a riot ensued.

In Purnea a young man appeared at a market and announced that cloth should be sold at eight *cubits* for one rupee, rice at nine *seers* for one rupee and fish at one *seer* for two annas. A clash developed between the merchants and the public and eight merchants had goods stolen from their stalls. The details of each market-looting incident varied, but they followed a broadly similar pattern. Those involved mostly came from the middle and lower reaches of north Bihar society. The incidents began when someone created a disturbance in a crowded bazaar by demanding, usually in the name of Gandhi and/or swaraj, that prices be lowered.[30]

It is not clear how far non-cooperation activists were involved in the initiation of market-looting incidents. Macrae, the Deputy Inspector-General of Police, thought that Congress workers held direct responsibility. His only evidence to support this conclusion was that after some of the incidents non-cooperators had arrived at the markets and attempted to act as mediators between the merchants and their attackers, seeking to reach some compromise which would make it unnecessary to call in the police and institute legal proceedings. Macrae thought that the non-cooperators had involved themselves 'with a view to concealing evidence.'[31] Forrest, the Tirhut Commissioner, contended that the non-cooperators had initiated the call for lower prices but now had second thoughts, after the lootings and disturbances, about the value of this tactic.[32]

These interpretations were unduly Machiavellian. The Bihar Congress did not want to create divisions within the Indian community and in particular did not wish to encourage disrespect for private property. It seems unlikely that local Congress leaders initiated market looting incidents, though some of their rank and file supporters may have done so.[33] Market looting in early 1921 resulted mainly from an extremely adverse price-supply situation, which had a disastrous impact upon the poor. After the price-supply situation improved from late February, market looting ceased.[34]

Nevertheless, market looting also reflected the messianic expectations that the initiation of non-cooperation had aroused in north Bihar. These expectations focussed on Gandhi, who by early 1921 had acquired a semi-divine status. In Saran during February 1921 the story spread that the God Jaganath had begun working with Gandhi and had made it known that anyone worshipping Gandhi was thus worshipping Jaganath himself.[35] Surely it is no accident that the market looting incidents occurred only a few weeks after Gandhi had toured Bihar.

The messianic expectations prevalent in north Bihar expressed themselves in other ways. In March 1921 Police Superintendent McNamara visited Dhanaha *thana* in the west of Champaran to investigate rumours that large crowds had been gathering. The local villagers told

McNamara that crowds had arrived from over the border with the United Provinces to the south-west, beating drums and shouting 'Gandhiji ki jai'. The United Provinces villagers told the local people that Gandhi, a Brahman, a cow and an Englishman had been put into a fire together, and that the Englishman had been burnt while the others escaped harm. They instructed the Dhanaha people to visit five other villages, shouting 'Gandhiji ki jai', and pass this story on; if they failed to do so their crime would be as serious as if they had killed five cows. This movement spread outwards from its point of origin in an indigo concern on the Gorakpur-Champaran border. From Dhanaha it moved on to the north-west and east and eventually died out.[36] The strength of the messianic sentiment typified in the Dhanaha movement encouraged one British official to conclude that 'there is no *economic* grievance behind all this agitation. It has been based on sentiment throughout.'[37]

The attitude of defiance towards British authority reflected in the development of messianic expectations also expressed itself in attacks on the police. In north Bihar the local police and *chaukidars* were the nearest and most visible representatives of state authority. By oppressive behaviour, moreover, the police had made themselves prime targets for defiance and aggression. On 19 February 1921, a force of six policemen and twenty *chaukidars* began investigating a case in the Kateya area in Saran. In Kateya and the neighbouring police circles thirty-five non-cooperation *panchayats* with a total of 219 members had been formed and 268 volunteers had been appointed. By these means the non-cooperation activists had brought thirty-three villages under their 'jurisdiction'. The police party had been ordered to investigate allegations that a non-cooperation *panchayat* had treated a Koeri woman unjustly and cruelly. While the police were interviewing witnesses a large group of men arrived armed with sticks, lathis and spears and shouting 'Gandhi ki jai'. The men ordered the policemen and *chaukidars* to kneel down and by shouting 'Gandhi ki jai' proclaim their acceptance of swaraj. When the members of the police party refused the men showered them with clods of earth and attacked them with lathis, forcing them to retreat. The sub-inspector in charge reported that the attacking force was 'about 2,000 in number' and included people from nineteen different villages. He listed thirty-two people as definitely having been among the rioters, and this list, which included names which are characteristically Brahman, Rajput, Koeri, Yadav and low status Muslim, indicates that they came from a wide social spectrum.[38]

Non-cooperation also encouraged villagers elsewhere in north Bihar to interfere with police operations. In June in the Bagaha *thana* in Champaran the police reported that serious crimes were not being reported.[39] Also in June the Bhagalpur Commissioner reported that in Purnea police officers were finding it hard to get accommodation while on tour. There had been little violence against the police, and the people were displaying an attitude of 'cold avoidance' rather than 'defiance'. They were also delaying rent payments, hoping that if swaraj came they would have less or even no rent to pay. The Commissioner remarked that the people were too shrewd 'to fully believe' either in the imminence of swaraj or that their rent burden might be lowered, but the belief was 'firm that under Gandhi Raj the necessaries of life would be much cheaper.'[40]

The arousal of messianic expectations and the trend towards violence worried the leaders of Congress, not least perhaps because people from the lower castes displayed particular aggressiveness.[41] By the early months of 1921 non-cooperation had managed to rally considerable mass support, but this support had often expressed itself in a manner inconsistent with the original aims of the campaign. The Congress leadership was uncertain about what to do next. There was no political mileage left in further calls for renunciation of honours, resignation from professional and government posts, and boycott of courts and other government institutions. The next step in the programme involved the initiation of massive civil resistance and the setting up of alternative government institutions. But the level of excitement and the tendency to violence indicated that as yet the movement was not sufficiently disciplined and organised to do this without risking the initiation of extensive disorder.

The Congress leadership temporised. On 31 March 1921 the All-India Congress Committee, the 'parliament of the Congress which had been strengthened in the general party reorganisation at the Nagpur meeting in December

1920, decided that henceforth the emphasis of non-cooperation would be on the production and use of swadeshi (i.e. 'Indian made') products and particularly on the production of cloth by means of the *charkha* (hand operated spinning wheel).[42]

This emphasis on spinning and on the production and consumption of swadeshi goods failed to capture the imagination of the people of north Bihar. Because of this, and because of police repression and the emergence of differences of opinion between the Congress and the Khilafat leaders the non-cooperation movement experienced a temporary lull during July and August of 1921. But the movement revived from September, and moved towards its high point in December 1921 and January 1922. At the All-India level the decisive development came in September when the British arrested the Ali brothers, the leading spirits of the Khilafat movement, for having called upon Indian troops to mutiny. In reaction to their arrest a wave of protest swept through India. The administration responded with further arrests, inspiring yet more protest. Gandhi heightened the excitement by publicly repeating the seditious words that had led to the arrest of the Ali brothers.[43]

In north Bihar the movement achieved its greatest strength in the Tirhut division where it interacted with anti-planter protest. The administration reported that the division 'was greatly disturbed' for the three or four months from October 1921 onwards.

> Defiance of authority was common... Europeans were frequently assaulted and insulted and Government servants were subjected to pressure of every kind to induce them to resign their posts in pursuance of the policy, for propagating which in its extremest form the Ali brothers were arrested... Speeches were delivered by irresponsible agitators calling for more volunteers ready to bear down by weight of numbers, and in complete disregard of casualties, the resistance which Government officers would be sure to put up against an attempt to stop public business. The imminence of civil disobedience was proclaimed and the announcement made that Mahatma Gandhi was about to wage war against the Government.[44]

The most dramatic incident in which activists brought pressure to bear on the administration occurred in late December 1921 when 200 men invaded the Sonbarsa *thana* on the northern frontier of Muzaffarpur. Apparently they had been inspired by the announcement of the All-India Congress Committee on 4 November that non-cooperation had reached a stage at which its climactic phase of full civil disobedience could be undertaken in selected and carefully prepared areas.[45] After invading the police station premises the non-cooperators called on the police to relinquish control and told them that 'they should leave Government service, as by remaining Hindus are eating cow flesh and Muhammadans are eating pig flesh'.[46] The police responded by arresting seven of the leaders of the demonstration. The remaining activists 'hung about from 4 o'clock till 11 at night' before finally dispersing. The District Police Superintendent commented that the demonstration had been made by 'a mob of high caste men', and said that this boded ill for the future.[47]

The non-cooperation campaign culminated in December 1921 and January 1922. On 16 January 1922 the Purnea Police Superintendent reported on incidents in which agrarian discontents were mixed in with nationalist fervour:

> Almost throughout the district there are rumours that Swaraj has been or very shortly will be obtained and this has resulted in certain specific outbreaks of lawlessness. In Rupauli P[olice] S[tation] the Sub-Inspector and police were openly defied by one of the parties in a land dispute. The party assembled in great numbers, forced the Sub-Inspector and the few police with him to leave the spot and in disregard of his warnings proceeded riotously to loot away the disputed crops with shouts of 'Mahatma Gandhi ki jai'. In Forbesganj P[olice] S[tation] some two or three hundred people attacked and demolished a pound at Dhanaha on 8.1.22...[and] raised the Swaraj flag over the ruins.[48]

In the Araria *thana* in Purnea on 5 February 1922 three policemen and several *chaukidars* arrested three picketers who allegedly had assaulted and robbed a liquor shop customer. While taking the prisoners to the Araria police station the police party was 'attacked by a large mob of a thousand people shouting the usual Non-Cooperation cries.' The *chaukidars* fled and the crowd surrounded the three regular policemen, inflicted slight injuries on them, and forced them to relinquish their prisoners.[49]

On the same day at Chauri Chaura in Gorakpur in the United Provinces, members of a non-cooperation procession massacred a group of policemen.[50] Gandhi and the All-India Congress Committee reacted to the massacre by calling non-cooperation off, on the grounds that if it continued extensive violence would result. The Chauri Chaura massacre provided an occasion for rather than the cause of the decision to suspend non-cooperation. Outbreaks of violence were merely a part of extensive popular turmoil over which by late 1921 Gandhi, the All-India Congress Committee and the provincial branches of the Congress party had very little control. Especially in the United Provinces and on the Malabar coast in south India, this turmoil challenged the social order as much as or more than the apparatus of imperial rule.[51] The Congress wanted to force the British out of India, but in doing so did not wish to demolish the existing social order.

The suspension of non-cooperation and heavy police repression brought protest to an end. But because the All-India Congress Committee sanctioned the continuation of swadeshi and prohibition propaganda and because the Bihar Congress held only tenuous control over many of its supporters the campaign took some time to grind to a halt. In the weeks after the suspension of non-cooperation several clashes developed between policemen and non-cooperation activists. In Darbhanga during March non-cooperators decided to ridicule drunken persons by tying them up. When some policemen tried to intervene, the non-cooperators tied them up and marched them into Darbhanga town.[52] On 8 April at a fair being held at Sitamarhi town in northern Muzaffarpur a constable quarrelled with a group of picketers of whom three attacked him with lathis. Some other policemen arrived, arrested the constable's assailants and took them off to a temporary *thana* that had been set up nearby. A crowd of 3,000 collected and confronted the police. Despite the arrival of further reinforcements the police could not restrain the crowd, members of which began throwing bricks and bal fruits. The police retreated and their three prisoners

escaped.[53] These incidents suggest that the decision to
suspend non-cooperation so as to avert violence and disorder had been made just in time.

III

In north Bihar in 1920-22 non-cooperation received
considerable support. Small landlords and rich peasants
took the lead in protest. It was 'a mob of high caste men'
which invaded the Sonbarsa *thana* in the north of
Muzaffarpur. Rajendra Prasad comments that in this area
Thakur Nawab Singh played a leading part. Singh had
'joined the non-cooperation movement under the Mahatma's
influence...with his sons, nephews and grandsons. A
prominent man in Sitamarhi subdivision, he took over the
direction of the movement there'.[54] In getting non-
cooperation under way the members of the village elite
rallied support from among their clients and retainers
within village society. And once agitation began middle
and poor peasants joined in, in an effort to advance their
interests and express their discontents. In the Kateya
thana in Saran in February 1921 Koeris, Yadavs and low
caste Muslims joined Brahmans and Rajputs in an attack
on the police, and those involved in the market looting
associated with non-cooperation came from the lower
reaches of north Bihar society. The non-elite participants
often lacked a sophisticated understanding of the nature
and aims of the movement, but their involvement added
greatly to the extent and weight of its impact.

In part support for non-cooperation came from small
landlords and rich peasants who wished to assert themselves against the allies of the British administration,
namely the great landlords and the indigo planters. The
movement perhaps also represented a successful attempt
by the village elite to dissipate popular dissidence – which
might threaten its own position – by directing antagonism
against the imperial state. More generally non-cooperation
provided a vehicle for the expression of widespread discontents, such as hostility to the police and anxiety over
the price-supply situation.

Non-cooperation challenged British rule over north Bihar but failed to ensure the defection of the key collaborators within the British administration, namely Indian officials, lawyers and policemen. The Bihar Congress provided the impetus for the movement, but eventually began to lose control over many of those who rallied to its support. In the absence of an alternative leadership and ideology to promote radical initiatives, the movement threatened to disintegrate into violence and disorder.

The Bihar Congress learnt from non-cooperation that it could rally mass support to put pressure on the British. But the tendency of the movement to drift out of control and its ultimate failure impressed Congressmen with the need to keep careful command over mass protest and further encouraged them to see it as a tactical alternative rather than as a substitute for constitutional agitation.

Before its eventual breakdown non-cooperation created considerable anxiety among British officials. During 1921, the year when anti-planter and non-cooperation agitation culminated, British officials discussed whether an extensive uprising was imminent.[55] They commented that north Bihar's population included 'many turbulent elements' and worried because north Bihar was 'cut off from the rest of the Province by the broad stream of the Ganges.'[56] The region contained 'a considerable European community', many members of which lived 'in lonely and isolated positions.'[57] If racial hostility became acute their position would be precarious. In theory the European population contributed to its own protection because its menfolk were organised into the Bihar Light Horse, an auxiliary body of some 120 mounted riflemen. But this unit was likely to be of limited use in a widespread rising because of the 'necessity of its members to stay close to their properties and families in order to protect them.'[58]

In December 1921 the provincial administration published a notification under the Criminal Law Amendment Act which allowed it to restrict the holding of public meetings.[59] And during 1921-22 it deployed an extra company of military policemen in the Tirhut division to reinforce the squadron of mounted military police stationed there; requisitioned the temporary services of a squadron of cavalry from the Eastern Command of the Indian Army; and posted a British infantry company at Muzaffarpur town.[60]

The implementation of these measures indicates that in north Bihar non-cooperation strongly challenged the stability of British rule. During the movement the British found themselves in a delicate position. Official policy aimed at making the Montagu-Chelmsford reforms work, and hence British officials had to tread carefully. Progressive opinion in Britain had to be placated, and the moderates of Indian politics had to be kept in sympathy with the regime. Law and order had to be preserved but undue repression, as the aftermath of the Amritsar massacre had shown, would create a politically costly backlash. In addition, the administration had to appear as an impartial arbiter.

In north Bihar the attempt to project an image of impartiality failed because of the favouritism the administration displayed towards the planters and the zamindars, whom it regarded as essential political allies. Unfortunately for the British, neither zamindars nor planters justified this special consideration. The great zamindars were passive rather than active supporters of the regime, and many small zamindars took part in non-cooperation. The planters strongly supported British rule, but their oppressiveness created grave problems. Indeed, the British found non-cooperation was particularly difficult to contain because of the repercussions of anti-planter protest. Antagonism to European planters easily translated itself into general anti-British and anti-administration feeling. Non-cooperation gathered greatest strength in the Tirhut division, the area where the anti-planter movement was strongest. In north Bihar in the early 1920s, the racial prejudices and colonial attitudes of British planters and officials were mirrored back at them in anti-colonial feeling.

The difficulties faced by the imperial state were increased because of the deficiencies of its police force. The police were trained merely to handle routine police work rather than to cope with the challenge of extensive civil disobedience involving large numbers of people who otherwise were law abiding citizens. Because of their corruption and arrogance the police lacked popular sympathy and support.[61] And because they were few in number and poorly equipped they found it difficult to handle large and hostile crowds.

The inadequacies of the police resulted in part from the financial weakness of Bihar and Orissa. In 1922 the police force was severely undermanned even though, since the foundation of the province in 1912, its share of the budget had increased by 50 per cent. The administration considered that no further increases could be made. The provincial finances were in a straitened condition, and the spending of more funds on the much criticised police force would be unacceptable to the more representative legislature which had been elected under the Montagu-Chelmsford reforms.[62]

The Bihar and Orissa administration could not even afford to pay its police constables a wage above that earned by ordinary labourers. In early 1921 an extensive agitation among the constabulary over their low pay disrupted police work over a wide area.[63] Nor could the administration afford to meet the extra expenses associated with the policing of the non-cooperation movement. In May 1921 the administration reported to the Government of India Army Department that it could not possibly maintain

> a force sufficient to cope unaided with the disturbances which may result from...Non-Co-operation... It would be unreasonable to plan the permanent arrangements for maintaining law and order on the assumption that the...movement is to go on indefinitely.[64]

The Bihar and Orissa administration found this problem of finance impossible to resolve. Under the Montagu-Chelmsford reforms the provinces had been given financial autonomy, and hence could solicit only limited help from the Government of India. Nor did the administration see any way of increasing its income from within the province itself. Land was the main source of wealth and because of the structure of agrarian relations underlying the framework of imperial rule most of the agrarian surplus was absorbed by the landed interest, and particularly by the zamindars. Only a small share went to the state. Because of its financial difficulties, the provincial administration maintained order on a shoe-string. In 1920-22 the administration displayed weaknesses in its capacity to handle unrest. In subsequent nationalist mass movements these weaknesses again would be revealed.

CHAPTER 5

THE CIVIL DISOBEDIENCE MOVEMENT, 1930-34

In March 1930, in obedience to the Working Committee of the Indian National Congress, the Bihar Congress initiated mass civil disobedience in protest against Britain's failure to grant Indians substantial advances towards self-government and independence. In the following months thousands of Biharis went defiantly to jail, tens of thousands participated in a variety of protest actions, and hundreds of thousands viewed nationalist agitation sympathetically and responded negatively to police and administrative repression.

Civil disobedience in north Bihar began slowly with agitation against the salt laws, but gained momentum with campaigns in favour of swadeshi and prohibition and against the *chaukidari* system. These campaigns depended for their effectiveness on the use by Congress activists of a limited amount of violence against people and property. The movement inspired great interest and excitement through a series of disturbances at Bihpur, an important rail junction in north Bhagalpur, during the middle months of 1930. However from late 1930 the movement had begun to decline.

The British maintained their position against the challenge of civil disobedience. But the movement greatly impeded normal administrative procedures, strained the jail system, made significant inroads into government excise earnings through agitation in favour of prohibition, and shook the foundations of British rule through the attack on the *chaukidari* system.

This chapter explores the context within which civil disobedience developed, discusses the use of 'limited violence', examines the course of events up to January 1931, focussing especially on the Bihpur disturbances, and surveys the movement in decline. The chapter concludes with an assessment of the movement's significance and impact.

I

In its aims, organisation and methods, civil disobedience was broadly similar to non-cooperation in 1920-22, but there were also important differences between the two movements. The Congress which joined battle with the British in the early 1930s was better organised and more deeply entrenched than that which had initiated non-cooperation a decade before. After the collapse of non-cooperation, Congress activists turned their attention to educational and charitable work and engaged in constitutional agitation. They achieved significant success in the sphere of local government by winning seats on District and Municipal Boards. Victory in local elections helped give Congressmen and the national movement publicity and prestige, while more concretely it meant that henceforth local Congress committees had powers of patronage at their command with which to rally supporters and reward the faithful.[1]

By December 1929, the month when the annual Indian National Congress session decided to wage mass protest in the pursuit of complete independence, Congress in north Bihar had created firm connections with many members of the village elite. From the time of non-cooperation onwards the Bihar Congress had sought to incorporate such people into its activities, and conversely, enthused by nationalist sentiment and perceiving advantages in the coming of more self-government, they had gravitated to the Congress.[2] Members of the village elite took the leading part in civil disobedience. Through their pivotal position in village society, and because of the attraction of the nationalist ideology which they espoused which embodied the hopes of many for a better future,[3] such people mobilised substantial support for nationalist agitation.

Partly because of the increased organisational capacity of its provincial units, and partly because during non-cooperation it had experienced difficulty in achieving effective central control, the Indian National Congress left much of the choice of issues and tactics during civil disobedience to the provincial congress committees.[4] Instead of being guided by a detailed programme similar to that promulgated during non-cooperation, during civil disobedience the Bihar Congress was free to exercise considerable initiative.

Non-cooperation began after many months of economic pressure and political uncertainty, whereas the period preceding the initiation of civil disobedience was relatively quiet. Moreover, non-cooperation developed in a context of high prices and scarcity, which encouraged participation by the poor. During the civil disobedience period, in contrast, the significant economic circumstance was the collapse in prices for agrarian produce consequent upon the great depression.[5] This slump put pressure on middle and poor peasants who sold cash crops to raise money to pay their rents and created difficulties for the landlords dependent on these rents. It also brought pressure to bear on the small landlords and rich peasants who dealt in agrarian produce. However the early 1930s had reasonable harvests and the price slump had little effect on sharecroppers or on poor peasants who were paid mainly in kind. Meanwhile, those poor peasants who were paid in cash for their labour benefited. Hence poor peasants tended to become less involved in civil disobedience than they had been in non-cooperation. Furthermore, the main impact of the price slump came from the last quarter of 1930 onwards,[6] when, because of heavy repression and the exhaustion of financial resources, the movement was already declining.

Throughout India, non-cooperation drew strength from the Khilafat agitation, and in north Bihar it also gained great momentum from anti-planter protest. In contrast civil disobedience developed without the impetus of other agitations, and failed to win Muslim support or the support of the broad social spectrum mobilised by anti-planter protest.

Another important distinctive feature of civil disobedience was that, much more than during non-cooperation, Congressmen employed a limited amount of violence to attain their ends.

II

The violence that Congressmen employed during the civil disobedience movement consisted of the use (or threatened use) of physical force against people and property. It incorporated sabotage, intimidation, physical assault, and also social boycott when it was employed to cause grave physical inconvenience.

The use of a limited amount of violence emerged from the nature of the Bihar Congress and from the social setting within which it operated. The socially conservative Congress sought to put pressure on the British without exacerbating existing tensions – and particularly those between peasants and landlords – which had the potential to disrupt the social order. To mobilise mass agitation and to keep it focussed upon the British, the Bihar Congress relied upon its adherents among small landlords and rich peasants. These members of the village elite exercised power through their high caste status and because of their control over land, labour and credit. Such men quarrelled both amongst themselves and with their social subordinates. Often such conflicts were resolved through compromise, through litigation, or through the intervention of the administration and the police. But these conflicts might also be resolved through force or the threat of force by kinsmen and clients and by *lathials*. Just as the police bolstered the position of the British administration in Bihar, the *lathials* bolstered the position of the locally powerful.

The members of the village elite who supported Congress had violence as one of the instruments at their command. However their use of violence during civil disobedience was limited, i.e. small scale and localised. It remained limited partly because these men had other, more subtle, means with which to exert influence, and partly because the repressive apparatus of the state operated to contain it.

In addition, violence remained limited because of the differential impact of the Great Depression on the people of Bihar. Because of the depression the prices of agrarian produce slumped dramatically. This slump put great pressure on landlords and rich and middle peasants but had less effect on or else benefited poor peasants. Economic considerations, therefore, affected the upper and middle rather than the lower levels of society. Both the non-cooperation movement of 1920-22 and the Quit India Revolt of 1942 incorporated the welling up, in response to high prices, of dissidence 'from below' on the part of the poor. But during civil disobedience this phenomenon did not develop. Had it developed in the early 1930s such dissidence might have erupted beyond the bounds of 'limited violence'.

During the civil disobedience movement in north Bihar violence was also constrained by the senior leadership of the Bihar Congress. These leaders adhered to the Gandhian, and official Congress, doctrine of *ahimsa* (non-violence). Rajendra Prasad whole-heartedly accepted Gandhi's moral authority, while Sri Krishna Sinha and most of the other senior leaders accepted *ahimsa* for more pragmatic reasons. The Bihar Congress sought to preserve the social order and to use open means of organisation to rally extensive support for protest against the British. Therefore it eschewed the adoption of openly violent methods which would invite heavy British repression and which might threaten the social order.

These constraints limited but did not stop the use of violent methods by local Congressmen. In north Bihar the centre of gravity of nationalist activity lay in the thousands of villages where the vast majority of the population lived. In the villages the principle of *ahimsa* won only partial understanding and uncertain allegiance. Through their experience in local agrarian and factional conflict, the small landlords and rich peasants who assumed the leadership of protest were well acquainted with the employment of intimidation and physical coercion. As the realisation grew that strict adherence to *ahimsa* could produce only meagre results, they began to use a limited amount of violence. Moreover the senior Congress leadership and most of the devoted followers of Gandhi among the rank and file were jailed in the first months of the movement, and thus could not exert their influence.[7]

III

Civil disobedience began with a protest against taxes levied by the administration on the production and sale of salt. This campaign was well suited to coastal areas, where sea-water could be processed by means of the heat of the sun. In landlocked Bihar the manufacture of salt was more difficult because it depended upon the availability of saline earth from which salt could be extracted by means of boiling and purification.[8]

Early in 1930 Bihar Congressmen began the illegal manufacture of salt. At first the breaking of the salt laws attracted considerable interest. When volunteers paraded through Samastipur town on their way to break the salt law in a nearby village the local merchants presented them with money, fruit, and garlands of flowers. 'All people', according to the *Searchlight's* report, 'gave hearty send off and showed great enthusiasm'.[9] But the excitement waned when the police confiscated and destroyed the utensils used by Congress volunteers for the production of salt and, at each salt manufacturing centre, arrested one or two of the leading organisers. The police kept arrests to a minimum, so as to limit as far as possible the interest and excitement that resulted.[10] These tactics succeeded. In north Bihar the large scale production of salt was difficult and, unlike some coastal areas, the region did not have a history of tension between the people and the administration over the salt laws.[11] In April the Saran Police Superintendent reported that 'so far...the ordinary masses are not taking the slightest interest in the [salt] movement, and it is confined almost entirely to school boys and youth'.[12] By May salt manufacturing had 'practically ceased'.[13]

After the failure of the salt campaign Congress workers lessened their adherence to the principle of non-violence and began using sabotage, intimidation and physical coercion. They agitated in support of the production and use of swadeshi goods, and boycotted vendors and users of foreign cloth. Because of aggressive picketing and the social pressure brought to bear by caste panchayats, this agitation had considerable success.[14]

Congressmen also campaigned vigorously against the sale of intoxicating drugs and liquor, the excise duty on which supplied a third of the provincial revenue.[15] They picketed drug and liquor stores and pressured both customers and vendors. On occasion they employed physical coercion. A sadhu who purchased a half *tola* of opium had it confiscated, and a man who ignored a picket line to buy liquor was beaten up and had his bottle of liquor broken.[16] In another incident picketers assaulted a liquor vendor, fracturing his skull, an injury from which he subsequently died.[17] When police interfered with the activities of picketers they often received a hostile response. In October 1930 four policemen and three *chaukidars* arrested nine Congress picketers at the Sarsi *mela*. As the police and their prisoners moved off to the railway station a large crowd assembled, jostled and abused the police, and rescued the picketers from custody.[18]

Congress workers also employed social boycott in support of prohibition. According to the principle of *ahimsa* such boycotts had to be carefully designed and implemented so as to convert rather than to coerce, but this proviso was often ignored.[19] In May 1930 the Purnea Police Superintendent reported that Congress workers had told licensees of liquor stores at Kesba village that if they continued selling liquor the services of barbers, washermen and food vendors would be denied them. And at Barhara bazaar in Purnea, Congressmen threatened to deny liquor vendors the use of the local supply of water.[20]

Congressmen also employed sabotage. They confiscated and destroyed supplies of liquor and diminished the future viability of liquor production by destroying the spathes of the toddy palms, thus making it impossible for toddy to be produced.[21]

Because of religious scruples against the use of alcohol and drugs the prohibition campaign won support from high caste people. It also drew support from lower caste people hopeful of improving their social status by abstaining from intoxicants.[22] Nevertheless many people did not display sympathy to the campaign. This was particularly true of the poor, for whom intoxicants provided some relief from a life of hardship. However the use of coercion helped contain opposition.

The producers, vendors and consumers of intoxicants, generally poor and of low social status, found it difficult to oppose the prohibition activists.[23] In Saran in May several toddy tappers assisted by some village watchmen confronted twenty Congress volunteers engaged in sabotaging toddy trees. A fight broke out and members of both parties were injured. The leader of the volunteers received a blow on the temple, and died a few hours later. No complaint was made to the police, but subsequently local Congress supporters took action against Sawal Chamar, the leader of the toddy tappers. A couple of nights later 'his house, straw rick, bamboo clump, mango trees, and everything he possessed were burnt to ashes, and he himself was forced to run away to Calcutta for fear of his life'.[24]

The Bihar administration had insufficient forces at its command to protect the interests of liquor producers, vendors and consumers by mounting guard over the numerous toddy trees and liquor and drug stores scattered across the countryside. Consequently its prestige and its income from excise duties suffered seriously.[25] Up to 30 December 1930 the total loss of excise revenue amounted to Rs.4,300,000, out of an annual excise income which totalled some Rs.20,000,000.[26] Nor did recovery occur quickly in the ensuing years, because the destruction of toddy spathes had a long-term effect on productivity. The drop in excise revenue came, moreover, at a time when the finances of the province were suffering from the impact of the great depression.

The prohibition campaign was complemented by a campaign against the *chaukidari* system under which the *chaukidars* acted as auxiliaries to the regular police force. In north Bihar this system was particularly crucial, because the province of Bihar and Orissa compared very unfavourably to the other provinces of British India in the amount it spent on its police force and in the ratio of its regular police to its population.

Activists in the anti-*chaukidari* campaign urged people to stop paying the taxes levied for the support of their local *chaukidars*, urged *chaukidars* to resign, and urged members of the *chaukidari* panchayats, which held the responsibility for the collection of *chaukidari* tax and the recruitment and direction of *chaukidars*, to relinquish their positions.

The call for a campaign against the *chaukidari* system found a receptive audience. The administration selected the members of the *chaukidari* panchayats from among landlords, rich peasants and from European landlords and sugar planters. Panchayat members often used the *chaukidars* as their own private police, bringing the system into disrepute. One Congressman described the *chaukidari* tax as 'the most hated of all taxes'. He commented that no villager 'likes this tax for the simple reason that the *chaukidar* is more an oppressor than a friend to the village folk'.[27] Moreover, the collectors of the *chaukidari* tax often acted oppressively. It was their custom to 'greatly harass the poor people and assess whatever tax they liked'.[28]

Because of the extra leverage it provided in local power struggles, members of the village elite competed keenly for panchayat membership. But the number of positions could not satisfy the demand. Those who did not gain membership tended to be hostile to the present incumbents, and sympathetic to anti-*chaukidari* protest, even if they themselves had sufficient prestige and power to be immune to harassment by panchayat members and their attendant *chaukidars*.

In addition, unlike a rent and/or revenue strike, an anti-*chaukidari* campaign seemed to be attended with few economic or political risks. The highest amount of tax levied on any individual was Rs.12, which seemed to limit the extent of individual liability.[29] A rent and revenue strike, in contrast, might lead to the confiscation of landholdings. And, a rent and/or revenue strike would exacerbate agrarian tensions and endanger the Congress small landlord-peasant alliance.

The campaign began in May 1930 and rapidly gained momentum. Many villagers readily agreed to suspend payment of the *chaukidari* tax and some pledged never to pay it while alien rule prevailed.[30] Congress supporters supplemented persuasion with limited violence to get *chaukidars* to resign their positions. The *chaukidars* came from the low status Dusadh *jati* and thus were easily subjected to pressure. Uncooperative *chaukidars* were refused access to village wells, and their womenfolk were harassed whenever they went out into the fields to relieve themselves. In some instances they encountered physical violence and complete social boycott.[31]

The campaign achieved greatest success when a substantial section of a locally powerful *jati* adhered to the Congress movement. At Ramdiri village in north Monghyr, where Bhumihars predominated, the 'entire panchayat as well as twelve out of the fourteen *chaukidars*...resigned'.[32] In Saran the *chaukidars* were 'prevented from carrying out their duties'.[33] It was reported from Saran that 'many of the defaulters of Chaukidari tax are rich and influential persons. They are Brahmans and Rajputs and consequently their lead is followed by the lower castes'.[34]

By mounting the anti-*chaukidari* campaign Congress struck at the foundations of British rule over Bihar. The *chaukidars* carried out the routine police work of the villages and, through their weekly reports at the police stations, operated as the 'eyes and ears' of the administration. When they ceased to perform these functions the whole edifice of police-administrative control became vulnerable. In the areas where the system did break down, the British were left groping in the dark and the local inhabitants were encouraged to believe that the days of British rule were numbered. The British reacted sharply to this challenge. Concerning Ramdiri village in north Monghyr, the Subdivisional Officer told his superiors that 'we shall not hestitate to use force, if this is found necessary in collecting the taxes'.[35]

The authorities responded to the non-payment of *chaukidari* taxes by sending a police party to the area. If the villagers continued to refuse payment, the police attached their movable property in lieu of the money owed. The police collected cattle, and had bedsteads, furniture and cooking utensils loaded into carts and carried away.[36] The value of the goods confiscated often greatly exceeded the tax owed, so the existence of a maximum liability of Rs.12 failed to protect the villagers. If the attachment of property failed to force the villagers to abandon their stand, the administration quartered additional police at the villagers' expense and jailed local activists. The police sent out to attach property and serve as additional police frequently acted oppressively.[37]

In the Bhorey and Kateya *thanas* in north-west Saran the threat to British rule became especially intense. The inhabitants of this locality had a tradition of conflict with the police and the administration.[38] They had taken an active part in the non-cooperation movement of 1920-22, and in 1930 their effective mounting of anti-*chaukidari* activity formed the leading component of their support for civil disobedience. High caste rich peasants seem to have taken the lead in protest, but were supported by people lower down in the social scale, some of whom were said to have criminal propensities. According to the Saran police superintendent the Bhorey *thana* was

> cursed with nearly 100 registered bad characters and suspected dacoits, almost all of whom have joined the civil disobedience movement and supply gangs of volunteers to distant places such as Chapra, Siwan, Gopalganj and Mirganj.[39]

In August 1930, in a request that additional police be posted in the area, the police superintendent listed incidents in which Congress supporters had acted violently and contended that the crime rate had greatly increased since the beginning of civil disobedience. He also claimed that regular policemen were being greatly hindered in the performance of their work, and that the *chaukidars* were being subjected to social boycott.[40]

The Saran police reacted harshly to these threats to their authority. On 4 October, Deputy-Police Superintendent MacKensie, accompanied by the Subdivisional Officer and some police, made a visit to Bhorey *thana*. He later reported that having come upon two Congress volunteers picketing the police station he and his party 'caught them and after giving them a good thrashing sent them home'. Next he and his men visited the bamboo and thatch hut which operated as the local 'Swaraj Ashram'. They demolished the hut and set fire to the wreckage. Later that day, according to Superintendent MacKensie, the police party descended suddenly and heavily on the picketers at the Hatuwa ganja shop. The proceedings may be described tersely as that the S[ub]I[nspector] got his own back (with interest) for the attempt to assault him on the second.[41]

Police action of the kind taken by Superintendent MacKensie helped contain nationalist protest, but created sympathy for the Congress and had adverse effects on the standing of the British administration. Of no area was this more true than Bihpur in north Bhagalpur.

In late 1929 Congress established an *ashram* at the important rail junction of Bihpur as the centre for nationalist activity in the north Bhagalpur region. Congress enrolled 300 volunteers at the *ashram* and gave them 'intensive training' along 'semi-military lines with formal parades held twice daily and ostentatious practice of fighting with lathis and daggers'. The activities at the *ashram* created great excitement among the local people many of whom were members of the pugnacious Bhumihar community.[42]

Congressmen initiated the salt campaign at Bihpur on 17 April 1930 and, a month later, began picketing liquor, drug, and foreign cloth stores. Congress workers also made intensive efforts to win over the local *chaukidars* to the nationalist cause. In response to both persuasion and to the limited use of violence many *chaukidars* resigned, while others stopped performing their duties. Congressmen also directed intimidation and coercion against the members of the regular police force. At the village of Sabour, Congress supporters attacked a senior policeman while he was attempting to enforce a prohibition order against volunteers who had started a market in competition with the market owned by a local zamindar. Fearing for their safety, many policemen became unwilling to go into the countryside.[43]

The Bhumihar Congressmen of the Bihpur area also broke up a district board election at Gopalpur village in an attempt to ensure the defeat of the loyalist candidate.[44] In the opinion of the Deputy-Inspector General of Police, Congress militance was consistent with the history of turbulence in the area. He referred to the murder in 1921 of the Gurkha watchmen on Grant's estate at nearby Sonbarsa and contended that 'Sonbarsa has in these parts become a war cry of rioters and it, with others, was used at Gopalpur'.[45]

By mid-May 'Congress had practically got the upper hand in this elaka and the police were hardly functioning'.[46] Faced with this challenge R.D.K. Ninnis, the District Superintendent of Police, consulted the District Magistrate and acted on instructions from the provincial government. On 31 May, in an effort to cripple Congress activities in the locality, he ordered his men to occupy the Bihpur *ashram*.

The occupation of the *ashram* elicited a sharp reaction. In the next few days, either out of sympathy for nationalist protest or because of increased Congress pressure, those few *chaukidars* who had still been performing their duties stopped doing so. Every day demonstrators gathered outside the *ashram*, only to be dispersed by lathi charges. By 4 and 5 June the level of tension had increased greatly. The crowds that gathered were larger than hitherto, and the speakers who addressed them assumed a more militant stance. On 4 June a speaker announced that Congress workers would bring pressure to bear on the families of the policemen who had occupied the *ashram*. The following day speakers urged the crowd 'to use all means in their power to compel the resignation' of those few *chaukidars* who still remained in their posts. According to Ninnis, one Congress activist

> got up on a table, turned to the constables who were on duty at the gate-way, lifted up his hands and denounced them as 'bloody butchers' for opposing their own countrymen; informed them that by doing so they were committing a deadly sin and said dramatically that their place was not where they stood but on the side of the Congress volunteers... Other leaders... addressed both the crowd and the constables in a similar manner...one of the prominent speakers was Chulhai Mahto who took a prominent part in the Gopalpur riot.[47]

Ninnis became anxious over these attempts to sway the police. He also worried over the rumour that soon an attempt would be made to rush the *ashram* grounds. Ninnis could not enquire effectively into the truth of this rumour. Because of the success of the anti-*chaukidari* campaign, he had no *chaukidars* to act as his informants and 'had to rely for all information upon one or two plain clothes constables'.[48]

Demonstrations outside the *ashram* culminated on 9 June, when Rajendra Prasad and other prominent nationalists arrived from Patna. By late afternoon large crowds had gathered at three different locations near the *ashram*. Ninnis, apparently acting on the assumption that the people assembled would move against the *ashram*, dispersed the crowds by lathi charges.[49]

The events of 9 June created a sensation. Many people did not believe the official assertion that the circumstances had obliged the police to disperse the crowds. One strong protest came from Anant Prasad, a local notable and a member of the Bihar and Orissa Legislative Council. On 11 June Prasad wrote to the private secretary of the provincial Governor and presented his own account of the events. He reported that on 9 June the prominent leaders Rajendra Prasad, Professor Abdul Bari, Baldeo Sahai and Murli Manohar Prasad had set out to investigate the circumstances surrounding the occupation of the Bihpur *ashram*. When they found their way to the *ashram* blocked by a body of police, Anant Prasad sent a message to Ninnis seeking permission to make an inspection. Ninnis refused permission and the politicians decided to return to the bazaar. Before doing so, Rajendra Prasad, Abdul Bari and A. Ariff addressed a crowd of about 10,000. After this assembly had begun to disperse the police began,

> the assaults on the sightseers which beggar description. I solemnly affirm that there was no justification for this... The crowd was perfectly peaceful...the indiscriminate assaults began, the Superintendent of Police running in front of a batch of constables...beating right and left and chasing the crowds...shouting *Maro Sala Ko*. [literally: "Kill the brothers-in-law".]

The police passed by Anant Prasad and entered the bazaar where a number of Congressmen and shopkeepers had gathered. They attacked this gathering, paying special attention to Abdul Bari and Rajendra Prasad. Next, before returning to the *ashram*, the police moved on and attacked the people collected nearby at the railway station. Prasad concluded his letter by resigning from the Legislative Council because he found 'co-operation with Government impossible under the present circumstances'.[50]

Anant Prasad's response to the events at Bihpur typified that of many who previously had been lukewarm towards the nationalist movement. The nationalist press highlighted the harsh action of the police, with emphasis on the injuries to Rajendra Prasad and on the contention that many members of the crowd were merely bystanders who were not involved with the Congress movement.[51] In the Bihpur *thana* itself, the actions taken by Ninnis failed to restore the position of the local administration. After the occupation of the *ashram* on 31 May those few *chaukidars* who were still performing their duties stopped doing so.[52] And after the violence of 9 June feeling against the authorities rose to a new level of intensity. Meanwhile, some policemen displayed misgivings about the harsh actions they had been ordered to undertake.[53] On 11 June – the same day that Anant Prasad sent his letter of protest and resignation – Ninnis reported that,

> All work outside Bihpur itself is at a standstill. The Sub-Inspector is unable to go out into the moffasal as threats have been made against his life and even when no active violence is shown to him he cannot obtain any assistance in making his enquiries. For the same reason it is not possible for the constables to go out... Summonses and warrants cannot be served. Cases are not being reported... In fact it is no exaggeration to say that this area is temporarily lost to the Government.[54]

This situation continued throughout the next few months. At Bihpur *ashram* Congress workers kept interest alive by sending groups of volunteers to the gateway. The volunteers attempted to enter the *ashram* but on each occasion the police drove them back. Elsewhere in the vicinity Congress agitation continued, and in previously inactive areas propagandists rallied support by reference to the events at Bihpur. Immediately to the north, in the Kishanganj *thana*, the movement had had little effect on the *chaukidars* until early June, but from then on 'almost daily up to the end of the month and well into July' complaints were made to the *thana* that *chaukidars* were being intimidated. In July and August the Bihpur region was isolated by severe flooding. But agitation continued indicating that 'the movement had taken root and did not need encouragement from outside leaders'.[55]

By sending strong police patrols to troublesome villages, by attaching property, and by arresting leading Congress workers the administration gradually regained control. In the second half of June *chaukidars* began to return to their posts, and by mid-July almost all had done so. By this time, too, 'the Sub-Inspectors had begun freely to move about their jurisdictions, but never without an armed escort'. Nor was it yet 'considered safe to send out night patrols for surveillance work'. Picketing continued throughout August and September, but volunteers mostly avoided confrontation with the police. By September collections of *chaukidari* tax had been brought more or less up-to-date but 'not without considerable trouble'. The *chaukidars* were functioning but they were still affected by 'the fear of social ostracism should they give out more information than the villagers wish'. In September the British consolidated their hold by posting 110 additional police at the expense of the inhabitants.[56]

The developments at Bihpur illustrate the contribution of limited violence to the impact of the Bihar civil disobedience movement. In the Bihpur area the limited use of violence crippled the *chaukidari* system, thus challenging the foundations of British rule. Ninnis reacted by investing the Bihpur *ashram* and by breaking up the crowds which subsequently gathered outside. Ninnis intended to restore the position of the local police but his initiatives had precisely the opposite effect.

By pushing Ninnis into a sharply repressive response the Bihpur Congress workers thwarted the policy, formulated in early 1930 by the Government of India, of dealing circumspectly with nationalist protest so as to avoid adverse publicity.[57] Ninnis himself probably was keen to come down heavily on nationalist activists, but he could not have done so had not the impact of limited violence upon the *chaukidari* system provided him with sufficient justification.

By making the very kind of response which the Government of India hoped to avoid, Ninnis provided a focus for protest and helped publicise the nationalist cause. Consequently it took months of time and the implementation of serious measures to restore British rule over the Bihpur area. In Bihpur and elsewhere in Bihar during 1930 official repression maintained British rule, but only at the cost of creating a long-term legacy of antagonism and disaffection.

Public dissatisfaction with official repression became heightened because of the character of the Bihar Police Force. Police Forces frequently display inadequacy in the handling of mass protest, but the Bihar force was particularly unsuited to the task. In part this inadequacy resulted from its small size. In February 1930 the Bihar and Orissa Governor commented that

> Taking the criterion of area or population, we have still the smallest police force in India; we spend less on our police per head of population than any other province. We cannot respond to the demand for new police stations; we cannot even man properly the stations we have whose jurisdictions extend in several cases from 300 to 800 square miles.[58]

Moreover, even in comparison to elsewhere in British India, the Bihar police force was badly paid. Policemen had to be corrupt to make ends meet, and this encouraged them to become exploitative and overbearing. Their bad reputation ensured that the police received vigorous criticism for their handling of nationalist protest. Even in instances when strong measures might have been justifiable in terms of the need to maintain public order, the tides of public sympathy flowed away from the police and towards those engaged in protest.

In addition, because they were so few in number the police could display little flexibility in their response to protest. The *chaukidari* system was vulnerable because the *chaukidars* were only incompletely under official control and protection, and hence could be subjected to pressure within the villages. Once the *chaukidari* system had come under attack the police found that often they could rely on the *chaukidars* neither for information nor for physical support. A few hundred policemen held responsibility for districts covering thousands of square miles and occupied by millions of people. Unable to awe dissidents by their numbers or by their wide dispersal, and often faced by large, excited, crowds, policemen tended to turn to the lathi and to the musket rather than risk a less combative approach, thus making violent clashes inevitable.

In December 1930 and January 1931 the inflexibility of the police response and the strength of nationalist feeling were revealed in five serious clashes. These clashes resulted in part from the excitement generated by civil disobedience in general and the incidents at Bihpur in particular. They may also have reflected the discontent caused, from October 1930 onwards, by the slump in agrarian prices.

At Bhorey in Saran on 16 December a force of thirty policemen, twenty of them armed with muskets, made twenty-one arrests and attempted to disperse a 2000-strong Congress meeting. More villagers arrived, swelling the crowd to 4000. A fracas developed. The police opened fire, but because of their inadequate training and the poor quality of the guns and ammunition inflicted few casualties. Under heavy attack with lathis and brickbats, they were obliged to take refuge in the *thana*.[59]

The other four clashes occurred during the observance by Congressmen of Independence Day on 26 January 1931. Two clashes occurred in northern Darbhanga. In the Harlakhi *thana* the local sub-inspector of police and his men arrested twelve members of a procession. Some bystanders reacted by assaulting the police with sticks and clods of earth. Assisted by some Muslims and by two of the headmen of the local *chaukidari* unions the police dispersed their assailants and subsequently arrested some of them. The Maithil Brahman names given in the police report indicate that the rioters were caste fellows of the men initially taken into custody.[60]

In the Khautana *thana* the sub-inspector, supported by a force of six constables and sixty *chaukidars*, stopped a small procession, confiscated the flags being carried and arrested three men. 'At the instigation of the local Marwari merchants' the crowd of spectators protested against the arrests and refused to disperse. Some members of the crowd, in which Yadavs were prominent, assailed the police with stones and lathis. Most of the *chaukidars* fled and the rest of the police party locked themselves into a building within the compound of the local dispensary.

The crowd continued to demonstrate and to pelt the doors and windows of the building with rocks, despite the efforts of the Marwaris who tried to dissuade its members from further protest. The demonstration only ceased with the arrival on the scene of a Muslim zamindar who, as a prominent figure in the locality, was able to persuade the crowd to disperse.[61]

A more serious Independence Day clash occurred at Goreakothi village in Basantpur *thana* in Saran. Sub-Inspector Chandrika Sinha, accompanied by three constables and about fifty *chaukidars*, ordered the members of a procession of some 3,000 people drawn from Goreakothi and eleven nearby villages to disperse. When they did not obey Sinha arrested two of their leaders. At this point the students of the nearby high school left their classes for their afternoon break and joined the crowd. The school was a centre of nationalist activity. It had been founded by Babu Narain Prasad Singh, a leading member of the locally predominant Bhumihar community. Singh had been active during the non-cooperation movement and in April 1930 had been sentenced to one year's imprisonment for breaching the salt laws. The arrival of the students gave the crowd a new impetus. Some members of the crowd began to throw stones and an affray began. The police fled, but were pursued determinedly. The rioters injured almost every member of the police party, thirty-four of whom afterwards required medical attention. To bring the area under control the British brought in a body of military police. Twenty-seven of the rioters were brought to trial, of whom eighteen were sentenced to six months' rigorous imprisonment, while the remaining nine were acquitted because they could not be positively identified.[62] The characteristically high and middle caste names of the accused suggest that the participants in the riot came from among small landlords and rich and middle peasants.

An even more dramatic Independence Day clash occurred at Beguserai town, an important rail junction and the principal town of north Monghyr. At Beguserai forty-five lathi-bearing constables supported by thirty-three policemen armed with muskets blocked the progress of a procession of 10,000 Congress volunteers and sympathisers. The police attempted to disperse the crowd by a lathi charge and some of its members, assisted by bystanders,

responded by hurling brickbats. The police party gave
ground, and the musket-bearing constables covered the
retreat with a disorderly fire. The police discharged 146
rounds, but were forced to retire to the *thana* building.
Thirty-two of the policemen sustained injuries. Among
the demonstrators, seven were killed and at least seven
suffered injuries. Four of the killed and three of the
wounded were Bhumihars.[63]

Senior police officers and the local police and officials
afterwards justified the action taken at Beguserai by
claiming that they had prior warning that the procession
intended to attack the police station. They pointed out
that since the early stages of civil disobedience there had
been growing tension between the police and the inhabitants of the locality, and particularly with the members
of the numerous and predominant Bhumihar community who
made up one-fifth of the population of the subdivision.[64]
These Bhumihars included amongst their number small
landlords and rich and middle peasants.

On four occasions Bhumihars had assaulted policemen,
and accordingly the police and the local authorities anticipated trouble on Independence Day 1931.[65] There was
'every indication', the Police Superintendent reported
'that it was not so much the inhabitants of Beguserai itself who were responsible for the riot, as the Babhans
[i.e. Bhumihars] from villages all over the subdivision'.
And according to the Deputy-Inspector General of Police,

> The mob consisted largely of Babhans, animated by
> an intense hostility towards the police, not merely as
> one tenet of a political creed, but also for more
> intimate and personal reasons arising from contact
> with the police during the last few months. There
> seems good ground for believing that a large part of
> the mob were deliberately seeking a trial of strength
> with the police... In the existing temper of the mob,
> an attack on the thana would have been almost in-
> evitable, whether deliberately planned or not.[66]

The senior administration of Bihar and Orissa did not
find the explanations of the police and the local officials
satisfactory, but did not indicate this uncertainty publicly.
The police and local officials had mishandled the situation,

but for the sake of the stability of British rule they had to be supported against their critics. After a confidential enquiry one senior official commented that

> I am not very satisfied that there was a real apprehension on the part of the officials, at the time, of an attack on the thana, and I am pretty sure that the procession itself started without any such intention.

Yet he did not think that 'the local officers were wrong in breaking up the procession'. If the processionists had been allowed to continue, they would have entered the bazaar area, where they may have caused much damage.[67]

Many members of the Indian community could not accept that the action taken by the police at Beguserai had been justified. An account by Bishundeva Narayan Singh claimed that the procession had merely wanted to pass along the road through the bazaar, and that it had wished to avoid clashing with the police. He pointed out that the procession had been stopped in a narrow stretch of road, and that therefore its leading members

> had no room to budge an inch either this side or that side in spite of the brutal lathi charge, because the entire procession was facing east and unless the men in the rear made room for them they could not disperse. In order to save themselves from being severely assaulted or killed on account of the indiscriminate lathi charge, they took recourse to throwing brickbats picked up from the vicinity of Ramtahal's shop, then under construction. The shower of brickbats resulted in scaring away the entire Police force to the thana.[68]

Moreover, having provoked the people into violence, the police responded with undisciplined, indiscriminate, and unnecessarily prolonged firing.

Editorially, the *Searchlight* compared police violence at Beguserai with that at Bihpur, and accused the Beguserai officials of acting as callously as General Dyer at Amritsar in April, 1919. Surely, it commented,

> in the face of this brutal episode it ill-becomes the officials of the province to talk about popular violence

and lawlessness. That such an obvious case of incompetence, such a flagrant instance of outrageousness, should be sought to be white washed...is but a reminder of the unspeakable humiliation of foreign rule administered by an arrogant bureaucracy.[69]

In addition to supplying the nationalist movement with valuable propaganda, the clashes at Beguserai and elsewhere in December 1930 and January 1931 helped illuminate the character of support for civil disobedience in north Bihar. The leading participants in protest came from high caste groups, namely Brahmans in Harlakhi *thana* and Bhumihars at Goreakothi and Beguserai. There is little indication of who else engaged in protest other than that at Khautana in Darbhanga Marwaris and Yadavs participated. In contrast to non-cooperation, Muslims did not engage in nationalist protest. Indeed, at Harlakhi they assisted the local police to disperse their assailants, while in Khautani a Muslim zamindar intervened to placate the demonstrators. On the basis of their caste affiliation, the demonstrators mainly seem to have come from among small landlords and from among rich and middle peasants. No evidence exists to indicate significant involvement by poor peasants, though no doubt some of them were among the bystanders who became drawn into attacks on the police. Among the participants, only the Marwaris in Khautana displayed a firm adherence to the doctrine of non-violence.

IV

The violent clashes between police and Congress supporters in late 1930 and early 1931 indicated that in some localities strong anti-police and anti-administration feeling had developed. However despite the drama of the clashes, by early 1931 civil disobedience in north Bihar had begun to decline. From late 1930 funds with which to support the movement had begun to dry up. In October the Bihar Congress advised the All India Congress committee

> of an immediate need for Rs.25,000 if civil disobedience was to carry on for six months more: volunteers could be fed in the villages with ease, but little cash was forthcoming locally and volunteers could not be moved about.[70]

By late 1930 the bourgeois elements who had previously funded the Congress stopped doing so because of their own economic difficulties and because mass agitation had become increasingly violent and threatened to run out of control.[71] The drying up of financial support to the All India Congress Committee from the Bombay bourgeoisie had a particularly deleterious effect on the Bihar situation, since all along the Bihar Congress had looked outside backward, agrarian Bihar for funds. Now, because of the effect of the slump in agrarian prices on the financial position of the small landlords and rich peasants who formed the backbone of the Congress organisation, the Bihar Congress was even less able than previously to rely on provincial sources of financial support.[72]

In addition, the hard measures taken against *chaukidari* tax defaulters and the posting of punitive police in areas which strongly supported the Congress had stifled the spirit of resistance in the villages. In July 1930 the Bihar Congress had reported that 'the movement is practically entirely in the villages and in the hands of the village people'.[73] From early 1931 this situation no longer continued. Henceforth the countryside generally remained quiet. Protest continued, but it was mainly the work of middle class urban people, and particularly of students.[74] Their activities did not pose as serious a challenge to British rule as the peasant dissidence of 1930.

Civil disobedience also declined because its momentum was broken by the Gandhi-Irwin Pact. On 5 March 1930 Gandhi and Irwin, the Governor-General, came to an agreement whereby, in return for the easing of restrictions on political activity and the release of Congress prisoners, Gandhi suspended mass protest pending the results of the second Round Table Conference on India's constitutional future, scheduled for London later in the year. From now on Congress workers would be instructed to restrict themselves to propaganda work and to peaceful, non-coercive picketing.[75]

At first the people of Bihar regarded the Gandhi-Irwin Pact as a victory for Congress. Irwin's treatment of Gandhi as an equal and his apparent acceptance, in doing so, of the legitimacy of the nationalist movement shook the morale of the police and boosted that of Congress supporters.

Congress activists, the Bihar authorities alleged, distorted the details of the pact and used its existence to drum up support.[76] In doing so they were assisted by the release of Congress prisoners. In Muzaffarpur, for example, the release of the prisoners inspired a new surge of activity.[77] By early April the people had come 'to understand that Swaraj has been obtained', and Congress workers were successfully collecting subscriptions. The Police Superintendent commented:

> The fact that such people as the Mahanth of Maniari, the Mahanth of Jaintpur, Rai Bahadur Shyamnandan Sahai and others are now helping to support the Congress indicates that *the general public are of the opinion that Congress has obtained authority and can seriously injure the interests of those who fail to lend their support.* [Emphasis added.][78]

Meanwhile, officials reported that villagers in the Bihpur area had been asking when the *chaukidars* and police 'are to be replaced by a Swaraj force'.[79] The authorities claimed that Congress activity involved numerous breaches of the Gandhi-Irwin Pact. In Saran, there was a renewed wave of sabotage of toddy palms, and in the Tegra *thana* of north Monghyr an old man who had purchased some *ganja* was attacked by Congress volunteers and subsequently died of his injuries.[80]

But before long the flurry of agitation died down. The national and provincial leaders of Congress urged their followers to observe restraint, pending the outcome of the Round Table Conference. Some nationalists felt dissatisfaction with the suspension of mass protest. In his reminiscences on the period M.N. Roy, the firebrand of the Patna City Congress Committee, notes that

> With the subsidence of excitement caused...by strict direction...not to offer provocation of any sort to the Police, the Congress Committee's income also fell sharply. We had to disband our Volunteer Corps.

He also complained, perhaps reflecting the attitude of many activists to the use of 'limited violence', that

> Picketing...had to be so peacefully and so persuasively
> conducted that it ceased to be effective; worse still,
> this wholly vegetarian enterprize also ceased to interest
> most of our young workers.[81]

In the absence of an alternative leadership and ideology
dissatisfaction such as this was not directed to constructive
ends. And meanwhile, having learnt that there was no
truth in the rumour that their past excesses were to be
scrutinised, the police dealt harshly with Congress activists.[82]

By July 1931 north Bihar had quietened sufficiently for
the British to withdraw the contingents of additional police
from everywhere except the Bhorey *thana*, where a detachment remained because even in normal times the area was
'turbulent and criminal'.[83] This state of inactivity persisted throughout the rest of 1931.[84]

Early in 1932 protest revived. By late 1931 the British
had become worried over unrest in Bengal, the United
Provinces and the North-West Frontier Province and had
failed to persuade Congress to disassociate itself from
agitation in these areas.[85] They also realised that the
Gandhi-Irwin Pact had effectively checked the momentum
of civil disobedience. Moreover, whereas previously they
had tried to avoid adverse publicity by dealing leniently
with protest, they now felt that it was essential to protect
police morale and administrative prestige by treating dissidents harshly.[86] The use of Congress of 'limited violence'
had contributed substantially to this hardening of attitude.

On 4 January 1932, the Government of India passed an
Emergency Powers Ordinance and threw the Congress
leadership into jail. Congress re-activated mass civil disobedience, a wave of protest erupted, and the police reacted sharply.[87] At Motihari town in Champaran on 26
January 1932 police fired on a group of Independence Day
demonstrators, killing one man and wounding another.
And in Muzaffarpur in February members of the Gurkha
Military Police Company fired four rounds of .303 rifle
fire into a crowd attempting to place Congress flags on
the Sheohar police station, killing four men and injuring
nine others, two of whom subsequently died.[88]

The police violence at Sheohar epitomised the harsh line now adopted by the authorities. Mass arrests, the confiscation of Congress funds and property and strong pressure against nationalist sympathisers delivered the movement 'a stunning blow'.[89] By mid-March the Viceroy reported that in Bihar and Orissa protest was on the 'downgrade', and he repeated this assessment throughout the year. On Independence Day in January 1933 there were numerous arrests but 'no serious incidents' and people displayed less interest than in previous years.[90] Civil disobedience died a lingering death, not finally being called off until April 1934. Until the end dedicated nationalists were willing to risk a lathi blow or a spell in jail by joining in a flag-waving procession or a noisy demonstration. But from mid-1931 on, with the exception of the brief flurry of excitement in early 1932, the movement did not attract widespread participation.

Despite the heavy weight of British repression the Bihar Congress perhaps could have re-invigorated civil disobedience in the 1932-34 period by initiating a rent strike. In the United Provinces in 1930 and 1931 such a departure — though not backed whole-heartedly by the provincial congress committee — won extensive support.[91] It has been argued that this option did not appear attractive in Bihar partly because the rent demand was lower than in the United Provinces.[92] This argument is ill-advised, since the heavy burden of *abwabs* meant that in real terms the demand on the ryots was substantially greater than the rent nominally charged. Moreover, the impact of the depression-induced slump in agrarian prices had made rents difficult to pay and caused much distress.[93] In north Bihar a rent strike probably would have achieved great support. However the interests of the strong landlord element in the Bihar Congress, the general conservatism of the Congress, and the absence of an alternative leadership meant that this tactic was not employed.

V

In north Bihar in the early 1930s the Bihar Congress initiated extensive civil disobedience against British rule. Members of the village elite took the lead in protest, rallying support from those below them in the social scale.

Because the months preceding the initiation of civil disobedience had been relatively quiet, because of prevailing economic conditions which reduced pressure on the poor, because of the absence of other movements to add impetus and supply supporters, and because of the care with which the Bihar Congress kept agitation focussed against the British, the civil disobedience movement lacked the social breadth and did not elicit the messianic fervour of non-cooperation. Accordingly, and because they had gained confidence from their handling of nationalist protest a decade previously, British officials in north Bihar grew less anxious over civil disobedience than they had over its predecessor.[94]

Civil disobedience reached its peak in the middle of 1930, with confrontations between police and Congress supporters in Bihpur in north Bhagalpur. In ensuing months it went through a process of decline. But despite its eventual defeat the movement strongly challenged the British administration of Bihar. This challenge became effective through the limited use of violence.

The salt campaign operated in strict accordance with the Gandhian principle of non-violence, but before long civil disobedience became characterised by the use or threatened use of physical force. Congress workers met with most success in their agitation against the sale of liquor and drugs and their campaign against the *chaukidari* system. Success in the prohibition campaign resulted from boycott, intimidation, physical coercion and sabotage. Strictly peaceful picketing and propaganda work would have been less effective. Similarly, the anti-*chaukidari* campaign had most success in those areas where Congress workers supplemented peaceful persuasion with intimidation and coercion.

The inroads of the prohibition campaign seriously sapped the revenues of the government. Meanwhile the campaign against the *chaukidars* shook the foundations of law and order. These threats to the income and stability of the British regime guaranteed a harsh reaction from the police. The Bihar police were always likely to act harshly. But, as the first, salt-oriented phase of civil disobedience had shown, they could exercise restraint when protestors remained non-violent and devoted themselves to an activity that issued only an indirect challenge to the regime.

Harsh police repression played into the hands of the Congress. Because the official Congress policy was one of non-violence, and because some nationalists adhered strictly to the policy while most gave lip service to it, Congress spokesmen could explain away incidents of violence on the part of Congress supporters as accidents, while pointing out that police violence was completely in accordance with the traditions of police work in the province.[95] Frequently, the police won the battle to maintain order but lost the propaganda and prestige war.

The limited violence of Congress supporters conflicted with the adherence of the leaders of Congress to the policy of non-violence. The Congress leaders responded to this problem by ignoring it. It may be instructive to draw a parallel with the workings of the British administration in India. British officials tended to indulge in noble words about bringing order to society and justice to the masses. Yet because of their reliance on local intermediaries the British in actuality were 'winking at the existence of a legal underworld where the private justice of faction settled conflicts with the blows of lathis'.[96]

The leaders of the Bihar Congress perhaps did not approve of the methods of their local supporters, but these methods had the merit of getting things done, of crippling the liquor trade, and of ensuring the resignation of *chaukidars*. Under the cover of the official policy of non-violence, the limited use of violence developed. An all-out, explicitly violent, attack on the British was not made, since such an enterprise would be both socially divisive and would stimulate massive and bloody repression, but the limited use of violence gained tacit acceptance. Limited violence put pressure on the administration and damaged its prestige, but encouraged it, for reasons of publicity, to delay making a repressive response. Limited violence, moreover, brought waverers into the Congress camp and prodded the police into harsh action which gave a publicity victory to Congress.

Individual Congress leaders attempted to ensure adherence to non-violent methods. In Patna in the weeks immediately after the signing of the Gandhi-Irwin Pact, Rajendra Prasad used his personal influence to ensure that Congress workers adhered to the provisions of the pact concerning picketing. Elsewhere, however, the intimidatory picketing characteristic of the pre-pact period continued for some time.[97]

And at times even such a devoted Gandhian as Prasad seems to have turned a blind eye to the activities of some Congress supporters. In the early months of 1931 Prasad responded to official complaints of Congress violence by enquiring from the Congress committees of the areas concerned. When the local Congress officials replied that there was no substance in the allegations, Prasad took them at their word and relayed a summary of their findings to the administration.[98] This action was disingenuous. Prasad had grown up in a Saran village, and he must have known that the official charges probably contained considerable truth.

The limited use of violence by Congress supporters operated within the quasi-liberal state structure established by the British in India.[99] The situation in India contrasted with that in other European empires where consistent and systematic repression occurred. To placate critics at home and to keep the support of collaborators in India, the British extended limited tolerance to social and political dissidence. They permitted constitutional political activity, gave some leeway to non-violent and non-coercive direct action protest, but vigorously and effectively repressed radical and violent protest. Because the British extended some tolerance to dissidence, and because for reasons of economy they kept their police forces (particularly in Bihar) to a minimum, limited violence had space within which to operate.

British repression of civil disobedience was selective and short-lived, and Congress supporters emerged from jail at the end of the movement to resume normal activities and, eventually, to campaign with great success for election to office in 1937. The limited tolerance permitted by the British made the limited use of violence feasible. Indeed, the merchants, lawyers, small landlords and rich peasants who ran the Congress found that, by choosing their targets carefully, they could bring significant pressure to bear within the framework of limited tolerance without jeopardising their own established position. In contrast to the situation during non-cooperation when a detailed programme was outlined, during civil disobedience the provincial congress committees were given autonomy in the choice of issues on which to focus. Unlike the United Provinces Congress Committee, which at least flirted with the notion of a rent strike, the Bihar Provincial Congress Committee carefully ensured that nothing was done to exacerbate agrarian relations and that all protest focussed exclusively upon the British.

The Bihar Congress's use of violence during civil disobedience was limited in the extent to which it received explicit sanction and selective in its choice of issues and targets. Even so, however, it combined effectively with the general upsurge of nationalist dissidence to reveal that the British lacked effective means with which to contain militant protest.

The regular police in north Bihar were under-manned and poorly armed. During the course of civil disobedience the members of the force were not always able to cope effectively with violent confrontations. At Beguserai and Bhorey for example the police suffered casualties and temporary reverses, and accordingly lost prestige. Such loss of prestige, the Chief Secretary complained to Rajendra Prasad, made it more difficult than previously for the police, with their limited numbers, to handle ordinary crime, let alone political disturbances.[100]

The *chaukidars* displayed even more weaknesses than the regular police. The *chaukidars* had always been subject to local pressure. In some areas in 1930 such pressure caused the temporary collapse of the whole *chaukidari* system. Nor did the *chaukidars* prove themselves reliable in clashes between police and demonstrators. Outside the Goreakothi school in Saran the chaukidars broke and ran before the onset of the crowd, while at Khautana in Darbhanga they left the regular police to their fate once stones began to fly. Overall, the conduct of both *chaukidars* and regular policemen during the period of the civil disobedience movement indicated that the whole police system needed drastic and extensive reforms. But such reforms would be costly, and because of the financial problems bedevilling the province they were not undertaken. A decade later, the inadequacy of the police system was to contribute to the collapse of British rule during the Quit India revolt.

CHAPTER 6

THE KISAN SABHA MOVEMENT, 1936-39

In north Bihar during the late 1930s, in a context of unrest deriving from the impact of the Great Depression, the Bihar Provincial Kisan Sabha led an extensive peasant movement. Dominated by the political *sanyasi* Swami Sahajanand, and strongly influenced by the Congress Socialist Party, the movement demanded the surrender to the peasantry of land held in the *bakast*, i.e. 'cultivating' possession of the landlords. Much land had recently passed into the landlord's *bakast* possession because, unable to pay their rents because of the depression-induced collapse in primary produce prices, tenants had had their holdings sold up in rent suits. Though dominated by the better-established peasantry the *kisan* movement also featured substantial middle and poor peasant involvement. Until its containment in mid-1939 the movement divided the Bihar Congress and created serious problems for the provincial Congress Ministry which had come into office in 1937. This chapter explores the context within which the movement arose, surveys its development, and concludes with an assessment of its significance and impact.

I

Peasant unrest in north Bihar during the late 1930s derived mainly from the depression-induced collapse in primary produce prices. By December 1931 the price of grain had dropped to half that of 1929. The price depression continued until the advent of the Second World War. The serious effect of the fall in the price of primary products was intensified because the prices of consumer items remained stable.[1] In 1928 one rupee could only buy $5\frac{1}{2}$ *seers* of rice, but in 1936 it was sufficient to purchase 10 *seers*. In contrast, during the same period the price of cotton had only decreased slightly, that of kerosene oil had remained constant, and that of salt had increased slightly. (Table 6.1).

TABLE 6.1

Primary Produce and Commodity Prices, 1928 and 1936

(a) Primary Produce Prices
(Quantities given could be bought for one rupee)

	1928	1936
Common rice	5 seers, 8 chataks	10 seers
Wheat	7 " , 8 "	12 "
Maize	11 " , 9 "	19 "

(b) Commodity Prices

	1928	1936
Kerosene oil per case of 2 tins.	8 rupees, 9 annas	Rs. 8 A. 9
Cotton per bundle of 8 to 9 pounds.	8 " 11 "	7, 11
Salt per maund.	3 " 2 "	3, 4

Source: 'Report of the Bihar Kisan Enquiry Committee', Prasad Papers f VII, 1937, microfilm 6, chapter 3, pp.1, 2. NML.

In 1934 the region also suffered from a major earthquake which demolished houses, disrupted communications, and reduced the productivity of the land because deposits of sand emerged from fissures that opened up in the earth. The earthquake also adversely affected drainage, a development which, combined with the effects of deforestation, made flooding more frequent and serious.[2]

The 1930s were difficult for most people, but the particular impact of hard times varied throughout the levels of north Bihar society. Poor peasants benefited from the lower prices for food-grains, but suffered in other ways. Among the poor peasants, labourers found themselves pressured to accept an even larger proportion of their wages in kind rather than in cash. The economic downturn also decreased the demand for labour, thus depressing

wages.[3] Sharecroppers now found that they could earn
less than previously for the purchase of consumer items
by selling a portion of their share of the crops they cultivated. During the period of high prices before 1930 some
sharecroppers had become short-term tenants by paying
a high cash rental instead of a produce rent, hoping
thereby eventually to establish occupancy rights. After
the price slump their position became extremely precarious.[4]

Peasants who held land as occupancy tenants had more
legal protection than short-term tenants and sharecroppers
against summary eviction, but they also found themselves
under great pressure, particularly as in the pre-1930 era
of high prices rents had been raised to a high level. In
1932-33 the provincial government reported that

> Prices are now on the whole, about half the average
> of the prices for the years 1920 to 1930 and the bur-
> den of cash rents has in consequence doubled, for in
> order to pay his rent the raiyat has to sell twice as
> much of the produce of his holding as he had to sell
> before 1930.[5]

The effect of the doubling of the rental demand varied
in accordance with the balance of power between a landlord and his tenants. Rich peasants had financial reserves
and local influence, and thus weathered the storm more
easily than middle and poor peasants. Absentee and petty
landlords sometimes did not have sufficient local leverage
to pressure their tenants effectively. Some landlords,
realising that in the prevailing price conditions the rental
demand could not possibly be covered by the produce of
the land, began

> freely giving remissions in return for prompt payment
> of the balance...Other landlords are contenting them-
> selves with realising arrears, so that the outstandings
> which remain will not be time-barred and can be re-
> covered by suit when better times come.

But tenants suffered

> severely in big estates where there is a mechanically
> efficient management and no intimate contact with the
> people...in spite of the prevailing conditions the
> Darbhanga Raj has collected a large portion of its rents.[6]

Indeed, as a result of stricter management, the Darbhanga Raj rent collections for the five years from 1932 to 1937 totalled Rs.28,349,000, an increase of Rs.3,071,000 on the total for the preceding five year period.[7]

Tenants who fell behind in their rent payments could be summoned to court to face a rent suit and might have their tenancy rights sold up at auction to pay for the arrears of rent owing.[8] In the event only a small proportion of the tenants were taken to court. (Table 6.2). But many were forced to protect themselves from this possibility by plunging deeply into debt.[9]

TABLE 6.2

Rent Suits in Bihar, 1928-1940

Year	Suits	Year	Suits
1928	100,246	1935	180,001
1929	123,458	1936	148,496
1930	122,030	1937	147,101
1931	122,116	1938	161,668
1932	121,936	1939	176,519
1933	149,036	1940	177,816
1934	157,321		

Source: GB(0) *Report on the Administration of Civil Justice in the Province of Bihar (and Orissa)* for 1928 through to 1940 (Patna, annual, 1928 to 1940).

Even when a tenant did have his holding sold up his position was not without hope. The Darbhanga Raj filed a large number of suits and bought up the holdings when they were auctioned by the court to pay off the rent arrears, with the intention of either settling them with other occupancy tenants or else of cultivating them by means of labourers, sharecroppers, or short-term tenants. But the legal and administrative task of acquiring possession of a sold-up holding was long and arduous, and the inefficient, corrupt lower-level officials of the

Darbhanga Raj often did not complete the process. Some judgement debtors (and especially those with enough wealth and influence to confuse and sway the local *amlas*), remained in possession of their sold-up holding for years, enjoying its proceeds without paying any rent whatsoever, and eventually managed to regain their occupancy rights at little expense.[10]

Only a minority of tenants lost the legal rights to their holdings through rent suits and some of these tenants retained possession of their holdings. Nonetheless, many had the threat of legal action and dispossession hanging over them, which added to the general anxiety of having to live through a period of financial stringency.

Many of the peasants of north Bihar had been aroused by the civil disobedience movement, and this experience encouraged them to seek political solutions to their problems. In 1936 the Congress-sponsored Kisan Enquiry Committee commented that when '...they were asked to assemble in any public meeting they would come in large numbers believing that a way out of their distress would be found out by the organisers...'[11]

The *kisan sabha* movement assumed the leadership of the peasantry. Bihar's first *kisan sabhas* (peasant associations) had been formed in the 1918 to 1923 period, but subsequently became moribund.[12] From 1929 a number of local *kisan sabhas* had become active under the leadership of Swami Sahajanand Saraswati, a *sanyasi* who hailed from a Jujhautia Brahman and small zamindari family from Ghazipur district in the United Provinces.[13] These *kisan sabhas* operated as front organisations for the provincial Congress movement. In 1934, Swami Sahajanand co-ordinated their activities into the Bihar Provincial Kisan Sabha.[14]

On paper the Bihar Provincial Kisan Sabha had an elaborate formal structure, but Walter Hauser comments that it could be 'more accurately characterized as a movement than an organization as such. Its primary instruments were numerous meetings, the rallies and annual sessions'.[15] The Bihar Provincial Kisan Sabha sought to protect the interests of all *kisans*, but did not define clearly who exactly it meant by the word *kisan*, which can be variously translated to mean 'farmer', 'cultivator', or 'peasant'. In his early years as a *kisan* activist Swami Sahajanand gave the word a broad application, and hoped to unite landless labourers, sharecroppers, occupancy tenants and small zamindars into a coalition against the great zamindars and the administration.[16] But in contrast to this ideal the main support and impetus for the movement came from among the occupancy tenants of Bihar. Rich peasants took the lead in protest, but middle and poor peasants also participated.

Swami Sahajanand Saraswati was a loyal Congressman who thought that the national struggle should take precedence over other political campaigns and who held that the Indian National Congress must play the central role in the achievement of the goal of national independence. But Sahajanand also worried over the harsh economic situation and lacked confidence in the ability and willingness of the conservative mainstream of the Bihar Congress to initiate substantial agrarian reforms. From 1934 Sahajanand and his followers began to differ increasingly from the mainstream members of the Bihar Congress. In doing so, they were much influenced by a continuing groundswell of popular discontent and by the ideological and organisational impetus supplied by the Bihari members of the Congress Socialist Party.[17]

The Congress Socialists were a bloc of young intellectuals who sought to capture control of the national movement and ensure that it led both to Indian independence and to the creation of a democratic socialist society. The Bihar branch of the party was initiated in 1931 during the period of the Gandhi-Irwin Pact. Most of its members were jailed after the resumption of civil disobedience in January 1932. After their release from jail in April 1934 the Bihar Congress Socialists involved themselves wholeheartedly in the *kisan sabhas*, which they looked upon as 'the mass base they needed to attain their objectives'.[18] They became the dominant force in the organisation of the kisan movement, establishing a strong majority in the Bihar Provincial Kisan Council, the chief executive organ of the provincial *kisan sabhas*.

The intervention of the Congress Socialists into the Bihar Provincial Kisan Sabha created three tiers of leadership. At the top was the single, dominating figure of Swami Sahajanand. In the middle were the young intellectuals of the Bihar branch of the Congress Socialist Party, among whom Jay Prakash Narayan exerted great influence. Beneath them were activists, often of only limited education and from middle rather than high caste groups, who operated within a restricted locality.

The new perspectives supplied through the intervention of the Congress Socialists in the *kisan* movement greatly encouraged support for the policy of zamindari abolition. In November 1935, bowing before pressure from both the Congress Socialist activists and the 'discontented tenantry', Swami Sahajanand included this policy as a major plank in the platform of the provincial *kisan* movement.[19]

Apart from the abolition of the zamindari system, the main aims of the Bihar Provincial Kisan Sabha were the cancellation of agrarian debts; the granting of ownership rights over their holdings to peasants; the exemption from taxation of all those whose income was below the minimum necessary to keep them and their families at a reasonable standard of living; and the provision of gainful employment for the landless.

In the interim before these major, long-term aims could be fulfilled, the *kisan* movement sought the implementation of nineteen short-term aims, which included the provision by legislation of common pasture in every village, the cancellation of arrears of rent, the limitation of interest rates to 6 per cent, the provision of cheap government loans, the right to vote for every adult, and the reinstatement of peasants in lands lost due to their participation in the 'freedom movement' or due to the failure to pay revenue or rent during the economic depression. Before listing these aims the manifesto claimed that the Bihar Provincial Kisan Sabha 'stands...for all who live by cultivation' and argued that the *kisan* movement, by organising the villagers, 'enables them to put a stop to the thousand and one harassments and extortionate practices of their landlords and their men and of petty government officials'.[20]

Kisan sabha activists complemented the strong demands of the Bihar Provincial Kisan Sabha platform with militance in their propaganda and demonstrations. The conservative majority of Congressmen viewed these developments with alarm.[21] Conservative dominance of the nationalist movement had managed to ensure that in Bihar during civil disobedience, in contrast to the United Provinces,[22] no landlord-peasant conflict emerged. By its practice of assertiveness and its policy of agrarian reform the *kisan* movement threatened to split the Congress movement asunder, and in particular to destroy that alliance between small landlord and rich peasant which hitherto had been central to Congress activity.

But despite considerable tension and occasional eruptions of conflict an open cleavage within the Bihar Congress did not develop until after the January 1937 elections to the provincial legislative assembly. Prior to the elections mainstream Congressmen and *kisan* activists were bound together in a relationship of mutual need. The elections were held in an electorate enlarged, under the terms of the Government of India Act of 1935, from 1.1 per cent to 9.3 per cent of the population. Many of the newly enfranchised rich peasants were more impressed by *kisan sabha* propaganda in favour of agrarian reform than by the orthodox Congress 'constructive work' programme which sought to foster village handicrafts and improve village sanitation. *Kisan* activism provided an electoral asset from which mainstream Congressmen were glad to benefit and against which they could not afford to protest too openly.

Yet while the *kisan* movement held the agitational and propaganda initiative the conservative mainstream of Congress maintained control over the party organisation. *Kisan* activists formed only a small minority within the Bihar Congress and had only minority representation on the provincial Congress committee. They held firm control over the Patna District Congress Committee and for a time controlled the Gaya District Congress Committee, but mainstream Congressmen controlled all the other district committees. However *kisan* activists formed substantial minorities in the Champaran, Muzaffarpur, Darbhanga and Monghyr district committees. Given their position in the Congress organisation, *kisan* activists needed to delay confrontation with their opponents. Meanwhile they sought to increase their leverage by rallying mass support.[23]

In the pre-election period the kisan sabhas won votes for the Congress and increased the expectations and militancy of the peasantry. After the election the provincial administration informed the Government of India that

> In the more advanced parts voters, who would normally have done what their landlords told them to do, are reported to have remarked that they voted for the Congress because they had noticed that the kisan agitation had led to a marked diminution in the amount of begari [i.e. forced labour] which their landlords dared to demand.[24]

While *kisan* activists busied themselves rousing the peasantry their opponents in the mainstream of the Bihar Congress actively wooed and were wooed by local notables who were much concerned to avert social change. According to Rajendra Prasad one important consideration in the selection of Congress candidates was whether a prospective candidate could cover his own election expenses. In addition, he commented, 'local circumstances compelled' the nomination of candidates who were adequately representative of the prominent caste groups. In many instances locally influential men who previously had been lukewarm about or even hostile to the national movement became absorbed into the Bihar Congress and won nomination as candidates.[25]

The Bihar Congress achieved dramatic success in the 1937 elections. It won more than 90 per cent of the seats it contested and finished with ninety-eight of the 152 seats in the Bihar Legislative Assembly. Thanks to the mainstream Congress domination of the candidate selection process, only seven of the newly elected members of the assembly came from what the provincial government described as the 'socialist element', whereas most of the others could 'be described as belonging to the right wing'.[26] With unity no longer a pressing concern internal tensions were more likely to find expression.

II

Once the Bihar Congress had won victory in the 1937 elections, controversy developed over whether it should form a government. The *kisan* activists called on Congress to boycott the legislatures and to press forward with a programme of mass protest. But the majority of Congressmen did not want to see the spoils and privileges of power thrown away and realised the potential dangers of mass agitation to social stability and to their entrenched position within the party organisation. After a period of some hesitation and uncertainty, they ensured that Congress assumed office.[27]

Soon after taking office in July 1937 the new ministry found that it could not keep the allegiance of all those who had supported its coming into power. In impoverished Bihar[28] the government's powers of patronage were limited. Not all those seeking jobs and favours could be accommodated, and some of those who were left out rebelled against the party establishment and henceforth sided with the *kisan* and socialist activists. Caste and factional rivalries also led to the squeezing out of several leading figures.[29]

Nor, by the policies it initiated, did the ministry silence criticism from the left-wing made up of *kisan* activists and disgruntled 'rebels'. The Bihar Congress Ministry sought to ensure that the Congress remained what McDonald has described as a 'multi-interest' party dedicated to the preservation of stability and social harmony. It therefore initiated policies designed to improve the position of the tenantry without substantially affecting the position of the small zamindars. The left-wing responded by claiming that the ministry was betraying both the general Congress policy and the specific promises made during the election campaign.[30]

Throughout 1937 the left-wingers, bereft of power within the Congress Ministry and the Bihar Provincial Congress Committee, took steps to bring pressure to bear on the government by means of mass protest.[31] Among the peasantry, the combination of harsh economic conditions and *kisan sabha* propaganda had created a readiness to engage in direct action. In Bhagalpur in March 1936 the local *kisan* organisers interpreted the teachings of the *kisan* movement as a call to stop paying rent. In north Monghyr landlord-peasant tension developed within the Bhumihar community. In December 1937, shortly after a visit by Swami Sahajanand, tenants displaced from their land after it had been sold up in a rent suit attacked and killed the servant of a zamindar while he was ploughing the forfeited holdings. In south Bihar, in the Gaya and Patna districts and in the Barahiya Tal area of south Monghyr, peasants and landlords clashed repeatedly.[32]

Sahajanand and his lieutenants took an active interest in and drew inspiration from these local struggles. But they displayed a reluctance to escalate these local conflicts into a broad-based campaign of direct action against the zamindars and the administration. Their reluctance derived partly from their acceptance of the primacy of the national struggle against alien rule and the primacy of Congress within that struggle. The *kisan* leaders also, it seems probable, realised that as yet their organisation and support base did not have the strength to make mass action feasible and effective. Instead, *kisan sabha* workers concentrated on defending their position and, where possible, increasing their strength within the Congress organisation.

The struggle that developed in 1937 between the left and the mainstream of the Bihar Congress reached its climax at the elections, held in late December 1937, of delegates to the annual session of the Indian National Congress, due to be held at Haripura in February 1938. These elections were of crucial importance, because under the terms of the constitution adopted at the Bombay Congress plenary session in 1934 the delegates who were elected to attend the annual all-India Congress session also served on the provincial, district, and local Congress committees.

The attempt by the left-wing to expand its influence was particularly strong in Darbhanga, the home district of the skilled activist Ramnandan Misra, the estranged son of a wealthy Bhumihar zamindar.[33] The left rallied substantial support, but its opponents benefited from their control over the party machinery and their links with the small zamindars. Tension sharpened on 13 December when the Bihar Provincial Congress Committee voted in support of initiatives already taken by the Champaran, Saran and Monghyr District Congress Committees and agreed that in view of the 'violent' propaganda of *kisan* activists, Congress members would be barred from participation in *kisan sabha* activities.[34] This meant that the delegate elections offered the last chance for the *kisan* activists to establish themselves in the Congress organisation.

The conservative Congressmen used unscrupulous methods to ensure success in the delegate elections. They impeded the enrolment of *kisan* voters, enrolled their own supporters after the final deadline, and appointed their partisans as polling officers.[35] In Darbhanga the elections were disrupted by extensive disturbances. The conservatives posted *lathials* at polling booths to stop *kisan* supporters from voting and dissuaded other potential *kisan* voters from attending the poll by threatening them with ejection from their holdings.[36] By means both fair and foul the conservatives triumphed in Darbhanga and throughout north Bihar. In addition to consolidating their hold over the district committees, their electoral victory permitted them to ensure that not one left-winger was appointed to the provincial working committee, and that only five of the thirty-six Biharis elected to the All-India Congress Committee came from the left.

In north Bihar and particularly in Darbhanga left-wing activists kept trying to capture control over the local party organisation until the final months of 1938. They even set up rival, parallel, district Congress committees in both Darbhanga and Saran.[37] But eventually, with orthodox Congressmen denouncing them for their militancy and shutting every door in their face the left-wing activists were forced to relinquish their attempt to gain control over the party machine. They also were obliged to look to the interests of the peasantry because of the heightening of agrarian tensions over the question of *bakast* lands.

In August 1938 Ramnandan Misra reported from Darbhanga that

> In the interest of the cause...we must get out of the party struggle at least for a year. Kisan problems require our immediate attention. Situation is very critical and serious, how can we leave the kidans, who are being assaulted, murdered, abused and their crops and property looted. In any case I cannot leave my district at least for a week. Yesterday morning one of my workers was attempted to be murdered. I think we shall be able to save his life, but I must proceed to the spot at once [sic].[38]

From late 1938 onwards *kisan* activists concentrated on leading the peasantry in mass protest against their landlords and against the pro-landlord policies of the Bihar Congress and the provincial administration. The annual conference of the Bihar Provincial Kisan Sabha, held at Waini in Darbhanga in December 1938, resolved to use satyagraha as the chief weapon of struggle in defence of the peasants' interests.[39] Henceforth the *kisan* movement was engaged in frequent direct action, with the focus of activity on disputes over those lands held by zamindars as their *bakast* holdings.

III

Under the zamindari system *bakast* (also spelt *bakasht*) was, along with *ryoti* and *zirat*, one of the three main categories of agricultural land. *Ryoti* lands, which generally comprised by far the greater part of a zamindar's property, were those in which an occupancy tenant had acquired protected rights. *Zirat* lands, which usually formed only a small part of a zamindar's property, were the 'homestead' lands of the zamindar in which no other rights could accrue. *Bakast* land consisted of holdings in which the zamindar exercised direct control over cultivation, but in which, under certain circumstances, occupancy rights could be acquired by short-term tenants paying a cash rental or by sharecroppers.[40] In common parlance, however, the legal and administrative distinction between *bakast* and *zirat* often was obscured because people used either term to refer to all the land over which the zamindar exercised direct cultivating control, whether or not it had the capacity to accrue occupancy rights. In the following discussion, the term *bakast* is used in its strict legal-administrative sense.

From the late nineteenth century the shortage of land in north Bihar had become increasingly acute. By the 1930s land was so scarce in some areas that landlords were able to rent out for cultivation lands formerly used for tanks, roads, and burning *ghats*.[41] With their property progressively dissipated through inheritance, zamindars competed fiercely with peasants over the control of land,[42] and disputes involving *bakast* holdings became common.

During the 1930s the *bakast* issue became particularly crucial because an unusually high number of tenants' holdings were sold up as a result of rent arrears suits. Often the purchaser of the holding was the landlord who was glad by this means to convert what had been *ryoti* land into *bakast* land, a category of land in which, for the time being at least, no rights other than those of the landlord existed. By having his *bakast* lands tilled by labourers, short-term tenants, or sharecroppers, a landlord could generally make a better profit, and be less hampered in doing so by legal and social restrictions, than he could by letting out the land to an occupancy tenant.

Small landlords who personally supervised cultivation profited most from *bakast* holdings, whereas large landlords often found that their *amlas*, who were indispensible for supervisory work in the large estates, soaked up most of the extra profits that could be derived from holding direct cultivating control. Large landlords generally attempted to resettle newly sold up land with an occupancy tenant. But because the administrative machinery of the great zamindari estates moved slowly and inefficiently the great landlords often held large areas as *bakast*.[43]

Often the former tenants of lands which had newly become *bakast* remained to till the land as sharecroppers or short-term tenants. Because of this development the legal position concerning the right to cultivate the lands often became 'exceedingly obscure'.[44] Former tenants who, during the depression period, had been pushed down a rung in the social ladder were deeply resentful. They viewed the coming of the depression not as one of the normal risks of agricultural life but as a highly unusual circumstance, equivalent to a major natural calamity, against the effects of which they felt they deserved protection and support from their zamindars and the administration, rather than harassment and the loss of the legal rights to their land. Even more resentful were those tenants who had actually been displaced from their holdings, which had been passed down to them through several generations, to make way for another occupancy tenant or for a sharecropper or short-term tenant. These resentments were articulated into a recurrent demand for the restoration of *ryoti* rights in *bakast* lands to tenants who had lost them during the period of the depression.

Once agitation began over newly *bakast* lands, moreover, poor peasants became inspired to claim possession of lands that had been held as *bakast* by landlords over a long period. To do so they appealed to a provision of the *Bengal Tenancy Act of 1885* which endowed sharecroppers and short-term tenants who cultivated *bakast* holdings continuously for a period of twelve years or longer with occupancy rights in the holdings. This provision had seldom been taken advantage of because of the ignorance, low morale, and lack of power of those it was intended to benefit. But in the 1930s, under the impetus of the *kisan* movement, poorer peasants began to campaign for the fulfilment of their rights in long-term *bakast* lands.

The distinction between protest over control of newly sold up *bakast* land and that over long established *bakast* land was not clearly defined. To strengthen their claim peasants, no matter what the facts were, tended to claim that they had only recently lost their occupancy rights in the land under dispute, and conversely landlords tended to claim that they had held the disputed land as their *bakast* over a long period. Because of the limitations of the evidence available, it is not always possible to clarify the position.[45] Throughout Bihar in the late 1930s campaigns seeking the granting of *ryoti* rights in both types of *bakast* land ran concurrently, reinforcing one another.[46]

In 1938 the importance of the *bakast* issue increased because, after detailed consultation with the zamindars to assure them that their essential interests were being protected, the Bihar Congress Ministry initiated ameliorative measures designed to defuse *kisan* protest. The measures included legislation allowing the reduction of rents in view of the low prices prevailing and legislation concerning newly *bakast* lands. The *bakast* restoration bill provided, under certain conditions, for the return to tenants of lands which had been sold up in the period from 1929 to 1936, if in return the tenant paid, within a period of five years, half the auction price of the holding as well as the legal costs.[47] The amount of land to be returned varied in proportion to the amount that had been sold up. (Table 6.3).

The *bakast* restoration bill was emasculated by clauses exempting from restoration those lands which were either (a) under the direct cultivating control of a petty zamindar,

TABLE 6.3

Formula for the Restoration of *bakast* Lands, 1938

Area Sold Up	Quantity Restorable
Less than 6 acres	All to be restored
More than 6 but less than 15 acres	Half to be restored
More than 15 but less than 30 acres	A third to be restored
More than 30 acres	A quarter to be restored

Source: *Indian Nation*, 31 July 1938.

who tilled the land by means of labourers, or (b) which had already been settled with another occupancy tenant. In the event the legislation benefited very few tenants. The term 'petty zamindar' was defined broadly, which meant that only a small minority of those landlords who held *bakast* land under direct cultivation were liable to have it restored. And in many cases former tenants who had remained associated with their former *ryoti* holdings as sharecroppers or short-term tenants were summarily displaced from them by zamindars anxious either to re-settle the holdings with other peasants willing and able to pay a better price for them than could be gained from the former tenants under the restoration provisions, or else to bring the holdings under their own direct cultivation.[48] It was reported that having learnt of the legislation 'the land-holders of Bhagalpur have settled every inch of restorable *bakast* lands benami or on acceptance of salami'.[49]

The *Bakast Restoration Act*, moreover, moved at a snail's pace through the legislature, which allowed zamindars additional time to find ways to avoid its provisions. Many tenants, furthermore, could not afford to pay the legal costs and half of the auction price for the *bakast* lands.[50] The efforts of former tenants to establish that *bakast* lands should be returned to them and the attempts of sharecroppers and short-term tenants to establish their occupancy rights over *bakast* lands also often failed because of the peasants' inability to bring convincing documentation before the courts. As the author of the provincial year book for 1938-39 commented

> the cultivator often finds it difficult to prove his claim even when it is just, because the conditions under which bakast land is let out by the landlord make it impossible for him to produce documents. In the absence of reliable oral evidence on either side, the courts have in the past been compelled to decide cases mainly on documentary evidence.[51]

Documentary evidence usually favoured the landlords because through their agents, the *patwaris*, they kept a strict control over the creation and distribution of documents and could usually ensure that their potential legal adversaries had little documentary evidence on hand. And even where their opponents had been able to collect some written evidence, the zamindar and his *amlas* always could bribe lower level officials and forge documents.

One example of forgery is revealed in a letter from a member of the Darbhanga Raj legal staff. The letter concerns the progress of court cases over a disputed area near village Raghopur in Darbhanga known as the Tinconwa zerat and reads in part:

> ...on account of the claim of the accused to the tinconwa lands the other two cases fixed for the tenth have become difficult...In order to explain away the receipts and prove that those do not refer to the disputed tinconwa [lands] and then to prove that the disputed tinconwa [area] is in Khas [i.e. direct] cultivation of the Raj, what labour I have been taking in examining and shifting documents and in getting maps and statements prepared can better be known from your Amlas. Today I had in my own hand given forms of statements to the Zirat clerk, Amin and others and they compiled them in part and to see whether they are doing rightly this evening I again examined them and compared them with registers and gave them further instructions to complete them and get other wanting papers. As desired by you, I am personally doing the whole thing and for reasons better known, [sic] we cannot safely rely on others for such matters.[52]

IV

Disadvantaged in the courts, and receiving no sympathy from the administration and the mainstream of the Bihar Congress, the peasantry had no alternative other than direct action. By having effects quite opposite to its nominal intentions the *Bakast Restoration Act* crystallised conflict over the *bakast* issue. The most important centre of agitation was the Padri circle of the Darbhanga Raj. In the Padri circle the discontented peasantry engaged in what the circle manager later described as 'a violent explosion of...agitation', in the course of which rent collections 'almost stopped' and the 'loot of Raj crops standing in Zirat and Dahnal [i.e. flood affected] lands was...a daily feature'.[53]

In the Padri (or Parri) circle in south-east Darbhanga the peasants demanded the return of *ryoti* rights in newly *bakast* lands. In the late 1930s the Padri area had a population of 40,000 people spread over fifty villages. 'Practically the whole population', Ramnandan Misra reported, 'consists of Koeris and Goalas who have been kept down under the iron wheel of the Hindu society'.[54] Until the 1930s the area had grown lucrative cash crops and the landlord had been able to raise the rents to a high level. But throughout the 1930s Padri suffered repeatedly from serious flooding because the local Darbhanga Raj officials had neglected to keep the dams earlier built for flood protection in good repair.[55] Flooding, combined with the collapse in primary produce prices, had a disastrous effect on the peasantry.

> Year after year, [they] would cultivate in the tragic hope of getting something. But nothing would come except the notice of the sale of their holdings. In this way about ten thousand bighas...became bakast lands...But the lands remained in the possession of the tenants.[56]

The Padri peasants received little sympathy from the agents of their landlord. On the contrary, the *patwaris* and other *amlas* of the Darbhanga Raj took advantage of the tenants' difficulties to bring extra pressure to bear on them. Nor were the Padri circle managers willing to ease their burden.[57] Consequently they turned readily to *kisan sabha* activists for assistance.

In June 1936 the local officials of the Darbhanga Raj broke up a large *kisan* meeting by driving an elephant into the crowd. Using this incident as a rallying cry, *kisan* workers continued their efforts to have the peasants' grievances redressed. In 1937, in response to continuing agitation, Sri Krishna Sinha, the Bihar Congress Chief Minister, visited Padri in the company of R.E. Russell, the Tirhut Commissioner. Subsequently the administration made representations to the top management of the Darbhanga Raj.[58] The Chief Manager, G.P. Danby, made a personal investigation and in May 1938 reported that

> The tenantry are generally in a deplorable condition... If we do not give immediate consideration to the tenants so distressed will they become that I cannot imagine their future. There has been considerable agitation. I am ashamed to say that it is due to some extent to the neglect and lack of sympathy shown to tenants...I believe the tenants are still loyal to the Raj and would become as good tenants as any other if now, and in the future, due consideration were given to them. [sic][59]

Danby tried to help the Padri peasantry by lowering rents and cancelling rent arrears.[60] However as chief executive of the Darbhanga Raj he also supervised determined efforts to ensure that all *bakast* holdings were settled on occupancy tenures.[61] The drive to settle holdings on occupancy tenures diminished the good done by rent remission and arrear cancellation. The settlement drive played into the hands of a small minority of 'money lending kisans'[62] who could afford to pay the high *salami* rates being levied (despite legislation passed in mid-1938 specifically abolishing *salami*), and could influence the local Raj *amlas* in their favour. In 1939 the circle manager reported that '35 per cent of the tenantry has become landless'[63] and Ramnandan Misra commented that

> by starting land settlement the Raj is forcing us to organize Bakast struggle. In several plots of land I found standing sugar cane crops but the land has been settled with another person. For instance in the village Sihma, a plot has been settled with Tribeni Raut, where still stands the crop of the tenant who has been cultivating it for long.[64]

In the Padri area peasants sought the return of lands which only recently had become *bakast*. Elsewhere however peasants sought control of holdings which had been *bakast* over a long period. For example in the Pandoul area in Darbhanga sharecroppers and short-term tenants, many of them Yadav by *jati*, began to claim rights to long established *bakast* lands. In the Pandoul area one piece of land which became the subject of a series of related disputes had been let out every year by the Darbhanga Raj for the growing of a *rabi* crop and had then been resumed so that the Raj could use it for the cultivation of sugar cane. The local villagers, if they could establish that they had tilled this land successfully for a period of twelve years or more, were legally entitled to be awarded occupancy rights over it.[65]

Walter Hauser and M.V. Harcourt have characterised the *bakast* struggle as a conflict between distinct social strata.[66] This assessment is certainly true of developments in Pandoul and Padri, where middle caste, poor and middle peasants struggled against the Darbhanga Raj, the centre of Maithil Brahman power and the greatest zamindari in Bihar. But elsewhere the class character of *bakast* protest was less clear-cut because the struggle was articulated through tensions within the village elite.

In Radhanager, the north Bihar village studied by Ramashray Roy, simmering discontent existed among the poorer peasants, who were under the thumb of an interconnected group of Brahman families. In the 1930s *kisan sabha* activists attempted to draw on this discontent to initiate a mass movement but found it hard to get protest underway because the poorer peasants feared reprisals from their landlords. But eventually, they succeeded by taking advantage of the fact that

> Some of the impoverished landowning Brahmana families had some old scores to settle with their richer brethren; others, seriously indebted [to them]... were in search of an opportunity to bring their indebtedness to an end – because debts were not legally registered – by breaking away from their benefactors.

The *kisan* organisers managed to win the support of these families, and the 'impoverished landed gentry...joined their social and economic inferiors in a common fight'.[67]

In north Bihar in 1939 intensified *bakast* protest culminated in the employment of satyagraha as a weapon of last resort. In principle *kisan* direct action was to be nonviolent, but in actuality violent clashes occurred.[68] In Radhanager village for example the struggle incorporated numerous law suits, the social boycott of landlords by their tenants, and the 'use of physical force'.[69] In north Bihar clashes over *bakast* holdings occurred on a small scale and in widely dispersed areas. Since the crucial issue was the ownership and possession of holdings the clashes occurred when one or the other party to a dispute attempted to exert what it claimed to be its rights in a particular plot of land. Such action might take the form of ploughing up and sowing the disputed land, or the harvesting of crops growing on this land. It might also involve the sabotage of crops previously planted by the opposition party. The peak months for *bakast* clashes, as for agrarian disputes generally, were those in which harvesting and/or ploughing and planting were under way - December/January, March/April, and June/July/August.[70]

The zamindars, knowing that they had the sympathy of the administration, generally called in the police when a confrontation seemed imminent. The administration posted extra police in particularly troubled areas and established a special police station in Darbhanga.[71] The small scale of the encounters, and their occurrence in the open fields, made it easier for the police and the zamindars to control them. Unlike those of the clashes of the civil disobedience period which had occurred in congested urban settings, there were fewer bystanders to be drawn into action against the police and there were few observers to carry away and publicise stories of police harshness. In addition the *bakast* movement got a bad press. It was unsympathetically treated and under-reported in the nationalist media and subjected to a tirade of criticism in the *Indian Nation*.

In February 1939 the *kisan* movement received a fillip when, at Reora in the Gaya district in south Bihar, the District Magistrate, after investigating a dispute that had been simmering for several months, made a settlement which awarded four-fifths of the disputed land to the tenants. The settlement subsequently created dissension among the peasants because the Bhumihar tenants resented 'Jadunandan Sharma's socialist distribution of the land in equal shares to the raiyats whether of high or low castes'.[72] However in the short term the success at Reora encouraged *kisan* workers in Darbhanga and elsewhere in north Bihar to continue with *bakast* campaigns. At Dekuli and Raghopore in Darbhanga, according to a Bihar government report, neither the local *kisan* workers nor the zamindars were cooperating with officially supported efforts to arrange a compromise settlement. The *kisan* workers, the report commented disapprovingly, seemed to be 'hell bent on satyagraha'.[73]

On 16 March, at Dekuli in the Bahera *thana* of Darbhanga, a group of villagers obstructed the progress of a cartload of rice which was being taken away on behalf of a local zamindar. A quarrel developed and one of the zamindars was assaulted. In retaliation the local zamindars and their supporters fired on the villagers, wounding nine of them. During April, elsewhere in the district, *kisans* 'divided the bakasht land of their malik between themselves without any opposition from the maliks'. In the first fortnight of June, with the beginning of the ploughing season, there occurred such a surge of activity that the administration reported that the 'kisan movement...appears to be working to a crisis'. A fortnight later the administration reported that 'the agrarian situation continues to deteriorate and reports of attempts or threats to seize bakasht land have come in from nearly every district in Bihar'.[74]

In the Raghopore and Dekuli areas of Darbhanga the *kisan* leaders were all set to initiate satyagraha, and only postponed its initiation pending the results of official efforts to arrange a settlement. At Raghopore the dispute was settled on terms which, according to an official view, were 'very favourable to the tenants'. But at Dekuli and elsewhere attempts at settlement failed, and tension increased. At Chitauli village in Saran *kisan* activists and supporters of the landlord clashed over disputed lands. Two of the *kisan* activists were beaten up, and the *kisan* leader, Jamuna Karjee, was arrested and sentenced to eight months imprisonment.[75] By the first weeks of July, in defiance of the All-India Congress Committee's ban on the initiation of satyagraha without the authorisation of the relevant provincial Congress committee, *kisan* activists were leading peasants in direct protest against their zamindars in a number of localities.

The storm centre of *kisan sabha* activity over the *bakast* issue during 1939 was Darbhanga, the district where *kisan* activists had made the strongest efforts to capture control of the Congress party machine. It was officially reported that in Darbhanga in early July

> Attempts to seize the land or to obstruct cultivation... have been almost daily occurrences and numerous clashes have occurred. There has been a large number of prosecutions and a number of the principal leaders...have been arrested. The agitation was intensified by the Provincial Kisan Sabha meeting which was held at Sakri close by on the 7th and 8th...Volunteers are now being imported from elsewhere to continue the attack which it is intended to enlarge into a general attack upon the bakast lands of the Darbhanga estate. It has been necessary to keep Magistrates and armed police continuously on the spot and a large number of arrests have been made. It is clear that this agitation is going to be made a provincial issue as the attack is upon the principal landlord of the province.[76]

In July, in the Pandoul area of Darbhanga, one confrontation began when some Darbhanga Raj *amlas* arrived with a tractor to plough a disputed holding. The local tenants bombarded the tractor driver with a volley of stones and attacked the Raj *amlas*.[77] Similar disturbances occurred in three Muzaffarpur *thanas*, while in the Gogri *thana* in north Monghyr police arrested several leaders for encouraging a crowd to plough disputed lands. In this area, according to an official report,

> most of the lands have been ploughed and settled by the landlords, but attempts have been made to re-plough the lands and uproot the seedlings.[78]

By the middle of July, according to a *kisan sabha* publicity officer, the 'agrarian situation was getting more serious day by day'.[79]

For some time it seemed that the *bakast* issue would lead to wider and more intensive disturbances, but a mixture of coercion and concession thwarted such a development. In Darbhanga by late July the police had arrested around 200 kisan protesters, thus striking a severe blow to the movement. When *amlas* of the Darbhanga Raj arrived at a village in the Pandoul area on 6 August to plough some disputed holdings only women, children and old men rallied to demonstrate against them, all the younger adult males already having been arrested. However, the protesters, most of whom came from the Yadav *jati*, put up a brave fight. They stopped the ploughing by sitting down in front of the plough bullocks, and only left after they had been jostled and beaten by the Raj *amlas*.[80]

With the immediate future of the Darbhanga campaign looking bleak, Jay Prakash Narayan intervened and made a fresh attempt, with official support, to arrange a compromise settlement. Success in containing the *kisan* campaign in Darbhanga, the provincial government later reported, was achieved through cooperation between the district officials and the members of the local district Congress Committee. The head of the district Congress Committee, Satya Narain Singh, MLA, the administration reported approvingly, had 'worked hard to counteract false propaganda by the Kisan Sabha and to infuse a more reasonable frame of mind among the tenants'.[81]

The imprisonment of *kisan sabha* activists and administrative initiatives to ensure the negotiation of settlements which made some concessions dampened the fires of peasant discontent. In addition to the granting of concessions in individual disputes, there was also the general effect of reforms in the tenancy law which allowed for the reduction of rents. The rent reduction operations carried out by the administration in the late 1930s, Hauser points out, affected only limited areas and did not always serve the interests of the tenants. Indeed in some instances, tenants were impoverished by the legal costs they incurred while trying to take advantage of the reduction legislation. But Hauser concludes that despite this the rent reduction operations did alleviate the situation in politically critical areas.[82]

By early August the situation had quietened considerably. The only exception to this general trend was a clash between landlords and *kisans* in the Laukaha *thana* in the Madhubani subdivision of Darbhanga district, during which the landlords' *amlas* opened fire, killing two men and injuring several others. At the end of the month the provincial government reported that

> There has been a general decrease in agitation partly
> owing to the fact that the ploughing and the sowing
> season is drawing to a close and partly due to ex-
> haustion and the success of local officers with the
> assistance of prominent non-officials in settling a
> large number of important disputes.[83]

A fortnight later, in mid-September, the government was able to report that kisan sabha activity had 'become much less pronounced',[84] and it was clear that the provincial government had effectively contained the movement. The government had achieved this success with relatively little trouble. In Darbhanga, the district where the movement attained its greatest strength, the police curbed protest by arresting some 200 *kisan* protesters. In Bihar as a whole only about 600 people were arrested during 1939 in connection with the *bakast* movement.[85] This figure pales into insignificance when compared with the figure of 10,889 arrests made in connection with civil disobedience up to November 1930.[86] Nor at any stage, and again in contrast to the civil disobedience movement, did *bakast* campaigners effectively challenge the local authority of the police by giving them a sound beating during small-scale clashes. The *bakast* movement was limited both in the areas and in the number of people it affected. The Bihar Congress Ministry viewed the campaign with anxiety, but found the mechanisms of control at its disposal adequate to deal with the challenge.

By September 1939 the campaign clearly was on the wane. Protest recurred in subsequent months, but not with the same intensity.[87] From September, with the coming of the Second World War, those *kisan* workers who were not in jail were distracted from the *bakast* issue by the question of what attitude to take to the war. The following month a settlement was reached in the long-standing Padri dispute, on terms which the government regarded as 'very favourable to the tenants'. Later in October there was an upturn in activity, and the administration remarked that more protests could be expected as the harvesting season approached.[88]

But these protests did not eventuate, partly because on 31 October, in obedience to an All-India Congress Committee resolution, the Bihar Ministry resigned. The decision to relinquish office in the provinces, according to the All-India Committee, was an act of protest against the way Britain had brought India into the war without consulting the nationalist leadership and without offering Indians further constitutional advance in return for help in the war effort.[89]

After the resignation of the Ministry the left-wing and mainstream members of the nationalist movement coalesced in opposition to the British. This development has inspired B.R. Tomlinson, M.V. Harcourt and G. McDonald to argue that the need to preserve party unity was the underlying reason for the decision to relinquish office. This suggestion may have some validity at the level of all-India politics, and in relation to other provinces, but in the context of political developments in Bihar in the late 1930s it cannot be supported.

B.R. Tomlinson contends that the prevalence of factional conflict over spoils and the resulting adverse effect on the prestige of the Congress movement encouraged the party leadership to decide that a spell out of office and a revival of anti-British propaganda would restore party unity and clean up the tarnished image of the nationalist movement. But though Tomlinson has demonstrated that since at least the early 1930s bitter factional conflict had been characteristic of provincial and local Congress activity, he does not present evidence in support of the view that in Bihar by late 1939 the problems of unity and image arising from factional strife had become compelling enough to force the Congress out of office.[90]

G. McDonald and M.V. Harcourt have suggested that the strength of the left-wing opposition to the mainstream of the Congress obliged the conservative Congress leadership to pay the price of office resignation in order to restore unity and preserve control.[91] But their claims are exaggerated: the challenge of the left-wing had only affected a limited area and involved only a limited number of people. By August 1939, weeks before the resignation decision, the movement had been contained by the Bihar Congress Ministry and the provincial administration and was on the wane.

In late 1939 mainstream and left-wing Congressmen agreed over the need to oppose British rule but differed

over the tactics which should be employed to express this
opposition. In the following months left-wingers called
for the initiation of mass protest against imperial rule,
and partly as a result of the pressure they brought to
bear the All-India Congress Committee adopted the compromise tactic of 'individual satyagraha'. The demands
of this debate over tactics took attention away from the
waning *bakast* movement. In November 1939 there was
one notable landlord/peasant clash, during which shots
were fired and a member of the peasants' party was killed.
Otherwise the situation remained quiet, and *kisan* workers
were reported to be 'marking time, waiting to see how the
political situation develops'. Concerning Darbhanga an
official report commented that 'where a few months ago
kisan agitation was causing grave anxiety the Kisan
Sabhaites are now quiet and are not speaking against the
Congress'.[92]

In the first fortnight of December the possibility of a
revival of *bakast* agitation was further reduced by a 20
per cent rise in food grain prices. This increase marked
the end of the long period of depression and took the
edge off *kisan* discontent.[93] In December, despite the
commencement of the harvesting season, the agrarian
situation remained quiet and 'nothing but ordinary disputes between landlords and tenants' were reported. And
in January 1940, the condition of the countryside was
officially estimated to be 'unusually quiet'. The *bakast*
campaign, which at one stage had caused 'grave anxiety'
in official ranks, had come to an end.[94]

V

In the late 1930s a strong peasant movement developed
in north Bihar. Its leaders claimed the right to shape
Congress policy because of their support among the
peasantry. 'Who does not know', Jay Prakash Narayan
asked in December 1937, 'that our Kisan Sabha workers
won the last general election for the Congress and are
asking for nothing more than the fulfilment of the Congress
Agrarian Programme?'.[95] The leaders of the movement
attempted unsuccessfully to capture control of the Congress and then, impelled by the repercussions of the
bakast legislation introduced by the Congress Ministry,

led a protest campaign in defence of the rights of peasants in *bakast* lands.

The Bihar Congress responded strongly to the challenge of this peasant movement. Though lackadaisical in their activity in other areas,[96] the conservative majority of Congressmen held firmly to the reins of power. In holding on to power they were much assisted by the prestige and sympathy gained for Congress during the nationalist struggle, by the administrative experience gained by many of them on district and municipal boards and in the reformed councils, by the strength of their links with vested interests in the localities, and by their close cooperation with the civil service and the police. They also benefited from the failure of their left-wing opponents to mount an effective campaign against them.

In Bihar, in the late 1930s, the main (indeed almost the only) alternative political institution to the left of the mainstream of the Congress was the Bihar Provincial Kisan Sabha.[97] The leaders of the Bihar Provincial Kisan Sabha, (like the provincial and local Congress leaders), were high caste men from zamindari backgrounds who accepted the primacy of the nationalist struggle over other agitation. The campaigns they led sought to transform the policy and activities of the Congress, not to pose a radical alternative. Their supporters were mainly middle caste peasants who sought to defend themselves against zamindari pressure. Such people held themselves distinct from the low caste, Harijan, and *Adivasi* peasants whom they often themselves oppressed.[98]

The aims of the *kisan* movement were essentially reformist. Because of the increase in the extent of *bakast* lands and because of the repercussions of the 1938 *bakast* legislation *kisan* activists were obliged to pay considerable attention to the *bakast* issue. Nonetheless, those involved in the *kisan* movement did have, but failed to grasp, the opportunity to initiate agitation over other issues.

Judging merely from the rhetoric of *kisan* activists and the contents of the *kisan sabha* manifesto the *kisan* movement might have been expected to engage in a rent strike or to call for a general moratorium on debt repayments. But this kind of initiative was not attractive because the main body of *kisan* supporters had property which could be confiscated in the course of a rent or debt suit. Moreover a rent or debt strike would create unrest among those at the bottom of the social scale.

An important component of the appeal of the *bakast* issue was its conservative connotation. Agitation over *bakast* lands, rather than being a radical initiative, comprised an attempt to work within the zamindari system, either to re-establish rights which had previously existed, or else to take advantage of rights under the law which had been established over the years. In a conservative society this call to defend rights which had been transgressed won substantial support.

The *bakast* issue had the potential to mobilise a variety of supporters drawn from a wide section of the social spectrum. But the Bihar Provincial *Kisan* sabha did not make use of the issue to cross the status line which divided Harijans and Adivasis from the rest of society, even though there were stirrings of dissidence among Adivasi sharecroppers over their rights in long established *bakast* lands.[99] Nor, though it claimed to represent 'all who live by cultivation',[100] did the Bihar Provincial *Kisan Sabha* take much interest in the plight of landless labourers, except to assure them that there was no need for them to organise themselves separately since it would protect their interests.

The Bihar Kisan Manifesto, rather than calling for the breaking up of large holdings and the distribution of land to the landless, instead called for the granting of full ownership rights over their holdings to tenants and for the provision of gainful employment for the landless. When, in 1937, under the leadership of the Harijan activist, Jagjivan Ram, the Bihar Provincial Khet Mazdoor Sabha (Agricultural Labourers' Association) came into existence, it received no support from the province's *kisan sabha* movement.[101] And when, in the mid-1930s, agrarian labourers began to protest against exploitation by their *kisan* and zamindar employers their protest was quickly curbed by intimidation and physical assault.[102]

Some years later, having become disillusioned with the movement that he had led in the 1930s, Swami Sahajanand pointed out that it was 'really the middle and big cultivators' who had been 'for the most part with the Kisan Sabha', and contended that such people were in the habit of 'using the Kisan Sabha for their benefit and gain'. He and his supporters, in contrast, had been trying to use these middle and big peasants 'to strengthen the Sabha, till the lower and lowest strata of the peasantry are awakened to their real economic and political interests and needs...'.[103]

During the middle months of 1939 *bakast* protest created difficulties for the Bihar Congress government. But ultimately the government, by combining coercion and concession, brought the situation under control. In its implementation of concessions the Bihar Congress consulted carefully with the zamindars and protected their essential interests, thus assuring their subsequent support. When the Bihar Congress Ministry relinquished office in October 1939 it did so from a position of strength rather than of weakness. Withdrawal from office reduced intra-party and agrarian tensions, but these results were by-products rather than conscious aims of the decision to resign.

Though contained, the *kisan* movement won some concessions and encouraged the peasants to defend their rights. The administration observed that 'a general awakening among the tenants as a result of the *kisan* movement' had made it more difficult for zamindars to impose *abwabs*, while one Darbhanga Raj circle manager noted that 'The tenants are not so submissive as they used to be.' Another Raj official commented that increased difficulties in rent collection were due to 'the process of transformation of 'Prajas' [i.e. subjects] to 'Kisans'.'[104]

The development of this consciousness meant that a decade subsequently, with the coming of Indian independence and universal suffrage, the demand for the abolition of the zamindari system became irresistible. But like the *bakast* legislation, the zamindari abolition legislation raised false hopes. Its implementation benefited the village elite at the expense, not only of large and absentee zamindars, but also of many middle and most poor peasants.[105]

After announcing that the Bihar Congress Ministry would relinquish office the Chief Minister, Sri Krishna Sinha, thanked the police and the administration for their cooperation during a period of agrarian turmoil.[106] By reacting conservatively towards an agrarian movement the Bihar Congress weakened its support among some people and used up some of the political capital it had gained through the sacrifices of the civil disobedience movement. But because the *bakast* movement had been limited in its extent and support, and because conservative Congressmen had acted as mediators and brought the peasants concessions, the Bihar Congress emerged from the period of *bakast* struggle with its prestige largely unimpaired.

The use by the Congress government of the police as a coercive force in support of landlords in their disputes with peasants over *bakast* lands increased hostility to the police. And the expectation that eventually Congress would return to government had a bad effect on the morale of Indian policemen and officials when British government was re-established after the resignation of the Congress Ministry. Lukewarm support for British rule manifested itself widely, particularly among those younger officials who had been appointed while the Congress Ministry held power.[107] This decline in morale was to contribute to the collapse of the police and administrative apparatus during the Revolt of August 1942.

CHAPTER 7

THE QUIT INDIA REVOLT, 1942

In August 1942, the All-India Congress Committee called on the British to 'quit India', and in an attempt to force them to leave, initiated mass civil disobedience. In response the British administration implemented a carefully worked out programme designed to cope with the challenge of large-scale civil disobedience in time of war. The British arrested leading Congressmen, declared the Congress organisation illegal and shut down Congress offices and printing presses. Throughout most of India these measures succeeded and after three or four days of angry demonstrations the situation quietened. But in Bombay city, in Gujarat, in the Deccan, in Midnapore district of Bengal, in the eastern United Provinces and in Bihar protest against the British intensified. In north Bihar British rule collapsed, and was only re-established by the deployment of large bodies of troops. Before it was curbed the 'Quit India Revolt' caused extensive damage to government property and greatly disrupted communications. In the opinion of the Viceroy the uprising provided the most serious challenge to British control over India since the Revolt of 1857.[1]

The success of the Bihar Congress in temporarily demolishing British rule over north Bihar resulted in part from the weakness of the police and administrative apparatus. This weakness had increased during the 1917 to 1942 period. Meanwhile, the depth and strength of support for the nationalist movement had increased greatly, particularly among the village elite. The upsurge of August 1942 received much impetus from the militance and determination of rich peasants and small landlords. Yet the strength of the movement also resulted from prevailing conditions of political uncertainty and economic pressure. This chapter examines the context within which the movement emerged, discusses its development and containment, and concludes with an assessment of its significance and impact.

I

The coming of the Second World War brought an abrupt end to the economic depression of the 1930s. By March 1941 the average price of coarse rice in Bihar had increased by 13.2 per cent over the average price in 1940 and by 32.5 per cent over the average price in 1939.[2] Primary produce prices rose steadily higher throughout the wartime period (Table 7.1). With rising prices and economic dislocation because of the war, many commodities became scarce. For the village elite, wartime conditions provided many opportunities to profit through grain dealing and black marketing.

The effect of the scarcity and high price conditions on the middle peasants was less clear cut. All middle peasants suffered from shortages of cotton, kerosene and other important consumer items, but some found it easier to pay rent and to profit from the sale of cash crops and rice. The prices for rice and other crops produced for the market generally rose higher than did the prices for the 'inferior' grains, such as gram, on which the middle peasant relied for the subsistence of himself and his family. Thus a middle peasant might manage successfully even when his harvests were below average. The circumstances in which a middle peasant found himself depended on his good or bad luck, the skill of his cultivation, the impact — which varied throughout the region — of flood, drought and crop disease, and of the particular conditions prevailing when he brought his crops to market.[3]

For the poor peasant, however, scarcity and high prices were as disadvantageous as they were advantageous for the rich peasant and small landlord. As prices rose the real value of cash wages diminished, while scarcity meant that those who received wages in kind found themselves under pressure to accept less. Given the abundance of labour and the extent of their indebtedness, poor peasants found themselves in a poor bargaining position. None the less, those whose labour was not tied to a landlord or rich peasant benefited from the increased availability of employment in the construction of aerodromes and in other projects associated with the war effort.

TABLE 7.1

*Official wholesale prices for rice and gram
1941-45, Darbhanga*

*(At three-monthly intervals. Prices given
in rupees per maund)*

Year and Month	Rice	Gram
1941 January	4-12-0	3- 4-0
April	4-15-0	3- 4-0
July	5-10-0	2-14-0
October	5-12-0	3-12-0
1942 January	5-12-0	3-10-0
April	5- 9-0	3-12-0
July	6- 7-0	4-14-0
October	6-12-0	6- 8-0
1943 January	7- 4-0	5- 0-0
April	9-10-0	5- 0-0
July	25- 0-0	13- 8-0
October	18- 4-0	11- 8-0
1944 January	12- 8-0	11- 8-0
April	17- 0-0	11- 8-0
July	15- 0-0	9- 8-0
October	12- 8-0	9- 0-0
1945 January	13- 0-0	7- 0-0
April	13- 4-0	7- 0-0
July	14- 8-0	7- 0-0
October	18- 0-0	9- 0-0

Source: *Darbhanga District Census Handbook* (1951 Census), pp.169-72.

Pressure on the poor resulted in a dramatic rise in the crime rate and helped inspire market looting. Crime figures, an official report commented in December 1940, had been rising steadily 'since 1939, if not before', and now indicated 'a disquieting position'. In April 1941 the Bihar government recorded ninety-two dacoities, an increase of 100 per cent on the monthly figure for the previous three years.[4] In June the following year dacoities reached a

record level, and a 'serious outbreak' of market looting
occurred at Raxaul town, Champaran, during which a
crowd of 500 looted three cloth shops. Subsequently looting incidents occurred at six other places in the district.[5]
The disturbances, the administration later established,
partly resulted from antagonism to local mill-owners who,
to avoid prosecution under the anti-hoarding regulations,
had shifted large quantities of grain into storage over the
border in Nepal.

To lessen discontent the government attempted to control price levels and to ensure the supply of essential
commodities. The measures taken averted a catastrophe
comparable to the Bengal famine of 1943, but also provided
opportunities for profiteering and corruption, thus increasing popular dissatisfaction.[6]

Politically, the 1939-1942 period was characterised by
increasing tension. The Congress leadership displayed
reluctance to initiate mass civil disobedience against the
British, but also did not intend to cooperate with them in
the war unless Indians gained a greater share of power.
But the British, engrossed in the war and unwilling to
surrender control over India's resources, were unwilling
to make substantial concessions.[7] To meet this challenge
and to placate those Congressmen who demanded that some
initiative be taken Gandhi launched, in October 1940, an
'individual Satyagraha' campaign. This campaign ran from
October 1940 to December 1941 and was intended to embarrass
the British without hindering the war effort. During the
campaign individual satyagrahis came forward and publicly
breached the government's wartime regulations restricting
the right of free speech.[8]

The campaign 'was not one of Gandhi's success stories'.[9]
In Bihar, many of the Congressmen designated as satyagrahis
did not wish to relinquish the influential positions they had
gained on municipal and district boards, particularly when
factional rivals were always ready to move into their places.
Consequently they refused or were extremely slow to court
arrest.[10] Nor, because of the individual, ritual quality of
the law breaking involved, did the campaign attract extensive support, though because of this it did succeed,
unlike previous campaigns, in adhering strictly to the
principle of non-violence.[11] But despite its limitations,

Individual Satyagraha kept alive interest in the nationalist movement and prepared the ground for the initiation of mass civil disobedience.[12]

The initiation of mass civil disobedience became increasingly likely with the worsening of the war situation and the repeated failure of the Government of India and the Congress to reach a compromise. In December 1941 Japan entered the war, and within three months devastated Britain's position in Asia. By March 1942, with the Japanese army thrusting through Burma and with Japanese ships and aeroplanes active in and over the Bay of Bengal, the invasion of India seemed imminent.[13] At this juncture the British attempted to gain Indian support with a new constitutional offer which was brought to India by Stafford Cripps, a long-time friend of the Indian nationalist movement. The offer was a substantial advance on previous initiatives. But it failed to give Indians an acceptable level of executive power and included a clause, inserted to placate the Muslim League, which allowed individual provinces to opt out of the proposed dominion. With the rejection by Congress of the Cripps offer the likelihood of mass action increased.[14]

In addition, Britain's disastrous military position encouraged Congressmen to conclude that now would be a tactically appropriate time to launch mass civil disobedience, and increased support for Gandhi's suggestion that the best way of averting Japanese invasion would be to force Japan's enemy, Britain, to relinquish control over the subcontinent.[15]

Anxiety intensified because of Bihar's proximity to the war zone. With the Japanese invasion of Burma, overseas Indians who originally hailed from Bihar returned to their native villages, impoverished and full of complaints about British mismanagement.[16] Trainloads of allied wounded from the Burma campaign travelled across north Bihar, arousing disquiet among the local population. Labourers, sick and war-weary after their exertions on the Assam border, returned to their homes in Bihar.[17] And from Calcutta, which seemed a likely target for serious Japanese attack, large numbers of casual workers returned to their Bihar homes, placing additional economic pressure on their families, swelling the petty crime rate and helping to encourage rumours of an impending British collapse.[18]

During the early months of 1942 the people of Bihar placed little faith in the future of British rule. People with liquid assets began buying buildings and land as a precaution against the collapse of the currency. In the first three weeks of February, savings banks withdrawals 'were nearly double those in the corresponding periods in the preceding years'.[19] Early in July the provincial government reported that 'the defeatism prevailing in political and particularly in Congress circles in its turn produces its repercussions on the uneducated classes. The impending collapse of Government is freely talked about even by villagers.'[20] Nor was the provincial government immune from the general decline in confidence. 'The usual depression!' was the comment of the Home Secretary to the Government of India on the provincial report for the second half of May.[21]

But pessimism on the part of the Bihar government was understandable. In January 1941, when there had been no threat of Japanese invasion and little immediate likelihood of mass civil disobedience, considerable doubt already existed about the ability of the police and the administration to fulfill their responsibilities. Indian officers in both the lower ranks of the civil service and in the police force were unwilling to engage fully and vigorously in their work. They felt that eventually a Congress government would return to power, and did not wish, for fear of future repercussions, to identify themselves overmuch as loyal servants of British rule. In the police force this lack of morale prevailed among sub-inspectors and their superiors, but had not yet extended to the rank and file.[22]

In addition to poor officer morale, the police were greatly hampered in their work by their sparse numbers. In the 1930s, increases in the numbers of the police had kept pace neither with the rise in the size of the population, nor with the increase in the number of serious crimes. In 1930 the ratio of police to population had been 1:2364, and there were 44,449 cognizable crimes reported. In 1939 the ratio had declined to 1:2625, but the number of cognizable crimes had risen to 53,903.[23] In 1941 the Director of the Government of India Intelligence Branch reported that even though

> a large proportion of the Province is very thickly populated and often contains as many as one thousand

persons to the square mile, the ordinary rural police station has as a rule no more than about 1 Sub Inspector and 6 constables, and it is not unusual to find that the Sub Inspector has to contend with crime which may run to as many as 200 cases registered in the course of a year. My own experience of crime conditions is limited to the United Provinces, and there, although the average rural population is not often in excess of about 600 persons to the square mile, it is the exception rather than the rule to find a police station with fewer than 2 Sub Inspectors and 8 constables.[24]

The inadequate number of police contributed to the rise in the crime rate and particularly to the increase in the number of dacoities.[25] In 1940, to assist the police in coping with dacoity the provincial government formed a Village Defence Organisation, a voluntary association made up of villagers willing to organise and train themselves, on a part-time basis, to defend their property. But unfortunately for administrative prestige the speakers who went on tour calling on people to join the organisation helped create 'the impression that the Police are not strong enough to tackle the dacoits'.[26]

Nor was it just the police force which was too small to meet its responsibilities. The Bihar districts were twice the size of those in Bengal and the United Provinces, which meant that Bihar had a lower ratio of district and subdivisional officers to the population.[27] The demands of war service, furthermore, siphoned off good officials, seriously affecting the quality of administrative personnel. Some district officials either were past their prime or else were young and inexperienced.[28] By the early 1940s the law and order apparatus in Bihar experienced serious strain in meeting routine responsibilities. It had nothing in reserve with which to meet a major crisis.

II

Within 24 hours of the acceptance, on 8 August, of the 'Quit India' resolution by the All-India Congress Committee, meeting in session in Bombay, the authorities arrested almost all of the leading Congressmen at the national provincial and district level, declared Congress an illegal organisation, and took steps to paralyse its operation. In Bihar, this government repression was greeted with consternation. At first the reaction centred in the towns, with students taking the leading part in rowdy flag-waving processions. At Patna on 11 August, police fired on a crowd trying to force its way into the grounds surrounding the Secretariat building, killing seven people, all of them students, and wounding several others.[29]

In reaction to repression unrest intensified. On 12, 13 and 14 August there were recurrent demonstrations in the towns, and disturbances began throughout the countryside.[30] Students hijacked trains and spread news of the uprising throughout north Bihar.[31] As the movement spread it became increasingly violent. In Darbhanga

> the villagers...cut all the roads and railways. The roads were cut where they were carried over embankments several feet high, trees felled across them, masonry bridges demolished, pontoons of the pontoon bridge on the main road sunk; railway lines torn up, 40-foot spans of the bridges removed and dropped into the rivers, the delicate and at that time irreplaceable electrical signalling apparatus at all stations destroyed; telephone and telegraph wires everywhere cut, rolled up and carried off home.[32]

Crowds of villagers invaded post offices, and destroyed furniture and papers.[33] They also attacked police stations. The police successfully defended some stations but elsewhere they surrendered or were overwhelmed. At Rupauli in Purnea and at Minapur in Muzaffarpur policemen were burnt alive while defending their *thanas*. In north Bhagalpur, all the *thanas* 'had been closed, locked and sealed by the Congress workers as early as the 13th August.' By 24 August in north Monghyr, all rural police stations had either been overrun or abandoned. Between 14 and 20 August, twenty of the twenty-five police-stations in Darbhanga came under attack and of these twenty, thirteen were taken by the rebels. By 19 August in Sitamarhi subdivision of Muzaffarpur, all the *thanas* except the *thana* at the subdivisional headquarters had been overwhelmed. Seventeen of the district's twenty-three police-stations came under attack and fourteen of these seventeen were taken. In Saran, the authorities abandoned nine police-stations.[34] Throughout north Bihar the *chaukidars* stopped functioning, either because of intimidation or because they sympathised with the movement. With the disruption of communications and the collapse of the police system the British lost control of most of the countryside. They retained control of the region's towns, in which they concentrated their forces, but elsewhere, according to one official account, 'Perfect chaos and anarchy were reported to be reigning.'[35]

This 'Perfect chaos and anarchy' had been created by a movement which itself was only very loosely organised.[36] The arrest of the senior Congress leadership and of the leading local nationalist activists resulted in a situation broadly similar to that which prevailed at the high points of official repression during the civil disobedience campaigns of 1930-34. At the local level, lower rank and less important activists and other nationalist sympathisers attempted to fill the leadership vacuum. In Saran the local activist Jubba Mallah led the attack on the Minapur *thana*. Judicial proceedings during 1944 recorded that:

> Until some three years or so ago...Jubba Mallah, who is a man in his middle thirties, appears to have earned an honest living...by exercising his craft as a fisherman. Some three years ago, however, he became a congress volunteer, and...moved about in the locality... preaching the creed of the congress party.[37]

The initiatives of local activists got protest under way, but no effective coordination developed between different areas. Because of the arrests the movement lacked experienced cadres, and the extensive sabotage of communications hampered the organisation of the insurgents as much as it did that of their opponents.

The absence of overall coordination meant that those involved had no very clear idea of what tactics to adopt. At first, in imitation of what had been done in previous nationalist civil disobedience campaigns, they engaged in slogan shouting processions behind the Congress banner.[38] At this early stage some sabotage of government property occurred, but extensive sabotage did not begin until the police had repressed demonstrations by means of lathi charges, gunfire, and mass arrests. In the initiation of extensive sabotage and of attacks on police stations throughout the countryside some part was played by the Congress left-wingers who had led the peasant movement during the 1930s. In 1938 and 1939 Congress Socialists had publicly emphasised the need, in any future mass nationalist campaign, to sabotage road and rail communications.[39] The Left was influential among students, who at first spearheaded the campaign, and during its course left-wingers distributed pamphlets calling on the people to sabotage communications and attack government property.

But the importance of left-wing influence should not be over-emphasised. The Left was strongest in Darbhanga, and had some influence in Muzaffarpur, but had little following throughout the rest of north Bihar. Both mainstream and left-wing Congressmen produced pamphlets calling for sabotage, and in both cases the pamphlets only seem to have appeared when sabotage was already under way.[40] Because the communications system was already in considerable disarray, these pamphlets did not have a wide circulation. The leading Left activist in the 1930s, Swami Sahajanand Saraswati, had gravitated towards the Communist Party of India. He supported Britain and the USSR in what he regarded as the 'People's war' against international Fascism, and hence he and his followers did not support the revolt.[41] Jay Prakash Narayan had spent most of the time since March 1940 in jail, and almost all of the other leading pro-revolt left-wingers were clapped into jail during the initial government clampdown. At the height of the movement only those less influential left-wingers whom the British had regarded as too unimportant to be taken into custody were still at large to engage in protest and propaganda.[42]

Ironically the authorities themselves were in part responsible for the tactics adopted by Congress supporters. The government, to justify its draconic response to the passing of the Quit India resolution, alleged that Congress had planned a wholesale programme of sabotage and disruption. In the first few days after the arrest of the All-India Congress Committee leaders the government widely publicised this allegation, encouraging Congress supporters to concentrate on disruption and sabotage.[43]

But overall, neither the role of the Left nor of the authorities decisively determined the measures adopted by the supporters of the Quit India movement. Sabotage was an established weapon in the armoury of the Congress, and had been used extensively against toddy tappers and liquor merchants during the 1930-34 campaign. In the 1920s and 1930s there had been incidents in which Congress supporters sabotaged communications.[44] Nor was strong antagonism to the police a new phenomenon. In north Bihar during previous mass civil disobedience campaigns there had been attacks both on policemen and on police *thanas*. On three occasions during the non-cooperation movement groups of demonstrators overran and occupied *thanas* and several times during the civil disobedience movement crowds of demonstrators attempted to raise the Congress flag over *thanas* but were repulsed with gunfire.[45]

The difference in 1942 was not that such events occurred, but that they occurred with a greater intensity and were concentrated within a shorter period of time than previously. The absence of the restraining influence [46] of the senior Congress leaders because of their imprisonment allied with the angry reaction to their summary arrest did much to cause this frequency and intensity of protest. The depth and extent of hostility to the authorities, and particularly to the police, meant that government property and personnel provided a natural target. And when, throughout the countryside, the administration buckled under the strain, many people who were not regular Congress supporters became further encouraged to participate in sabotage, assault and disruption.

The Quit India revolt reached its height during the ten days after 14 August. At this time the insurgents dominated the countryside and the authorities had to bring in large bodies of troops to recapture control.[47] During this period the revolt drew support from a broad section of the social spectrum. M.V. Harcourt, on the basis of information about the backgrounds of those taken prisoner during the movement, has concluded that, among those actively involved, young, high caste men predominated, but that many representatives from lower status groups were also included.[48] This finding is supported both by contemporary accounts[49] and by the evidence supplied by the official lists, compiled in 1953, of the 'Martyrs' who died as a result of police and military violence.[50]

Information on prisoners and casualties does not give a completely reliable picture of those involved in the movement. No doubt a number of prisoners were wrongfully or maliciously arrested.[51] When the police and the military opened fire, their shooting was not always accurate, and sometimes it was indiscriminate. Nonetheless, the evidence on prisoners and casualties, reinforced by contemporary accounts, does indicate who was in the forefront of protests and demonstrations. But this evidence does not give a fully accurate portrayal of those who, without necessarily being in the front line of agitation, did become actively involved. It seems that in north Bihar in August 1942 there developed not one but two overlapping insurgencies, one a 'nationalist revolt' by Congress supporting, high caste peasants, and the other a 'rebellion of desperation' by the poor, low caste people of the region.

The first insurgency began with the circulation of the news of the arrest of the Congress leaders and the initiation of heavy repression of the Congress party, and intensified after the harsh official reaction to the first series of protests. Students, who mainly came from among the village elite, took a leading part. The essential motivation of this 'nationalist protest' was political.

The 'rebellion of desperation' got under way when the success of nationalist revolt in temporarily paralysing the mechanisms of British rule stimulated the poor to join in attacks on government buildings and property. Often their main object was loot: indeed they were very much the same people who had engaged in market looting in the earlier months of the year and who recently had swelled the figures for petty crime. The Madhubani subdivisional officer reported that

> Most of the Hindus who took part in the movement were from the higher castes...There were agitators from other castes also. Generally people from lower castes or those belonging to the agricultural labourer class did not take part in the movement at first. They joined the movement in its later stage when they hoped that they would be able to make something out of it by looting...[52]

In north Monghyr, according to the Beguserai subdivisional officer, the

> Congress had their organisation in every village more
> or less: the young men...specially the Bhumihars,
> had an inherent tendency to work as volunteers under
> Congress flag. These village organisations were in
> the best form at the time of Congress government.
> After the fall of Congress government there was marked
> decline but in many villages they maintained it; the
> village teachers played an important part in maintaining
> the organisation...the school students started the
> [Quit India] movement; they were joined by all sections
> of Congress workers. The sober section of Congress
> tried to keep the movement under control, but when
> they allowed the village mass to join, it became an
> economic question: the vast properties, specially
> foodgrains at the railway station attracted them...Of
> the villagers the Bhumihars and the poor labourers
> took prominent part in the loot. The merchants class
> in outlying stations were at the mercy of the Congress...
> But somehow, they managed to get the leaders on their
> sides and thereby saved their property from loot: at
> some places, they got hold of the leaders by making
> payment to the Congress cause: at some places they
> joined the movement to some extent...[by 14 August]
> the situation was completely out of the hands of the
> students: the looters got complete upperhand: in
> order to keep the hold the younger section of the Congress began to support the action of the looters and
> even joined: the sober section did not approve it but
> they had no hold at the time. [sic][53]

It seems probable that those who joined in the revolt mainly because of economic necessity began taking part last and withdrew first when repression began. Because of this they are under-represented in the casualty and imprisonment figures. The breakdown of law and order, it also should be noted, supplied great opportunities for 'professional criminals'. The crime figures during the period ran at a high rate,[54] and it is impossible to discover what proportion of 'crimes' were committed by 'professional criminals', and what proportion were the work of impoverished villagers driven by economic necessity. Indeed, these categories overlap extensively, since every year in impoverished, inegalitarian north Bihar dire poverty forced many to make crime their profession.

Many of those active in the Quit India revolt were driven by economic hardship, and for a period they operated in a context in which British rule had temporarily broken down. This might seem to have been an appropriate situation for the development of agrarian radicalism. The British administration had always supported the zamindari system, and during the 1930s officials and police had worked to contain peasant protest over the *bakast* lands. Surely the absence of an apparatus to maintain public order and protect rights in property offered an ideal opportunity for the initiation of agrarian protest? But despite these apparently favourable circumstances, no agrarian protest developed during and immediately after August 1942. Quit India activists made no attacks on property other than on that belonging to the government.[55] Impoverished villagers and 'professional criminals' made some attacks on zamindari property, but these attacks were not given ideological justification as part of an agrarian movement.

The non-development of radicalism at the time of the Quit India revolt resulted partly from the dominant role in initiating and directing protest played by small zamindar members of the Bihar Congress. It also resulted from the attitude taken by left-wing activists. Left-wingers were divided over the question of whether or not to support the insurrection. Swami Sahajanand, the left-wing leader who had commanded the most extensive support in the 1930s, opposed the revolt on the grounds that India should support Britain and the Soviet Union in their 'People's War' against the threat of Fascism. Jay Prakash Narayan and other left-wingers who supported the revolt emphasised the primacy of the nationalist struggle over the struggle for agrarian reform.[56] The authorities, moreover, clapped many of the pro-Congress left-wingers into jail in their initial pre-emptive wave of arrests. If they had been left at large some of these left-wingers may have decided in the heat of battle that the opportunity to engage in anti-landlord protest was too good to miss.[57]

Anti-landlord protest also remained latent because, to the chagrin of the British who had always looked to them for support, most zamindars either remained strictly neutral or else supported the Congress.[58] The Maharaja of Darbhanga, for example, refused to supply the authorities with the assistance of the armed guards whom he employed to protect his treasury. He justified his refusal by claiming that the guards could not be relied upon to fire at demonstrators who might perhaps include their kinsmen, caste fellows or fellow villagers. But, no doubt another reason for this refusal was that he had no wish to direct popular discontent against himself and his property.[59] In the event those involved in the Quit India revolt took no action against the Darbhanga Raj. The manager of the Parihar circle, which lay in the Sitamarhi Sub-division of Muzaffarpur, subsequently reported that

> In the month of August last there was an unprecedented congress movement in this sub division. The Sub Divisional officer and several Sub Inspectors of Police were murdered...There was no agitation whatsoever against the Raj and in spite of the above movement Raj works were never suspended.[60]

From Padri circle, a storm centre of *kisan* protest in the 1930s, the manager reported that

> an unparalleled congress rebellion of terrible magnitude reared its head and within a week crippled and paralysed the Govt. ... Hasanpore road railway station was burnt down and looted, fish plates [were] removed, wires [were] cut and roads breached [and] culverts smashed ...

The manager does not mention, however, any occasion on which this popular fervour was directed against the Darbhanga Raj.

Indeed, it would seem that the activities of the insurgents received sympathy from the Darbhanga Raj management. The Padri manager's report continues with the comment that after order had been restored the Padri

> tenants were saved...from military and police atrocities by very prompt action taken by the Chief Manager and his constant attention towards this bringing pressure on [the]S[uperintendent of]P[olice], [the] District Magistrate and [the] Samastipur S[ub] D[ivisional] O[fficer]...Protection from military tortures brought [the] tenants under very heavy obligation to the Raj. As a consequence [the] Padri tenants willingly con-

tributed rupees 6,000 towards [the] Christmas fund. Not a single Padri tenant was allowed to be arrested although a huge number was made accused...whose names still appear in the absconders printed list.[61]

The dominance of mainstream Congressmen, the attitude taken by the zamindars and the lack of effective left-wing leadership contributed to the absence of an anti-landlord campaign. Moreover many of the peasants who had taken part in the *kisan* movement in the 1930s were, in the early 1940s, benefiting from the high prices prevailing for agricultural produce. In the 1940s they found it easy to meet their rent obligations, and through money-lending and grain dealing they profited handsomely from the acute wartime credit and grain shortage. Hence their involvement in the Quit India revolt did not result from economic pressure. In contrast, their participation derived from loyalty to the Congress, sympathy with nationalism, antagonism to the police, and the feeling that the collapse of British rule was at hand.

III

The Quit India movement in north Bihar drew in a broad cross-section of the population and temporarily succeeded in crippling the apparatus of British rule. But despite this striking initial success the British, by deploying large bodies of troops, soon re-established themselves. Initially they used troops to secure the headquarters towns and the lines of communication, and then they sent them out to pacify the villages and to support the Police in the imposition of heavy collective fines. (Table 7.2). Within a few days of the arrival of troops in an area, the mass participation phase of the movement ceased,[62] to be replaced by a lengthy phase of sporadic guerilla warfare. The British re-established control quickly partly because at their disposal at the time of the insurrection they had a massive military force which had been concentrated in order to face the Japanese. And under war censorship, they could repress revolt ruthlessly without worrying about domestic or international opinion. By this crucial stage of the war, moreover, they had developed a siege mentality, and had determined to cope relentlessly with internal dissidence.[63]

TABLE 7.2

Collective fines imposed and realised in north Bihar to end of November 1942 and February 1943.
(Amounts in Rupees)

District	To End November 1942 Imposed	Realised*	To End February 1943 Imposed	Realised*
Champaran	94,500	40,643	94,500	55,207
Saran	151,700	150,080	159,800	151,433
Muzaffarpur	367,700	304,391	368,878	345,744
Darbhanga	461,100	385,255	462,200	391,515
Monghyr[§]	201,450	97,995	206,092	97,995
Bhagalpur[§]	325,350	333,100	349,259	337,384
Purnea	86,500	60,332	86,500	84,518
TOTAL	1,688,300	1,371,229	1,727,229	1,463,796

* To nearest rupee

§ Figures for both north and south gangetic portions of these districts

Source: GB, [Secret] *Report on the Civil Disturbances in Bihar, 1942* (Patna 1944), p.22.

The rebels were handicapped by their poor armament. Armed with spears, lathis, and axes they first challenged policemen armed with muskets and then encountered soldiers armed with magazine rifles and machine guns and supported by air power.[64] Lack of effective organisation also contributed to the failure of the revolt. The usual procedure before an attack on a police station was for some meetings to be held nearby, at which speakers whipped up feeling against the police and the authorities. Next would come an all-out frontal assault on the police station, almost always by broad light of day. This meant that the rebels lost the advantage of surprise.[65]

Nor need the imbalance in weaponry between the two
sides have been as great. The rebels captured guns in
many of the early successful attacks on police stations,[66]
and fire-arms were also held by some private citizens.
There was also an extensive arms 'underground' which
supplied arms to professional criminals. It seems that the
arms confiscated from policemen and officials were generally
taken away by individuals and hidden. In the early stages
of the revolt, the rebels made little effort to gather arms
from various sources and train people in their use.[67] The
rebels could not hope to match the armament of the military,
but they could have armed themselves more effectively to
carry on guerilla war. In addition, if the rebels had been
able to organise themselves sufficiently to direct effective
attacks against district headquarters towns, the short-
term success of the movement could have been even greater.

Until the arrival of the military, the towns were held
only by small groups of officials and policemen. In the
early days of the revolt many of the police were wavering,
and a number of police officers relinquished their posts.
In the Madhubani subdivision of Darbhanga a Sub-Inspector
gave up his *thana* and his pistol to the insurgents and de-
camped to Nepal.[68] The Champaran Police Superintendent
reported his dissatisfaction with the Mounted Military
Police, an elite unit within the Bihar Police force. On 24
August he ordered them to disperse a crowd but

> There was a marked reluctance on their part to take
> any action and even after my order to clear the crowd
> with sword sticks this was not done and they merely
> waved their sticks over the heads of the crowd...I
> also ordered them to dismount and to protect our flank
> during the mass attack on our force but without any
> orders they retired without firing a single shot...the
> whole troop should be disbanded and replaced.[69]

In Saran, lathi-bearing constables were moved by the use
by demonstrators of the slogan, 'Police *Hamara Bhai Hai*'
(the police are our brothers) and showed great reluctance
to break up a march led by several leading women nationalists.[70] In Muzaffarpur, the rebels killed a Subdivisional
Magistrate and an Inspector and a sub-inspector of Police
during the first fortnight of the uprising. On 1 September
the District Officer reported that these deaths had 'completely

demoralized the police...and it is not possible for them to function in any police-station unless they have the assistance of troops for a few weeks'.[71]

Even those policemen whose morale remained high were not always effective when faced with a determined attack. Some of the older constables called upon to use guns during the revolt had little knowledge of fire-arms and were terrified of them.[72] Nor did all the subordinate Indian officials, when faced with a crisis, prove to be loyal and reliable servants of the British.[73] Official buildings, furthermore, had been built to suit the climate. They had wide verandahs and large windows and doors and could not be easily defended.[74]

If, in the first days of the revolt, the rebels had made determined attacks on the towns, using sheer weight of numbers and all the available fire-arms, the short-term success of the movement could have been considerably greater. Such a massed attack was attempted at Katihar in Purnea district on 26 August. Congress workers assembled a large crowd, brought in Santal bow-men to provide fire-power and placed women and children to the front to discourage the police from opening fire. Unfortunately for the members of the crowd a military detachment had arrived at Katihar a couple of days earlier and dispersed them with fire from a Bren gun.[75]

If the rebels had been able to take over the towns, even if only until the arrival of the military, the whole complexion of the revolt could have been changed. In the suppression of the revolt the police and officials who retained control of the headquarters towns acted as the 'eyes and ears' of the military. They pointed out the focal points of nationalist resistance and lessened the ruthlessness of military repression.[76] If the local police and officials had either been killed or driven out of the towns, then the military repression would have been both less effective and more brutal and indiscriminate. The reaction to such repression might have been an intensification and lengthening of mass resistance which would have greatly helped those who carried on guerilla activities in the months after the initial rising was quelled.

The rebels, in addition to being ineffectively organised, also displayed great tactical naivety. There were few attacks under cover of night and little attempt at concealment. An exception occurred at Marhowrah village in Muzaffarpur district, where a crowd of villagers emerged from the cover of a tall standing maize crop and massacred five British soldiers and an Anglo-Indian civilian.[77] Only later, after the high point of the movement had passed, did greater tactical sophistication develop. The influence of Gandhian ideology also played a part in the collapse of the mass movement. Rebel activists who were devoted Gandhians eschewed efforts to damage their opponents.[78] They thought that dedicated activists should be ready to sacrifice themselves and therefore encouraged suicidal frontal confrontation.

After the first phase of the Quit India revolt was brought to a speedy end by the arrival of troops, the expression of unrest rapidly declined. By early September officials reported that the situation was returning to normal.[79] Extensive arrests, large collective fines on rebellious villages, military route marches and police and military reprisals successfully intimidated the mass of the population. Often harsh measures were employed, and to protect its agents from subsequent prosecution the government had to enact a retrospective Act of Indemnity.[80]

From September onwards small bands of rebels engaged in guerilla warfare. They often allied themselves with professional dacoits, and not infrequently politically inspired banditry became difficult to distinguish from its non-political counterpart. The most successful band of rebel dacoits was led by Siaram Singh. Singh's band was active for several weeks in the south Monghyr and south Bhagalpur area, where it received considerable support from his Bhumihar caste fellows. In April 1943 police pressure forced the band to move north of the Ganges, where it operated successfully in the jungly country of the Kosi basin.[81]

Siaram Singh's band, until apprehended by the police in 1944, engaged in a series of fund-raising robberies, waged a campaign of terror against *chaukidars* and other collaborators with government, and made a well planned, though abortive, attack on a police outpost situated on the Gangetic *diara* lands in the Sonbarsa police circle in Bhagalpur. The reason for the failure of the attack is instructive, since it reveals that support for the rebel bands was limited: the police were given prior warning of what had been planned as a surprise, pre-dawn attack by a member of a low caste group which suffered oppression from the local Bhumihars.[82]

Other bands of rebels frequently took refuge over the border in Nepal. At first the Nepal authorities took no action against them, apparently because they had sympathy for the rebellion and wished to wait and see how the conflict developed.[83] In response to strong pressure from the British, the Nepal authorities eventually began rounding up the rebels, but their measures against them were never as vigorous and effective as those south of the border. The guerilla movement received a great fillip on 9 November when Jay Prakash Narayan, Ramnandan Misra and four other Left activists managed to escape from Hazaribagh jail in south Bihar.[84] After getting in touch with rebel activists throughout India, Narayan made his way to Nepal, where he attempted to coordinate guerilla activity and to lay the foundations for a renewal of mass agitation. He kept in touch with underground workers by special courier, and set up a training camp to give workers instruction in military tactics and in the use of fire-arms and explosives.[85]

The Nepal authorities, prodded by the British, eventually arrested Narayan and some of his supporters and confined them in the Hanumannagger jail. But in May 1943 a force of fifty rebels raided the jail and rescued Narayan and six other activists. Narayan returned to India and continued his underground work until captured in September 1943.[86] As M.V. Harcourt has pointed out, Narayan's arrest marked the end of the main period of underground activity.[87] By the end of 1943 the British had arrested most of the important underground workers and had broken up most of the rebel bands. Siaram Singh and his men evaded capture until the following year, but this was an exception to the general trend. By late 1943 the British had also managed to bring down the crime rate, which had been running at high levels throughout 1942 and 1943.[88]

To achieve these results the British had been obliged to keep detachments of troops in the region and to improve

the size and efficiency of the police force. Within three
weeks of the initiation of the revolt they raised the pay of
the police, recruited a large number of additional police,
procured arms from far and wide to ensure that every
police station was equipped with at least six efficient fire-
arms, and gave the police more training in the use of these
weapons. In north Bhagalpur, where rebel bands were
especially active, the authorities set up the new sub-
district of Saharsa, and in north Monghyr and north
Bhagalpur they established five new armed police posts.[89]
In late 1942 and early 1943 the Bihar police system came
under critical scrutiny, and the authorities overhauled the
arrangements for the collection of intelligence, further increased the pay of the police, began paying the *chaukidars*
a special war bonus, undertook in subsequent years to increase the size of the police force from 13,250 to 21,600
and set out to increase the force by the end of 1943 by at
least 2,400 men, of whom 1,600 would bear fire-arms.[90]

IV

The events of August 1942 revealed the considerable
success which the Bihar Congress had achieved in harness-
ing popular turbulence to weaken the British hold over
north Bihar. In 1920-22 and 1930-34 the Bihar Congress
led civil disobedience movements which strained the apparatus of British rule, while in August 1942 it initiated a
revolt which temporarily demolished this apparatus.

At the height of the Quit India Revolt the *chaukidars*
stopped functioning, some regular policemen gave in to the
rebels, and many more temporarily wavered. Among Indian
officials, many were lukewarm in their support of the British
administration. During the guerilla phase of the revolt,
many policemen and *chaukidars* were lackadaisical in their
performance of anti-rebel operations, and low morale was
all-pervasive. In future, so the administration decided in
November 1942, every effort would be made to recruit
policemen from outside the province, since Biharis could
no longer be relied upon. More and more during the war
years, Bihari policemen and officials began to wonder about
their future once Congress returned to power, which was
regarded as an inevitable development once the war was
over. Among the mass of the population, nationalist feeling

continued to prevail. A large cross-section of the population had been actively involved in the revolt, and many of the rest of the people had been sympathetic to it. In the months after the revolt pro-British speakers seeking support for the war effort had to trade on the future by promising the coming of Swaraj immediately after the war.[91]

Because of its success in attracting extensive support and because in north Bihar and elsewhere it temporarily dissolved British rule the Quit India revolt has attracted considerable scholarly interest. Writers of the nationalist school have promulgated what has been called 'The Myth of the '42 Rebellion'.[92] To supply Indian nationalism with a myth of heroic armed struggle these writers have exaggerated the extent, intensity and success of the movement in north Bihar and elsewhere and have neither looked closely at the social groups involved in the insurrection nor analysed why they became involved.[93] More recent writers, such as Bhuyan and Hutchins,[94] have used their material more rigorously but have still arrived at the conclusion that the revolt was essentially a 'nationalist revolt', failing to perceive that it also incorporated a 'rebellion of desperation'.

M.V. Harcourt offers another perspective. Harcourt sees the 'small-holder peasant' as playing a central role both in the peasant agitations of the late 1930s and in the revolt in 1942. He describes the 'small-holder peasant' as occupying the middle range of the social hierarchy and as producing both for subsistence and for the market.[95] Harcourt's interpretation cannot be accepted, either for the late 1930s[96] or for the period of the Quit India movement.

In the early 1940s many 'small-holder' peasants profited from high cash crops and from high food-grain prices. The wartime harvests were below average and contributed to the conditions of scarcity caused by war induced economic dislocation. Harcourt contends that from mid-1942 onwards the threat of worsening scarcity created anxiety among the peasantry so that they launched themselves into protest when the initiation of the Quit India revolt provided them with an opportunity to express their discontent.[97]

Harcourt's argument fails to recognise that in a situation of increasing scarcity and rising prices some at least of the middle peasants could afford to sell a smaller amount than hitherto of their crop to earn cash to pay their rent, and thus could have either more disposable income from the sale of the rest of their surplus or else could perhaps store a portion of their crop as insurance against an adverse future season. His argument also ignores the fact that peasants could get good returns for their high quality grains and could then purchase a larger quantity of the cheaper, low quality grains for their own consumption.

In July 1943, when the scarcity was even worse than in the previous year the provincial administration commented that

> The cultivator and the petty landlord who are prospering as a result of the high prices of grain are expected to remain aloof if there is any revival of trouble. But the daily wage earner in urban areas and the landless agricultural labourer in the interior might be a source of trouble.[98]

Skill in cultivation, good or bad luck, changing market conditions, and variations throughout the region in the impact of flood, drought and crop diseases all contributed to the circumstances in which smallholder peasants found themselves. Some middle peasants were under economic pressure, but others did well out of high grain and cash crop prices. Many middle peasants participated in the revolt not because of economic pressure but because of antagonism to the police and the administration, because of sympathy for the nationalist cause, and because of encouragement from those above them in the social scale. Harcourt suggests that peasant small-holders took the leading part in the Quit India revolt. The evidence indicates, however, that the role of these middle peasants was secondary to that of groups from opposite ends of the social spectrum, namely the Congress-supporting rich peasants and small landlords at one extreme and the poor and the landless at the other.

Harcourt also errs in his suggestion[99] that *kisan sabha* activists played a leading part in the organisation of the insurrection. His suggestion is perhaps true of Darbhanga, where socialist/*kisan sabha* activity had been intense in the late 1930s, and where *kisan* activists had done considerable propaganda work in the months preceding the uprising. (Their propaganda, it should be noted, stressed the need for a united front against British rule rather than class conflict.) But *kisan sabha* activists did not do much in the way of preparation and propaganda for insurrection in the rest of north Bihar, throughout which there was extensive unrest in August 1942. Harcourt contends that the politicisation and radicalisation of the late 1930s paved the way for the 1942 revolt. In Darbhanga, and to some extent throughout the region, *kisan* activism in the 1930s helped develop anti-government feelings, and particularly anti-police feelings. But the 1942 movement was also intense in areas that had only been slightly touched by *kisan* agitation. In Purnea, and in the Bihpur *thana* in Bhagalpur, for example, the main politicising force had been mainstream Congress activity from the 1920s on. Throughout the region, indeed, the nationalist upsurge in August 1942 was a compressed version of the civil disobedience campaign of 1930-34, with its intensity and fast-moving pace being a reaction to harsh and immediate official repression. This politically motivated 'nationalist revolt' overlapped with an economically motivated 'rebellion of desperation' akin to some aspects of popular participation in the non-cooperation movement of 1920-22. These two upheavals combined to produce an insurrection which temporarily demolished the fragile framework of imperial rule.

The collapse of British rule seemingly provided suitable conditions for the development of agrarian protest. But prevailing economic conditions made rich peasants and many middle peasants disinterested in agitation against their landlords. Without their leadership and despite harsh economic circumstances the poor peasants failed to initiate agrarian protest. Moreover, agrarian protest failed to develop because of the success of the Bihar Congress in containing and directing popular turbulence. The Quit India revolt perhaps provided a 'safety valve' which directed discontent amongst the poor peasants against the British. By its actions during the 1937 to 1939 period, the Bihar Congress had weakened the Left and consolidated its support among the zamindars. The non-appearance of an effective alternative leadership in the 1937-42 period encouraged many potential left-sympathizers to accept the conservative leadership of the Bihar Congress in 1942.[100] In addition, the failure of the zamindars actively to support the British in 1942, which was based on an accurate assessment that their best interests lay with the Congress, helped ensure that the nationalist rising did not broaden into an agrarian movement.

CONCLUSION

AGRARIAN REFORMISM, NATIONALIST AGITATION, AND THE ABSENCE OF RADICALISM

Between 1917 and 1942, six major peasant movements developed in north Bihar. The movements were unprecedented: previously socio-economic and cultural conditions in general and the dominance of the landed interest in particular had kept dissidence sporadic, small-scale and localised. Under the direction of rich peasants and small landlords the movements commanded wide support among the less powerful members of north Bihar society. Some of these less powerful people participated because they were the clients or retainers of members of the village elite, while others took part of their own accord to air their grievances and protect their interests.

Agrarian stagnation provided the foundation for dissidence. The population had increased under British rule, but the conservatism of British social and economic policies thwarted the transformation of the agrarian economy. This transformation was necessary to produce an increase in wealth at least commensurate with the expansion of the population. Increased impoverishment raised tensions which were channelled into peasant dissidence. This dissidence took various forms: the movements emerged within particular contexts and had distinctive features.

The eruption of mass movements in an impoverished and inegalitarian society increased the potential for the emergence of challenges to the established social order. The non-fulfilment of this potential owed much to the actions of the Bihar branch of the Indian National Congress.

The Bihar Congress succeeded in controlling and directing mass turbulence. The Bihar Congress was dominated by small landlords and rich peasants and sought to unite a broad social spectrum in opposition to alien rule. It sought to ensure that agrarian protest and nationalist agitation did not coalesce, because such a fusion would both challenge the conservative, landed interests which it represented, and threaten the stability of the small landlord/rich peasant alliance which was the foundation of its strength.

The presence of the zamindari system of land-holding facilitated the efforts of the Bihar Congress to keep nationalist agitation and agrarian protest separate. Under this system most of the people had very limited contact with the representatives of the alien administration in connection with rent and revenue matters. Hence agrarian protest did not necessarily involve the administration. In Bihar, moreover, most of the zamindars were small men with effective local ties. Since the administration sought their support, and was reluctant to repress them, these people could easily adopt an attitude of ambivalence or antagonism to British rule. And even the great landlords avoided close identification with the British. For example Kameshwar Singh, who became Maharaja of Darbhanga in 1929, kept on good terms with the British but also presented himself as a moderate nationalist, maintained a friendship with Rajendra Prasad, and donated covertly to Congress funds.

In the neighbouring United Provinces, in contrast, Congress was less successful in keeping agrarian protest and nationalist agitation separate. Much of the United Provinces was only temporarily settled, and the revenue administration regularly impinged upon the peasant consciousness when it engaged in settlement operations to assess productivity and increase rents. In addition, in the United Provinces a highly visible group of large landholders had become clearly identified as a bulwark of British rule.[1]

The Bihar Congress managed both to keep the nationalist struggle distinct from agrarian conflicts and to discourage agrarian reform movements. In 1919-20 Swami Vidyanand led an extensive movement against the Darbhanga Raj. The Bihar Congress gave the grievances publicised by Vidyanand only scant attention. The Congress did not wish to encourage anti-zamindar protest by supporting Vidyanand in criticism of the Maharaja of Darbhanga, the largest landlord in the region. Rajendra Prasad denounced Vidyanand, accusing him of being a charlatan.

In the 1917-23 period, the Congress displayed more sympathy for anti-planter protest. Criticism of the predominantly European planter-landlords was grist to Congress's anti-British mill. But Congress gave only limited support to anti-planter protest, lest attacks on the planter-landlords develop into attacks on landlords in general.

In the 1930s a small group of 'left-wingers' within the Congress directed a peasant movement motivated by the disastrous effects of a slump in primary produce prices. They sought to fuse agrarian protest with nationalist agitation, but were outmanoeuvred by the mainstream members of the Congress. The left-wingers made only moderate demands and failed to develop a coherent, radical critique of their society. They were contained easily; if they had developed a sound analysis and adopted a radical stance they may have had greater success.[2]

Congress efforts to discourage and contain agrarian movements succeeded partly because the well-established peasants who led them had limited, reformist aims. These rich peasants displayed ambivalence to their landlords. They quarrelled with them over particular issues, but also aspired to join their ranks by purchasing zamindari property. And, because people from high caste *jatis* predominated among zamindars and big tenants, the two groups were meshed together by caste affiliation.

Though eschewing the use of agrarian grievances to fuel anti-administration protest, the Bihar Congress nevertheless mounted agitations which strongly challenged British rule. Because of the financial weakness of the province the hold of the British was tenuous. The turbulence of the 1917 to 1923 period strained the skeletal British police/administrative apparatus. During these years the Bihar Congress shunned Vidyanand's campaign. But it turned the anti-indigo planter movement to propaganda advantage, and drew on a variety of discontents to fuel the non-cooperation movement of 1920-22.

The next challenge to British rule came with the civil disobedience agitation of 1930 to 1934. Congress activists employed 'limited violence' to harass the British administration. By means of 'limited violence' Congress hamstrung the *chaukidari* system, brought waverers on side, cut at

government revenue from excise duties, and helped elicit
a harsh police response which was of great propaganda
value.

The greatest challenge to imperial rule came in August
1942, when the Indian National Congress launched mass
civil disobedience. The ensuing revolt temporarily demolished the police/administrative apparatus, thus increasing
the potential for the development of an agrarian upheaval.
This potential did not develop into reality, partly because
many peasants had benefited from the prevailing price in-
flation conditions, but mainly because of the organisational
and ideological dominance of the Congress.

The British policy of limited tolerance for dissidence
reinforced the defence by Congress of the social order.
The British administration allowed people to engage in constitutional political activity, gave some tolerance to non-
violent and non-coercive agitational politics, but vigorously
repressed militant and violent protest. This policy suited
the interests of the village elite. Small landlords and rich
peasants wished to capture governmental and administrative
control without altering the social structure. Violent revolt
and the violent repression it would elicit might polarize
society and encourage radical initiatives. Hence members
of the village elite made only a limited use of violence. The
area of tolerance allowed by British rule, which contrasted
with the absence of tolerance under other colonial rulers,
allowed the village elite to dissipate popular discontents in
movements which challenged the alien regime without
threatening the social order.

More fundamentally, a challenge to the social order did
not develop because of the limited impact of imperial rule
on north Bihar society. After the 1857 Revolt the British
attempted to secure their position by conserving existing
social structures. This policy was carried out especially
well in north Bihar. In north Bihar, the British administered, to use Anand A. Yang's perceptive phrase, a 'limited
Raj' which left traditional structures intact and which
relied on the support of the great landlords and on the
acquiescence of the village elite. When, during the course
of the twentieth century, this acquiescence began to be
replaced by opposition, the days of the British Raj were
numbered.

The British did little to modernise the agrarian economy of north Bihar, and long established socio-economic relationships persisted. The only significant European entrepreneurs in the region, the indigo planters, operated within the existing social and productive structure. The impact of the indigo industry, C.M. Fisher points out,

> can be summarised as distortion rather than fundamental destruction. The indigo factories created... difficulties in the...operation of the indigenous economy, but did nothing to alter or undermine the structure... The indigo industry created tensions... but instituted no radical change.[3]

Similarly British rule distorted, rather than transformed, the structure of the agrarian society of north Bihar.[4] Traditional patterns of deference, allegiance and leadership continued. The north Bihar peasantry took part in movements which sought either agrarian reforms or an end to alien rule. But they did not engage in radical protest against the oppressive social structure which provided the basis for both agrarian exploitation and imperial domination.

APPENDIX

The Darbhanga Raj Archives

In recent years our understanding of Indian history has been enriched by researchers who have moved beyond newspaper collections and government record rooms and delved into a variety of records previously little used for historical research. One important body of records, which only recently has been made available to scholars, is held in the Darbhanga Raj Archives in Darbhanga town, north Bihar.[1]

Until the abolition of the zamindari system in the early 1950s the Darbhanga Raj covered more than 2,000 square miles and comprised the largest landed estate[2] in Bihar and, after the Burdwan Raj, the second largest estate in the vast area incorporated within the former Bengal Presidency. Amidst a mass of small land-owners the Maharajas of the Darbhanga Raj dominated north Bihar. The Bihar administration was content merely to maintain public order, contain crime, and ensure the successful collection of revenue, partly by indirect taxation and partly through the raising of land revenue from the Maharaja of Darbhanga and his fellow zamindars. The British only exacted a small portion of the agrarian surplus and most of the remainder flowed into the zamindars' purses. The Maharaja of Darbhanga had a massive income and lived in grand style.

To a villager tilling land under the Darbhanga Raj, the British administration was a distant entity which intervened only rarely in his life. In contrast, the Darbhanga Raj exerted much more frequent influence. The villager paid rent in cash or produce to the Raj, and endured the harassment and illegal exactions of its servants. In its estates the Raj held the right to sell goods in the markets, to fish in ponds and streams, and to conduct ferry services over streams and rivers. Villagers eagerly sought positions in the large Darbhanga Raj bureaucracy, knowing that they could acquire wealth and power by climbing through its rungs. In the areas it owned and more generally throughout much of the region the Darbhanga Raj exerted pervasive influence. Historians are indeed fortunate that the records of the Raj have survived. The Darbhanga Raj was one of several great estates which existed in pre-independence India. But of the record collections – when they survive – of these estates, only that of the Darbhanga Raj is both well organised and open for scholarly research.[3]

The Darbhanga Raj of north Bihar was established in the time of the Emperor Akbar. Some of the material held in the Raj Archives dates back to the sixteenth, seventeenth and eighteenth centuries, but most of it dates from 1860 onwards. In 1860 Maharaja Momeshwar Singh died, leaving his son Lakmeshwar Singh as the minor heir to the estate. Until Lakmeshwar attained his majority in 1879 the estate was administered by the provincial government. The British officials responsible for the Darbhanga Raj reorganised its administration and established procedures for the manufacture and storage of records of administrative decisions and processes. They set up archives and appointed a record keeper and several assistants. The archives were divided into two parts: a section holding rent and tenure records written in Hindi and Persian, and an English language section holding general administrative records. This note deals with the materials held in the English language section.

The English language section comprises General, Law, Rent and Revenue departments. The materials held in the General Department are by far the most voluminous and are most directly useful for the historian. But the materials in the other departments are of considerable value: for example, perusal of the Law Department holdings reveals much about the conduct and context of particular criminal and civil cases and about the legal machinery of the Raj and the legal system within which it operated. The Rent and Revenue files, which deal mainly with the administrative and technical details of rent collection and revenue payment, also contain valuable information.

The holdings of the General Department comprise over 1,100 large cloth-bound bundles, each containing numerous files. As with the materials held in the other departments, the files are grouped under various categories and have been listed under these category sub-headings in ledgers prepared year by year. The most useful materials in the General Department are 'Darkasht' (Petition) files, Annual Administrative Reports, Head Office Inspection Reports, Head Office Conference Proceedings and Associated Papers, and Management and Miscellaneous correspondence between different levels of the Darbhanga Raj management.

The Darkasht files consist of petitions from tenants and employees of the Darbhanga Raj. In many cases these are accompanied by comments and replies from the responsible Darbhanga Raj officials. These files illuminate the operation of the Raj administration and summarize many of the grievances of the tenantry, improving our understanding of agrarian relations in the region. And where a petition is accompanied by a counter-petition, we gain insight into factional conflict in the villages.

The Annual Administrative Reports were compiled by the managers of the fourteen Darbhanga Raj administrative circles. According to the regulations of the Darbhanga Raj, each circle manager had to submit a yearly report. Many managers failed to fulfil this requirement, and others fulfilled it in a very cursory fashion. Nevertheless, some managers submitted lengthy and regular reports which yield much information. These reports provide background material on the climate, inhabitants, and agricultural conditions of the various localities in which the Maharaja of Darbhanga was the dominant land-owner. They also contain accounts of the repercussions of important political events. For example the reports dealing with the period of the Quit India Revolt provide information on the development of the insurrection in north Bihar and indicate that despite a background of agrarian protest in the late 1930s, the 1942 revolt remained purely nationalist in character.

The Annual Administrative Reports also contain details about the land-control and rent-collecting activities of the circle manager and his assistants. They provide information on the amount of rent and other dues collected, and frequently comment on particular problems of management. They also discuss the exercise of a variety of landlord rights held by the Darbhanga Raj, notably the lease of fishing rights and of the rights to conduct markets. The Reports also give information about agrarian disputes and the manner in which they were handled, and about the general tenor of agrarian relations. In some instances the correspondence held with the reports and the marginal comments made on the reports by head office officials yield further valuable insights and information.

The Inspection Reports were compiled from time to time by senior Raj officials, and often by the Chief Manager himself, after personal enquiry into the administration of particular circles. Inspection Reports dealt with much the same topics as the Annual Administrative Reports but from the critical perspective of the senior management of the Raj. In reports prepared in the 1930s, for example, the Chief Manager, the Englishman G.P. Danby, criticised Circle Managers and their staff for inefficiency, high-handedness and corruption.[4]

From time to time management conferences were held at the head office of the Darbhanga Raj. In January 1920, Raj officials assembled to discuss the challenge posed by Swami Vidyanand's Movement. This movement received only limited coverage in the press and in government records and hence the Darbhanga Raj Conference proceedings and papers provide indispensable evidence. At another conference, held in May 1937, the Chief Manager criticised some Circle Managers for their ineffectual handling of development funds.[5]

Much useful material can also be found in the Management and Miscellaneous sections of the General Department holdings. Most of this material consists of correspondence between the head office of the Raj and the circle managers. When it relates directly to the administration of the Raj this material is held in the Management section, whereas when it is of more general interest it is held in the Miscellaneous section.

The General Department records of the Darbhanga Raj have proved invaluable for research on peasant movements in north Bihar. The records also could be employed for research on many other topics. For example, they could

form the basis for a study of the administration of the
Darbhanga Raj, and could contribute substantially to research into the economic history and development problems
of north Bihar. In addition to the General Department
records, moreover, the Rent, Revenue and Law records
in the English language section of the archives and the
Rent and Tenure records in the Indian language section
will amply repay investigation.

Unfortunately not all of the papers held in the archives
are in good condition. A harsh climate has taken its toll,
and some of the papers dating from the pre-1910 period
urgently need restoration. This circumstance does not
reflect on the management and staff of the archives but
results rather from a lack of funds with which to tackle
the large and expensive task of restoration and preservation. In view of the crucial historical importance of the
Darbhanga Raj records, it may be hoped that the necessary
funds will soon be found.

NOTES

1 I gained access to the Raj archives through the courtesy
of the trustees of the Darbhanga Raj estate. After the
archives came under state control in mid-1976 I continued research in them through the courtesy of the
Bihar State Government. For help in gaining access
to the archives I am much indebted to Chetkar Jha,
M. Mishra, and the Director of the Bihar State Archives,
Taran Sharan Sinha. My only predecessor in using the
Darbhanga Raj archives for a major research project is
Jata Shankar Jha of the Jayaswal Research Institute.
His major publications are *Biography of an Indian
Patriot. Maharaja Lakmishwar Singh of Darbhanga*
(Patna 1972), which deals with the Darbhanga Maharaja
who reigned from 1879 to 1898, and *Beginnings of
Modern Education in Mithila. Selections from Educational
Records of the Darbhanga Raj 1860-1930* (Patna 1972).
Qeyamuddin Ahmed has drawn on the archives for his
'Origin and growth of the Darbhanga Raj (1574-1666)
based on some contemporary and unpublished documents',
Indian Historical Records Commission Proceedings,

XXXVI, II, 1961. For other reports on the archives see Clive Dewey, 'The History of Mithila and the Records of the Darbhanga Raj', *Modern Asian Studies*, 10, 1976, and Jata Shankar Jha, 'A Peep into the Darbhanga Raj Records Office', *Indian Archives*, XII, 1958. For his contribution to the preservation of the archives historians owe a debt to Clive Dewey, who in 1976 intervened to stop the records being sold for waste paper. For a more detailed version of the following remarks see the appendix to my 'Agrarian Relations in North Bihar: Peasant Protest and the Darbhanga Raj, 1919-20', *Indian Economic and Social History Review*, XVI, 1, 1979.

2 The term 'estate' is used here as a collective noun, referring to a number of dispersed properties. A large portion of the total Darbhanga Raj holdings lay within the jurisdiction of Darbhanga, but the Raj also held properties in Muzaffarpur, Bhagalpur, Purnea and Monghyr.

3 The fate of the records of the Balrampur Raj is typical. Until zamindari abolition the Balrampur Raj comprised some 500 square miles and was the premier estate in the United Provinces. In the 1950s its records were sold for waste paper. Thomas R. Metcalf, 'Notes on the Sources for Local History in North India', *Journal of Asian Studies*, 26, Nov. 1966-Sept. 1967, pp.672-3; 'Landlords Without Land: The U.P. Zamindars Today', *Pacific Affairs*, XL, 1 & 2, 1967, pp.8-9. Concerning the other great estates, I have only incomplete information. According to Sailen Ghose's *Archives in India. History and Assets* (Calcutta 1963) the records of the Burdwan Raj have been preserved in a well organised repository. But so far scholars have not been given access to them. In his *Agrarian Problems of Permanent Settlement. A Case Study of Champaran* (New Delhi 1978) Girish Mishra reports (p.324) that 'Whatever records are available at [the] Bettiah [Raj] are very difficult to handle because they are neither serially arranged nor are they catalogued'. I am informed reliably that the available Hawhwa Raj papers are also not organised.

4 Inspection Report, 7 May 1938, f 6H2, C. Padri, G 1938-39; Inspection Report, n.d., f 12B2, C. Birnager, G 1939-40, RDA.

5 Conference Proceedings, f 10C, C Management, G 1937-38, RDA.

NOTES

Chapter 1

1 For information on north Bihar see J. Byrne, *Bengal District Gazetteers: Bhagalpur* (Calcutta 1911); Sir John Houlton, *Bihar: The Heart of India* (London, Calcutta 1953); Maori (pseudonym for James Inglis), *Sport and Work on the Nepaul Frontier* (London 1878); L.S.S. O'Malley, *Bengal District Gazetteers* for *Champaran* (Calcutta 1907), *Saran* (Calcutta 1908), *Muzaffarpur* (Calcutta 1907), *Darbhanga* (Calcutta 1907), *Monghyr* (Calcutta 1909), and *Purnea* (Calcutta 1911); O.K.H. Spate, A.T.A. Learmonth and B.H. Farmer, *India, Pakistan and Ceylon: The Regions* (London, 3rd ed. 1967); and Minden Wilson, *History of Behar Indigo Factories.* (Calcutta, 1885 and 1908).

2 The following account of the social structure of north Bihar in the early 20th century draws conceptually on Hamza Alavi's 'Peasants and Revolution', in Kathleen Gough and Hari P. Sharma (eds), *Imperialism and Revolution in South Asia*, (New York, London 1973) and his 'Rural Bases of Political Power in South Asia', *Journal of Contemporary Asia*, 4,4, 1974. For information I have drawn on the *Bengal District Gazetteers*, the *Survey and Settlement Reports* and the decennial *Census* reports. For a preliminary discussion which emphasises the fluidity of the social structure for those above the subsistence level see Peter Robb, 'Hierarchy and Resources: Peasant Stratification in late Nineteenth Century Bihar', *Modern Asian Studies*, 13, 1, 1979. Robb's analysis raises some interesting points, but deals only briefly with the relationship between indebtedness and social position and neglects the tendency in traditional society for kinship and factional networks to help protect cultivators against fluctuations in their individual fortunes.

3 It should be noted that middle peasants of high caste status were subject to ritual sanctions against the per-

formance of various agricultural tasks. Hence they were obliged to employ labourers for these tasks. However since the amount of land they controlled was small and they had limited resources these high caste middle peasants generally employed only one or two labourers, and hired them only on a short term basis.

4 See Padri Annual Administrative Report [hereafter AAR], 10 August 1920, Collection [hereafter C] XXXIV, f 2A, General Department [hereafter G] 1919-20, Raj Darbhanga Archives [hereafter RDA].
5 O'Malley, *Saran*, p.123.
6 Interview, Umarpathi Tewari, Dumari village, Darbhanga, 17 October 1976. See also Rajendra Prasad, *Autobiography*, (Bombay 1957) pp.1, 20.
7 For a study of the local elite in one north Bihar village see Ramashray Roy, 'Conflict and Co-operation in a north Bihar Village', *Journal of the Bihar Research Society*, XLIX, 1963.
8 At the turn of the century the two largest zamindars in north Bihar after the Maharaja of Darbhanga were the Maharaja of Hathwa and the Maharani of Bettiah, who held respectively 561 and 1,824 square miles of property and paid Rs.250,000 and Rs.500,000 in land revenue. O'Malley, *Saran*, p.153, *Champaran*, pp.151-2. By 1907, in the north Bihar districts of Saran, Champaran, Muzaffarpur, Darbhanga and Purnea, there were only 75 estates which paid more than Rs.5,000 in land revenue. Only six of these estates paid more than Rs.100,000; 21 paid between Rs.15,000 and Rs.100,000, and 48 paid between Rs.5,000 and Rs.15,000. In the Bengal Presidency as a whole by 1907 only 590 estates paid more than Rs.5,000 in land revenue. The ownership of these 590 estates was shared between 11,378 people, of whom only 504 paid, as individuals, more than Rs.5,000 per year. Government of Bengal [hereafter GBEN], Land Revenue Proceedings [hereafter LR], 19 S/4, B 107-10, July 1907, West Bengal Archives [hereafter WBA].
9 On the Darbhanga Raj and its rulers see Qeyamuddin Ahmed, 'Origin and growth of the Darbhanga Raj (1574-1666), based on some contemporary and unpublished documents', *Indian Historical Records Commission Proceedings*, XXXVI, Part II, 1961; Clive Dewey, 'The History of Mithila and the Records of the Darbhanga Raj', *Modern Asian Studies*, 10, 1976; Jata Shankar Jha,

A History of Darbhanga Raj, (Patna 1968) and *Biography of an Indian Patriot, Maharaja Lakmishwar Singh of Darbhanga* (Patna 1972); O'Malley, *Darbhanga,* pp.143-6; Ishvari Prasad Singh, *The Youngest Legislator of India: The Biography of the Hon'ble Maharajadhiraja Sir Kameshwar Singh, Bahadur, K.C.I.E. of Darbhanga* (Patna 1936); and Shyam Narayan Singh, *History of Tirhut from the earliest times to the end of the nineteenth century* (Calcutta 1922). See also the Maharajadhiraj Dr. Kameshwara Singh Memorial Volume, *Journal of the Bihar Research Society,* XLVIII, 1962. For information about the Maithil Brahman Community, see Paul R. Brass, *Language, Religion and Politics in North India,* (London 1974) and Hetukar Jha, 'Nation Building in a north Indian region. The Case of Mithila', unpublished manuscript. (Hetukar Jha of the Sociology Department, Patna University kindly permitted me to use this manuscript.) For details of Rameshwar Singh's activities as a leader of orthodox Hinduism, see Richard Gordon, 'The Hindu Mahasabha and the Indian National Congress, 1915 to 1926', *Modern Asian Studies,* 9, 2, 1975, pp.155, 160, 181. For the income and expenditure of the Darbhanga Raj see O'Malley, *Darbhanga,* p.145; 'Extracts from the Annual Report of the Officiating Manager', GBEN LR 48-49, May 1878, p.7, Bihar State Archives [hereafter BSA]; 'Report on the Administration of the Darbhanga Raj, 1914/1915', C XXXIV, G 1915-16, RDA.

10   O'Malley, *Darbhanga,* and *Saran;* Girish Mishra, *Agrarian Problems of Permanent Settlement. A Case Study of Champaran* (New Delhi 1978).
11   See Ronald J. Herring, 'Radical Politics and Revolution in South Asia', *Journal of Peasant Studies,* 7, 1, 1978.
12   In all of the north Bihar districts except Purnea, Muslims formed around 12 per cent of the population. In Purnea, they comprised 43 per cent of the population, and were particularly numerous in the eastern half of the district. O'Malley, *Purnea,* pp.58, 60. Centuries of Mughal rule had helped shape one aspect of north Bihar social life: the subjugation of women. Bihar was 'the most Pardah ridden province in India' and women from better-off families rarely moved outside their homes. Women were second class citizens, and any initiative to improve their lot elicited a hostile reaction. Sexual exploitation was allied with social and

economic exploitation and poor and low caste women were preyed on by money lenders, zamindars and rich peasants. Circular from Ramnandan Misra, All India Congress Committee Papers [hereafter AICCP], G 43 (wi) (wii) 1935, Nehru Memorial Library [hereafter NML]; *Searchlight*, 24 Jan. 1930; Jha, 'Nation Building in Mithila', pp. 94-5.

13 In 1907, Muslims owned nine of the 75 estates in the districts of Saran, Champaran, Muzaffarpur, Darbhanga and Purnea that paid more than Rs. 5,000 in land revenue. Separate figures for the north Gangetic sections of Monghyr and Bhagalpur districts are not available. GBEN, LR 19S/4, B107-10, July 1907, WBA.

14 *Social Origins of Dictatorship and Democracy. Lord and Peasant in the Making of the Modern World* (London 1967), p. 383.

15 See Ravinder Kumar, 'The Political Process in India', *South Asia*, 1, 1971. In 'North Bihar Village' Ramashray Roy examines the history of factionalism in the village of Radhanager from 1900 to 1960. For details about two factional conflicts in areas under the control of the Darbhanga Raj, see 'Brief of case of Charanjib Jha versus Naubat Jha', f. 10E, C V (Criminal), Law Department [hereafter L], 1920-21, RDA; Alapur Manager, Diary 28 May 1923, f 5, C XXV, G 1922-23, RDA. For a perceptive analysis of factionalism in village India see A.T. Carter, 'Political Stratification and Unstable Alliances in Rural Western Maharashtra', *Modern Asian Studies*, 6, 4, 1972.

16 Roy, 'North Bihar Village', p. 298; Bihar Government Communique, *Searchlight*, 10 Feb. 1931; O'Malley, *Saran*, p. 32.

17 O'Malley, *Monghyr*, p. 63. See also Byrne, *Bhagalpur*, p. 52.

18 M.N. Karna, Health, Culture and Community in a North Bihar Village, Ph.D. thesis, Patna University, 1970; Parihar AAR, C XXXIV G 1919-20, RDA: Maori, *Nepaul Frontier*, pp. 137-8.

19 G.E. Owen, *Bihar and Orissa in 1921* (Patna 1922), pp. 142-4. See also Naredigar AAR, f 10J4, G 1937-38, RDA.

20 Maori, *Nepaul Frontier*, p. 21.

21 Nor was the extent of literacy increasing rapidly. As of March 1921'...only 4.27 per cent of the male, and 0.65 per cent of the female, or 2.43 per cent of the

total population of the province was undergoing instruction'. Owen, *Bihar 1921*, p.112.
22 For general accounts of rioting see the annual GB(O), *Report on the Administration of the Police in the Province of Bihar (and Orissa)* (Patna, annual, various dates). The argument that follows draws on Anand A. Yang's 'The Agrarian Origins of Crime: A Study of Riots in Saran District, India, 1866-1920', *Journal of Social History*, XIII, 2, Winter 1979.
23 Dharampur AAR, 13 March 1920, f 20 C XXXIV, G 1919-20, RDA. See also O'Malley, Purnea pp.130-1.
24 Roy, 'North Bihar Village', pp.301-4.
25 Yang, 'Riots in Saran', p.12. Unfortunately, however, our knowledge of clashes between distinct strata is limited because, as Frank Perlin points out, 'Only that conflict interfering with administration or manifested on such a scale as to be noticeable outside, is likely to be recorded, while conflict within the village, between castes or privileged and under-privileged landholders, is only too likely to escape the accounts'. See his 'Cycles, Trends and Academics among the Peasantry of North-West India', *Journal of Peasant Studies*, 2, 3, April 1975, p.367. Walter Hauser refers to an area in Patna district, south Bihar, where disputes within zamindari estates did not usually reach the courts because the zamindars decided the disputes and enforced their decisions with the aid of lathials. The Bihar Provincial Kisan Sabha, 1929-1942, a Study of an Indian Peasant Movement, Ph.D. thesis, University of Chicago, 1961, p.52.
26 J. Beames, *Memoirs of a Bengal Civilian*, (London, 1961), p.134.
27 See her *Agrarian Conditions in Northern India. Volume One: The United Provinces under British Rule, 1860-1900*, (Los Angeles, London, 1972), p.241.
28 Government of Great Britain [hereafter GGB], *Indian Statutory Commission*, (12 vols, London, 1930), XII, p.388.
29 B.H. Baden-Powell, *The Land-Systems of British India* (3 vols, London, 1892), I, pp.389-442; Ranajit Guha, *A Rule of Property for Bengal. An Essay on the Idea of Permanent Settlement* (Paris, 1963); Sir William Wilson Hunter, *Bengal M.S. Records* (2 Vols, London, 1894), I, pp.74-84.
30 Baden-Powell, *Land Systems*, 1, p.440; Hunter, *Records*,

I, pp. 89-104; O'Malley, *Champaran*, p. 125, *Muzaffarpur*, p. 114, *Purnea*, pp. 116-17; J.H. Kerr, *Final Report on the Survey and Settlement Operations in the Darbhanga District 1896 to 1903*, (Patna 1926); Mishra, *Agrarian Problems*, pp. 9-18.
31 Guha, *Rule of Property*, pp. 167-86; Hunter *Bengal Records*, pp. 74-84.
32 Walter C. Neale, 'Land is to Rule', in R.E. Frykenberg, (ed.) *Land Control and Social Structure in Indian History* (London 1969) pp. 9-15; Mishra, *Agrarian Problems*, pp. 34-47.
33 A. Earle, Resolution 147T-R, 20 June 1904, appended to Kerr, *Darbhanga Settlement Report;* O'Malley, *Monghyr*, p. 159; Baden-Powell, *Land Systems*, I, pp. 438-40; Mishra, *Agrarian Problems*, pp. 15, 28-29.
34 Moore, *Social Origins*, p. 360. See also Daniel and Alice Thorner, *Land and Labour in India* (London 1962), p. 109.
35 GGB, *Statutory Commission*, XII, pp. 372-5, 387; B.R. Tomlinson, 'India and the British Empire, 1880-1935', *Indian Economic and Social History Review*, XI, 2-3, 1974.
36 GGB, *Statutory Commission*, XII, p. 375.
37 *Ibid.*, p. 391.
38 Secretary of State for India, *India Office and Burma Office List, 1911*, (London, 1911).
39 Pierre Proudhon, quoted in Barbara W. Tuchman, *The Proud Tower: A Portrait of the World Before the War, 1890-1914*, (New York, 1970, first pub. 1966), p. 74.
40 Byrnes, *Bhagalpur*, pp. 115-19; Maori, *Nepaul Frontier*, pp. 152-3, 163, 165; Owen, *Bihar 1921*, p. 113; Parihar AAR C XXXIV, G 1915-16, RDA; letter 4, C IX G 1921-22, RDA: Alapur Manager, Diary, 9 May 1923, C XXV, G 1922-23, RDA: District Magistrate Johnson to Bhagalpur Commissioner, 21 February 1921, Government of Bihar and Orissa [hereafter GBO], Political Special Department [hereafter PS], f 66, 1921, BSA. See also Walter C. Neale, *Economic Change in Rural India. Land Tenure and Reform in Uttar Pradesh 1800-1955*, (London 1962), pp. 192-7.
41 Quoted in Byrne, *Bhagalpur*, p. 117.
42 Byrne, *Bhagalpur*, p. 147; O'Malley, *Champaran*, p. 139, *Saran*, p. 136, *Muzaffarpur*, p. 126, *Darbhanga*, p. 129; *Monghyr*, pp. 182-3, *Purnea*, p. 147; Owen, *Bihar 1921*; H.C. Prior, *Bihar and Orissa in 1923*, (Patna 1924) p. 75.

43 Maori, *Nepaul Frontier*, p.156; Owen, *Bihar 1921*, p.103; Byrne, *Bhagalpur*, p.52.
44 Yang, 'Riots in Saran', pp.3, 7.
45 Owen, *Bihar 1921*, p.103. For consistently critical remarks, see the annual *Police Administration Reports*.
46 O'Malley, *Darbhanga*, pp.1, 129.
47 Rainey to Secretary, GOI, 29 May 1921, PS f 29, 1921, BSA: Dundas to GBO, PS f 218, 1922, BSA; E.L.L. Hammond to Army Secretary, 10/11 March 1922, HP f 49, 1921, NAI; PS f 572, 1921, BSA; Memorandum, HP f 49, 1921, NAI; GBO to Scroope, Tirhut Commissioner, 17 Apr. 1922, PS f 29, 1921, BSA.
48 Owen, *Bihar 1921*, p.99; Secret Report by Mr. R.J. Hirst, PS f 159, 1929, BSA [hereafter Hirst Report], pp.14-15; Special Branch Inspector's report, 21 June 1930, PS f 140, 1930, BSA; *Searchlight*, 20 Dec. 1922; Report of the Committee appointed to devise measures to deal with corruption in the Police, p.10, PS f 159(B), 1929, BSA [hereafter Corruption Report].
49 Corruption Report, p.6; Hirst Report, pp.6, 17, 18, 28.
50 GBO PS f 140, 1920, BSA.
51 See also HP f A 159-170, Aug.1910, NAI; Gertrude Emersen Sen, *Voiceless India*, (Benares, 1946), pp.169-82; Maori, *Nepaul Frontier*, pp.161-9; Prasad, *Autobiography*, p.14.
52 H.C. Prior, *Bihar and Orissa in 1922*, (Patna 1923) pp.89-92.
53 C.S. McDonald, Bahora Division Manager to Chief Manager, 19 June 1923, f 20, C XXV G 1922-23, RDA.
54 Yang, 'Riots in Saran', pp.7, 13.
55 Hauser, 'Bihar Kisan Sabha', p.7, note 2. See also Ira Klein, 'Population and Agriculture in Northern India, 1872-1921', *Modern Asian Studies*, 8, 2, 1974.
56 O'Malley, *Muzaffarpur*, p.27.
57 Quoted in Kerr, *Darbhanga Settlement Report*, p.84.
58 *Ibid.*, pp.80, 81, 85.
59 O'Malley, *Purnea*, p.72.
60 Spate, et. al., *India*, pp.564, 565, 569.
61 Amiya Kumar Bagchi, 'Reflections on Patterns of Regional Growth in India During the Period of British Rule', *Bengal Past and Present*, XLV, Part 1, No.180, Jan.-June 1976, p.272.
62 *Ibid.*, pp.260-267. See also Rajat. K. Ray, 'The Crisis of Bengal Agriculture, 1870-1927 – The Dynamics

of Immobility', *Indian Economic and Social History Review*, X, 3, 1973, pp.272-9.
63 Bagchi, 'Patterns of Regional Growth'; Ray, 'Crisis of Bengal Agriculture'; Mishra, *Agrarian Problems*, Chapter 4; C.M. Fisher, Indigo Plantations and agrarian society in North Bihar in the nineteenth and early twentieth centuries, D.Phil. thesis, Cambridge University, 1976.
64 Ray, 'Crisis of Bengal Agriculture', pp.244-5; Bagchi, 'Patterns of Regional Growth', p.265.
65 Fisher, 'Indigo Plantations', pp.109-10.
66 One typical instance was their handling of the affairs of the Darbhanga Raj after the death of Momeshwar Singh, who was Maharaja of Darbhanga from 1829 until his death in 1860. During his reign Momeshwar Singh supported a host of kinsfolk, lived in great state, and spent lavishly on ceremonies. Many of his relatives held posts in the administration of the Darbhanga estates, and displayed an inefficiency only surpassed by their venality. When Momeshwar Singh died, leaving behind a minor heir, the Darbhanga Raj was verging on bankruptcy. But the provincial government stepped in, took over the administration of the estates and, by careful management, restored prosperity before handing them back to the heir, Lakmeshwar Singh, when he came of age in 1879. J. Burn, 'Report on the Administration of the Darbhanga Estates, 1860-1879', GBEN, LR 49-53, August 1880, BSA. See also Anand A. Yang, 'An Institutional Shelter: The Court of Wards in late Nineteenth Century Bihar', *Modern Asian Studies*, 13, 2, 1979.
67 Amiya Bagchi, 'Foreign Capital and Economic Development in India: A Schematic View', in Gough and Sharma, *Imperialism and Revolution*, p.53.
68 Anand A. Yang, 'Peasants on the Move: A Study of Internal Migration in India', *Journal of Interdisciplinary History*, X, 1, Summer 1979. See also O'Malley, *Muzaffarpur*, pp.87-8 and *Saran*, p.92 and Fisher, 'Indigo Plantations'.
69 For discussion of the relation between economic conditions and the crime rate see GBO Fortnightly Report Number Two [hereafter FR(2)], August 1920, PS f 8, 1920; G.E. Owen, *Bihar and Orissa in 1928-29*, (Patna 1930), p.61.
70 Owen, *Bihar 1921*, pp.100, 109.

71 James R. Hagen and Anand A. Yang, 'Local Sources for the Study of Rural India: The 'Village Notes' of Bihar', *Indian Economic and Social History Review*, XIII, 1, 1976, p.78.
72 Kerr, *Darbhanga Settlement Report*, p.101; O'Malley, *Darbhanga*, p.120.

Chapter 2

1 O'Malley, *Champaran*, pp.108-11; Maori, *Nepaul Frontier*, p.7.
2 B.B. Misra (ed.), *Select Documents on Mahatma Gandhi's Movement in Champaran 1917-18* (Patna 1963) 'Introduction', p.8.
3 B.B. Kling, *The Blue Mutiny. The Indigo Disturbances in Bengal 1859-1862*, (London, 1966); Ranajit Guha, 'Neel-Darpan: The Image of a Peasant Revolt in a Liberal Mirror', *The Journal of Peasant Studies*, 2, 1, October 1974.
4 Fisher, 'Indigo Plantations', p.35.
5 G. Mishra, 'Indigo Plantation and the Agrarian Relations in Champaran during the Nineteenth Century', *Indian Economic and Social History Review*, III, 4 Dec. 1966; Byrne, *Bhagalpur*, p.129; O'Malley, *Champaran*, p.111, *Saran*, p.102-3, *Muzaffarpur*, p.101, *Darbhanga*, p.99, *Monghyr*, p.140-1, *Purnea*, p.130-1; K.K. Datta, *History of the Freedom Movement in Bihar* (3 vols, Patna, 1957), I, pp.179-80.
6 O'Malley, *Muzaffarpur*, p.126.
7 Gorakh Prasad to Editor, *Searchlight*, 31 Dec. 1920; 'The Voice of the Tenant', *Searchlight*, 22 Sept. 1922; Judith M. Brown, *Gandhi's Rise to Power: Indian Politics 1915-1922* (London 1972) p.64; Datta, *Freedom Movement*, II, p.224.
8 Maori, *Nepaul Frontier*, pp.5-6; Fisher, 'Indigo Plantations', pp.55, 232.
9 Maori, *Nepaul Frontier*, Ch.2.
10 Fisher, 'Indigo Plantations', Ch.5.
11 Maori, *Nepaul Frontier*, p.18.
12 *Ibid.*
13 GBO, *Champaran Committee Report*, p.9.
14 'An Ex-Civilian', *Life in the Mofussil: or, the Civilian in Lower Bengal*, (2 vols, London 1878), I, pp.249-51;

Notes to pages 40-42

Fisher, 'Indigo Plantations', pp.87, 89; G. Mishra, 'Socio-Economic Background of Gandhi's Champaran Movement', *The Indian Economic and Social History Review*, V, 3, Sept. 1968; Jacques Pouchepadass, 'Local leaders and the intelligentsia in the Champaran satyagraha (1917): a study in peasant mobilization', *Contributions to Indian Sociology*, New Series, 8, 1974.
15 Fisher, 'Indigo Plantations', pp.85-89, 103.
16 *Ibid.*, pp.64, 104, 105, 109, 310; Datta, *Freedom Movement*, II, p.223.
17 Fisher, 'Indigo Plantations', p.312.
18 *Ibid.*, pp.111, 112. For the particular circumstances in which this antipathy found political expression during the 19th century, see *ibid.*, Ch.3 and the same author's 'Planters and Peasants: The Ecological Context of Agrarian Unrest on the Indigo Plantations of North Bihar', in Clive Dewey and A.G. Hopkins (eds), *The Imperial Impact. Studies in the Economic History of Africa and India*, (London 1978).
19 Fisher, 'Indigo Plantations', pp.46-7.
20 Beames, *Memoirs*, pp.172-3.
21 An Ex-Civilian, *Life in the Mofussil*, pp.251-2; Maori, *Nepaul Frontier*, pp.153, 223.
22 Wilson, *Behar Indigo Factories*, pp.100-1, 122-3, 138-9, 242-3, 329-31; Datta, *Freedom Movement*, II, p.175; Fisher, 'Indigo Plantations', pp.59, 60, 103, 176-8.
23 Quoted in Yang, 'Riots in Saran', p.15.
24 O'Malley, *Champaran*, p.117; J.A. Sweeney, *Final Report on the Survey and Settlement Operations (Revision) in the district of Champaran 1913-19* (Patna 1922) p.25; Maori, *Nepaul Frontier*, p.22; Fisher, 'Indigo Plantations', p.217; Mishra, *Agrarian Problems*, pp.37-8.
25 Fisher, 'Indigo Plantations', pp.310, 311.
26 See Stephen Henningham, 'The Social Setting of the Champaran Satyagraha: The Challenge to an Alien Elite', *Indian Economic and Social History Review*, XIII, I, 1976, pp.63-4, 66-7, 72.
27 Fisher, 'Indigo Plantations', p.64; O'Malley, *Champaran*, pp.109-10.
28 *British Parliamentary Papers*, 1890-91, 59, 157, p.8; T.R. Filgate, 'The Behar Planters' Association Ltd', in Arnold Wright (ed.), *Bengal and Assam, Behar and Orissa*, (London 1917), pp.268-71.
29 Fisher, 'Indigo Plantations', p.311.

30 *Ibid.*, pp. 35, 37, 51.
31 D.J. Reid, 'Indigo in Behar', in Wright, *Bengal and Behar*; Filgate, 'Behar Planters' Association'; and Wilson, *Behar Indigo Factories*.
32 Wilson, *Behar Indigo Factories*, p. 101; O'Malley, *Purnea*, pp. 130-31.
33 Reid, 'Indigo in Behar', p. 238.
34 Fisher, 'Indigo Plantations', p. 280.
35 *Ibid.*, Filgate, 'Behar Planters' Association'.
36 'Rutherfordism at Bettiah', *Searchlight*, 18 Aug. 1920; 'Rutherfordism', *Searchlight*, 1 Sept. 1920; Pouchepadass, 'Local Leaders', pp. 73-4.
37 Misra, *Select Documents*, p. 13; Filgate, 'Behar Planters' Association', p. 349.
38 Misra, *Select Documents*, pp. 13-14; Mishra, *Agrarian Problems*, pp. 274-6; K.K. Datta (ed.), *Writings and Speeches of Mahatma Gandhi Relating to Bihar, 1917-1942*, (Patna 1960), p. 97; Prasad, *Autobiography*, p. 89.
39 See Mishra, *Agrarian Problems*, p. 286.
40 Sweeney, *Champaran Settlement Report*, p. 19; M. Razi Ahmad, Indigo Unrest in Champaran and Mahatma Gandhi, 1867-1918, Ph.D. thesis, Patna University 1966, p. 97, note 27.
41 Sweeney, *Champaran Settlement Report*, p. 20.
42 *Ibid.*, Misra, *Select Documents*, p. 15.
43 About 15,000 peasants assembled and shouted, in the local Bhojpuri variant of Hindi, slogans that outlined their grievances. According to Tendulkar their efforts miscarried: when George asked the meaning of the slogans a quick-witted aide told him that they were expressions of joy and welcome. D.G. Tendulkar, *Gandhi in Champaran* (Patna 1957) p. 18.
44 Sweeney, *Champaran Settlement Report*, p. 21.
45 The previous survey and settlement operations were conducted from 1892 to 1899.
46 Sweeney, *Champaran Settlement Report*, p. 23.
47 *Ibid.*, p. 25.
48 Misra, *Select Documents*, pp. 18-20.
49 *Ibid.*, p. 20.
50 *Ibid.*, 'Biographical Notes'; Mishra, *Agrarian Problems*, pp. 286-90; Pouchepadass, 'Local Leaders', pp. 71-73.
51 Mishra, *Agrarian Problems*, pp. 288-90; Pouchepadass, 'Local Leaders', pp. 74-75.
52 Datta, *Freedom Movement*, II, pp. 193-5; Brown, *Gandhi's Rise*, p. 65.

53 R.A. Huttenback, *Gandhi in South Africa, British Imperialism and the Indian Question, 1860-1914*, (London 1971); Brown, *Gandhi's Rise*, Joan Bondurant, *Conquest of Violence, The Gandhian Philosophy of Conflict*, (New Jersey 1958).
54 Brown, *Gandhi's Rise*, pp.60-1.
55 The Champaran District Officer, W.B. Heycock, was directed to pass the order by L.F. Morsehead, the Commissioner of the Tirhut Division. Morsehead to District Magistrate, Champaran, 13 Apr. 1917, and Heycock to Gandhi, 16 Apr. 1917, Misra, *Select Documents*, pp.61-2.
56 Telegram, GBO to Tirhut Commissioner, 19 Apr. 1917, H. McPherson to L.F. Morsehead, 20 Apr. 1917, Misra, *Select Documents*, pp.73, 75-6.
57 M.K. Gandhi, Statement filed before Subdivisional Magistrate, Motihari, 18 Apr. 1917, Misra, *Select Documents*, p.69.
58 Pouchepadass, 'Local Leaders', pp.69-71; Brown, *Gandhi's Rise*, p.77.
59 M.K. Gandhi, *An Autobiography. The Story of My Experiments with Truth*, (London 1966); Brown, *Gandhi's Rise*, pp.73-75; Pouchepadass, 'Local Leaders', pp.70-71; Rajendra Prasad, *Mahatma Gandhi and Bihar. Some Reminiscences*, (Bombay 1949), pp.19, 35.
60 Sweeney, *Champaran Settlement Report*, p.23.
61 W.H. Lewis, Subdivisional Officer to W.B. Heycock, District Magistrate, 29 Apr. 1917, Misra, *Select Documents*, p.99.
62 For the interaction of the Government of India and the provincial government see Brown, *Gandhi's Rise*, pp.70-2.
63 H. Cox, Secretary Bihar Planters' Association, Champaran, to H. McPherson, Chief Secretary GBO, n.d., Misra, *Select Documents*, p.219.
64 Rajendra Prasad, *Satyagraha in Champaran* (Madras 1928); Tendulkar, *Gandhi in Champaran*.
65 Sweeney, *Champaran Settlement Report*, p.25.
66 *Ibid.*
67 Speech by Hammond, Legislative Council Proceedings, transcript in PS f 159, 1922, BSA.
68 Mishra, 'Gandhi's Champaran Movement', p.271; 'The Voice of the Tenant', *Searchlight*, 22 Sept. 1922.
69 Sweeney, *Champaran Settlement Report*, p.23.
70 *Searchlight*, 19 Aug. 1921.

Notes to pages 50-55

71 Prasad, *Satyagraha in Champaran*, pp.16-17; Brown, *Gandhi's Rise*, p.63.
72 Sweeney, *Champaran Settlement Report*, p.25; GBO FR(1) Jan. 1918, PS f 8 1918, BSA.
73 GBO Police Abstract 419, Champaran, 7 March 1919, BSA.
74 *Searchlight*, 31 July 1921; 'Note on the situation in village Sonbarsa in Thana Bihpur', HP f 315, 199 NAI [hereafter Note on Sonbarsa], paras 2, 5; O'Malley, *Monghyr*, pp.74, 129.
75 Note on Sonbarsa, para. 2.
76 Judgement by Justice Das, HP f 315, 1922, pp.40, 54-5, NAI.
77 Note on Sonbarsa, paras 1 and 3.
78 *Ibid.*
79 *Ibid.*, paras 5, 6; 'Note on the agitation in Grant's estate', HP f 315, 1922, NAI.
80 Note on Sonbarsa, para 9.
81 *Ibid.*, para 10.
82 *Ibid.*
83 *Ibid.*, paras 4, 5.
84 *Ibid.*, paras 5, 7.
85 FR(2) June 1920, PS f 8, 1920, BSA.
86 Judgement by Justice Das, HP f 315, 1922, NAI, p.43.
87 Note on Sonbarsa, paras 7, 8; Chief Secretary GBO to Secretary European Association, 2 Nov., 1921, HP f 315, 1922, NAI.
88 'Special Branch Officer's Report', 4 Feb., 1921, HP f 315, 1922, NAI; Report by Drake-Brockman, Deputy Inspector-General Police, 7 Feb., 1921, HP f 315, 1922, NAI [hereafter Drake-Brockman Report].
89 *Ibid.*
90 Drake-Brockman Report, pp.19-20.
91 Memorial presented to the Government of Bihar and Orissa by the north Bihar branch of the European Association, HP f 315, 1922, NAI; GBO Chief Secretary to Secretary, European Association, 2 Nov., 1921, HP f 315, 1922, NAI; Judgement by Justice Das, HP f 315, 1922, NAI.
92 Secretary, European Association to GBO Chief Secretary, 8 Nov., 1921, HP f 315, 1922.
93 GBO Chief Secretary to Secretary European Association, 2 Nov., 1922, HP f 315, 1922, NAI.
94 GBO, *Report of Land Revenue Administration of the Province of Bihar and Orissa, 1921-22*, (Patna 1922), p.18; K.S. Coombe, Manager, Luttipur Concern,

Notes to pages 55-60

Narayanpur, to Rajendra Prasad, 26 Sept., 1936, f XII, 1936, Mf 4, Prasad Papers [hereafter PP], NM1.
95 *Searchlight*, 25 Apr. 1920; Vaidyanath Jha, 'Confidential Purnea Report', 7 Apr. 1920, f 14H, C XXVI, G 1919-20, RDA [hereafter Purnea Report].
96 Purnea Report.
97 W. Johnson, District Magistrate Purnea to Assistant Manager, Kabur factory, quoted in *Searchlight*, 25 Apr. 1920.
98 Purnea Police Superintendent's Report, circa 30 Apr. 1920, held with the Purnea Report. The presence of this and other police reports in the files of the Darbhanga Raj indicates either police corruption or police collusion with the Raj authorities.
99 Purnea Report.
100 *Ibid.*
101 *Ibid.*
102 *Ibid.;* Confidential CID Reports, held with Purnea Report.
103 Purnea Report.
104 A.K. Khan, Gondwara Circle Manager, to His Highness the Maharaja, 18 August 1920, held with Purnea Report.
105 Commissioner Bhagalpur to Chief Secretary, 1 June 1921, PS f 184, 1921, BSA.
106 Purnea District Magistrate, 'Terms of Settlement', 29 May 1921, PS f 184, 1921, BSA.
107 Commissioner Bhagalpur Division to Chief Secretary, 1 June 1921, PS f 184, 1921, BSA.
108 *Ibid.;* Purnea Police Superintendent to Deputy Inspector General Police, GBO, 10 Apr. 1921, and Purnea District Magistrate, report dated 29 May 1921, PS f 184, 1921, BSA.
109 Police Superintendent's and Commissioner's letters, cited in notes 105 and 108 above.
110 Purnea District Magistrate's Report, and his 'Terms of Settlement', 29 May 1921, PS f 184, 1921, BSA.
111 Champaran Police Superintendent to 1st assistant to Deputy Inspector General Police, 21 June 1921, PS f 287, 1921, BSA.
112 *Searchlight*, 19 August 1921.
113 Toplis, Muzaffarpur District Magistrate, quoted in Tirhut FR(1), August 1921, PS f 93, 1921, BSA.
114 A *mahant(h)* held the right to officiate in a village temple and also controlled the landholdings which wealthy villagers had donated to provide for the upkeep

of the temple and its staff. Because he combined religious leadership with control over land a *mahant* held considerable power in village society. Toplis, Muzaffarpur District Magistrate, quoted in Tirhut FR(1), Sept. 1921, PS f 93, 1921, BSA.
115 *Ibid.*
116 Champaran Police Superintendent, Confidential Diary for week ending 24 Oct., extract quoted in PS f 93, 1921, BSA.
117 Hammond, GBO Chief Secretary to GOI Home Secretary, HP f 357, 1921, para.5, NAI.
118 Champaran Police Superintendent, Confidential Diary for week ending 24 Oct., extract quoted in PS f 93, 1921, BSA.
119 *Ibid.*
120 Champaran Police Superintendent, report on situation in Champaran, 3 Nov., 1921 [hereafter Champaran Police Report]; Special Report Case 29, Report II, 2 Nov., 1921 [hereafter Special Report II], both in PS f 539, 1921, BSA.
121 Champaran Police Report.
122 *Ibid.*
123 *Ibid.* and Hammond, GBO Chief Secretary to GOI Home Secretary, para.2, HP f 357, 1921, NAI.
124 Champaran Police Report.
125 Hammond, GBO Chief Secretary to GOI Home Secretary, paras 3 and 5, HP f 357, 1921, NAI; Council speech by Mr. Hammond, PS f 159, 1922, BSA; Champaran Police Superintendent's Report, 13 Nov. 1921, GBO PS f 539, 1921, BSA.
126 Hammond, GBO Chief Secretary to GOI Home Secretary, para.3, HP f 357, 1921, NAI.
127 Special Report II.
128 Champaran Police Report.
129 Hammond, GBO Chief Secretary to GOI Home Secretary, paras 4 and 6, HP f 357, 1921, NAI; PS f 216, 1922, BSA; *Searchlight*, 23 Aug. 1922.
130 Hammond, GBO Chief Secretary to GOI Home Secretary, para.2, HP f 357, 1921, NAI; GBO *Police Administration Report 1922*, (Patna 1923), p.7.
131 J. Pearson, Risaldar Mounted Military Police to Champaran Police Superintendent, 27 Dec. 1921; Champaran Special Report Case 35, Report II, 3 Jan. 1922; Extract from Fortnightly Confidential Report, 17 Jan. 1922; Champaran District Officer to Tirhut

Notes to pages 63-71

> Commissioner, 10 Jan. and 28 Feb. 1922; all in PS f 69, 1922, BSA.
132 Champaran Police Superintendent, Demi Official letter, 4 Jan. 1922, PS f 69, 1922, BSA.
133 See for example the press clipping from *Prajabandhu*, 11 Jan. 1922, held with *ibid*.
134 H.K. Gray, Mia Chapra Indigo Concern, to Police Sub-Inspector, Patepur, n.d., and Tirhut Commissioner to GBO Chief Secretary, 24 Jan. 1922, both in PS f 3, 1922, BSA.
135 Muzaffarpur Police Superintendent, Supplementary Confidential Diary, 23 Jan. 1922, PS f 3, 1922, BSA.
136 Petition by ryots of Khawaspore and other places, 16 Oct. 1922, C XXV, f 18C, G 1922-23, RDA.
137 See A.V. Khan, Gondwara manager to MacDonald, indigo manager, C XXV, f 18C, G 1922-23, RDA.
138 C.S. McDonald, Bahora manager to chief manager, 19 June 1923, C XXV, f 20, G 1922-23, RDA.
139 Conference papers 7 June, 1 Sept. 1923, f 7A, C XXV, G 1922-23, RDA; Instructions from Head Office, 12 June 1923, f 18ZF, C XXV, G 1922-23, RDA; Fisher 'Indigo Plantations', pp.285-7.
140 Filgate, 'Behar Planters' Association'; Houlton, *Bihar*, p.118; Behar Planters' Association Report for 1937-38, Political 2, f 52, 1939, Commissioner's Record Room, Muzaffarpur town.
141 See Prasad, *Autobiography*, p.97, *Mahatma Gandhi*, pp.23-4, and *Satyagraha in Champaran*, p.vii.

Chapter 3

1 An earlier version of this chapter appears as 'Agrarian Relations in North Bihar: Peasant Protest and the Darbhanga Raj, 1919-20', in the *Indian Economic and Social History Review*, XVI, 1, Jan.-March 1979. For details of economic conditions see GGB, *Statutory Commission*, XII, p.9; and the annual GBO, *Land Revenue Administration Reports*.
2 Baden-Powell, *Land Systems*, II, pp.630-1.
3 *Ibid*., pp.641-56.
4 Byrne, *Bhagalpur*, pp.115-19. See also Dietmar Rothermund, 'Government, Landlord and Tenant in India, 1875-1900', *Indian Economic and Social History Review*, VI, 4 Dec. 1969.

5 See Wilson, *Behar Indigo Factories*, pp.332-4.
6 *Ibid.*, p.191; Maori, *Nepaul Frontier*, pp.216, 220-1; Dietmar Rothermund, 'A Survey of Rural Migration and Land Reclamation in India, 1885', *Journal of Peasant Studies*, 4, 3 April 1977, p.239.
7 C.J. O'Donnell, *Ruin of an Indian Province. An Indian Famine Explained*, (London 1880).
8 O'Malley, *Purnea*, p.113; C. Vowell, 'Report on the Census of the District of Purnea, 1891', para 145, Miscellaneous Papers, BSA.
9 See for example, J.A. Sweeney, 'Statement on Ramnagar', in GBO, *Report of the Committee on the Agrarian Conditions in Champaran*, (2 vols, Patna 1917), II.
10 Kerr, *Darbhanga Settlement Report*, p.101; Lila Rai to Editor, *Searchlight*, 24 Sept. 1922.
11 However though they had large incomes, the large zamindars of Bihar often lived beyond them and became embroiled in financial difficulty. See 'Review of 1896', *Behar Times*, 1 Jan. 1897, and 'Triennial Review', *Behar Times*, 5 Jan. 1900.
12 For example Umarpathi Tewari, who became a clerk in the Darbhanga Raj in 1936, was the son of Ram Sakhi Tewari, who held about 50 acres of land, some as a tenant and some as a zamindar. Palat Mishra, who was a Darbhanga Raj jeth ryot in the Madhubani subdivision of Darbhanga in the late 19th and early 20th centuries, held about 12 to 15 acres of high quality land. Interviews, Jageshwar Mishra, Darbhanga town 23 Sept. and Umarpathi Tewari, Dumari village, Darbhanga, 17 Oct. 1976.
13 O'Malley, *Darbhanga*; 'Extracts from the Annual Report of the Officiating Manager', GBEN LR Proceedings, 48-49, May 1878, BSA; 'Report on the Administration of the Darbhanga Raj, 1914/15', C XXXIV, G 1915-16, RDA; Raj Darbhanga, *Raj Darbhanga Directory, 1941*, (Darbhanga 1941), RDA.
14 G.P. Danby, Chief Manager, Memorandum 9 Mar. 1933, f 16D27, C Management, G 1941-42; 'Rules Regarding Patwaries and Jethrayats', f 16D39, C Management, G 1941-42, RDA; Interview Jageshwar Mishra, Darbhanga town, 20 Sept. 1976; Maori, *Nepaul Frontier*, p.147.
15 'Rules regarding Patwaries and Jethrayats', f 16D39, C Management, G 1941-42, RDA; Parihar Manager to Chief Manager, 9 March 1920, letter 9, f 2, C XXXIV,

Notes to pages 74-76   225

G 1919-20, RDA; see also Alapur AAR, 1326 F (1918-19), f 2, C XXIV, G 1919-20, RDA.
16 Chief Manager, Memoranda dated 6 Aug. 1937, 25 Aug. 1939, f 16D27, C Management, G 1941-42, RDA. See also P.J. Musgrave, 'Landlords and Lords of the Land: Estate Management and Social Control in Uttar Pradesh, 1860-1920', *Modern Asian Studies*, 6, 3, 1972.
17 For details of earlier conflicts see the Darkasht files RDA; and see O'Malley, *Purnea* pp.130-1.
18 Badrinath Upadhya, *Reply to 'The Open Letter' Printed in the Searchlight Steam Press with a foreword from an alleged Sanyasi calling himself Swami Vidyanand*, (Bankipore, n.d.), p.1. This 52-page pamphlet, which was written by the manager of the Rajnager circle of the Darbhanga Raj, supplies much information about Vidyanand's activities. The author of the pamphlet quotes Vidyanand's letters and petitions in detail before presenting arguments against them.
19 *Ibid.*; GBO Police Abstract 1868, 14 Nov. 1919, BSA; *Searchlight*, 15 Dec. 1920.
20 See Vidyanand to the Lieutenant-Governor of Bihar and Orissa, 17 Nov. 1919, para 14, quoted in Upadhya, *Reply to Vidyanand*, pp.33-6.
21 GBO Police Abstract 1356, Darbhanga, 5 July 1919, BSA; GBO FR(1) Oct. 1919, GBO PS f 8, 1920, BSA.
22 Memorial to the Lieutenant-Governor of Bihar and Orissa, quoted in Upadhya, *Reply to Vidyanand*, pp.2-3.
23 Five of these petitions are quoted in *ibid.*
24 *Ibid.*, pp.12-14, 47.
25 Note by Onraet, Manager Rohika circle, 11 Aug. 1920, on the contents of a letter from Lakshmi Kant Jha, f 14H, C XXVI, G 1919-20, RDA.
26 GBO Police Abstracts 1842, Bhagalpur, 14 Nov. 1919, and 1944, Bhagalpur, 22 Nov. 1919, both in BSA; Upadhya, *Reply to Vidyanand*, pp.34-6.
27 GBO Police Abstract 1981, Bihar Special Branch, 13 Dec. 1919, BSA; GBO FR(2) Dec. 1919, GBO PS f 8, 1920, BSA.
28 Swami Bidyanand, 'Timely notice to cultivators', leaflet quoted in GBO Police Abstract 1680, Bihar Special Branch, 11 Oct. 1919, BSA; GBO Police Abstract 1786, Bihar Special Branch, 1 Nov. 1919, BSA; Manager, Naredigar Circle, Raj Darbhanga to Supaul Sub-divisional Officer, 20 Nov. 1920, f 10E, C V, L 1920-21, RDA.

29 GBO FR(1) Jan. 1920, PS f 8, 1920, BSA; Onraet, Manager Rohika Circle to General Manager, 7 Jan. 1920, f 14 H, C XXV, G 1919-20, RDA.
30 GBO FR(1) Feb. 1920, PS f 8, 1920, BSA.
31 GBO FR(1) Mar. 1920, PS f 8, 1920, BSA.
32 GBO FR(1) Dec. 1919, PS f 8, 1919, BSA.
33 GBO FR(1) Apr. 1920, PS f 8, 1920, BSA.
34 GBO FR(1) Sept. 1920 and FR(1) Dec. 1920, PS f 8, 1920; Sunder to Maharaja, 2 May 1920, f 10E, C V, L 1920-21, RDA.
35 Wilson, Muzaffarpur Police Superintendent to District Magistrate, 12 August 1920 and Russell, Report for Samastipur, 7 Aug. 1920, both in GBO PS f 333, 1920, BSA.
36 GBO FRS for May-Sept., PS f 8, 1920, BSA; GBO FR(1) July 1920, PS f 9, 1920, BSA.
37 GBO FR(1) May 1920, PS f 8, 1920, BSA.
38 Guise, Darbhanga Police Superintendent, Notes, GBO PS f 333, 1920, BSA; Naredigar Manager to Head Office, 20 Mar. and Pandoul Manager to Babu Nath Bannurjee, 12 Mar. 1920, f 14H, C XXVI, G 1919-20.
39 GBO Police Abstract 1756, Bihar Special Branch, 25 Oct. 1919, BSA; GBO PS f 333, 1920, BSA.
40 GBO, *Instructions for the preparation of the electoral roll*, (Patna 1920), BSA; GBO FR(1) Dec. 1920, PS f 8, 1920, BSA.
41 See for example the *Darkasht* files in the General Department holdings of the Darbhanga Raj and the conference papers, f 14S C XXVI, G 1919-20, RDA.
42 Naredigar AAR 1318 F (1910-11), f 16D3, C Naredigar, G 1941-42, RDA; Dharampur Manager to Chief Manager, 13 Mar. 1920, f 2, C XXXIV, G 1919-20, RDA; Upadhya, *Reply to Vidyanand*, p.13, para 5.
43 Pouchepadass, 'Local leaders', pp.74-5; Alapur AAR 1326 F (1918-19) f 2, C XXXIV, G 1919-20, RDA; Interview, Jageshwar Mishra, Darbhanga town, 15 Sept. 1976.
44 Naredigar AAR 1318 F (1910-11), f 16D3, C. Naredigar, G 1941-42, RDA; Upadhya, *Reply to Vidyanand*, p.12, para 2; Interview, Jageshwar Mishra, Darbhanga town, 15 Sept. 1976.
45 See the petitions quoted in Upadhya, *Reply to Vidyanand*.
46 GBO Police Abstract 1756, Special Branch, 25 Oct. 1919, BSA; GBO FR(1) Feb. 1920, PS f 8, 1920, BSA.
47 GBO Police Abstract 1756, Bihar Special Branch, 25 Oct. 1919, BSA.

48 GBO Police Abstract 1786, Bihar Special Branch, 1 Nov. 1919, BSA.
49 Rohika AAR, 1326 F (1918-19), f 2, C XXXIV, G 1919-20, RDA.
50 Padri manager to Chief Manager, 10 Aug. 1920, f 2A, C XXXIV, G 1919-20, RDA. See also, Alapur AAR 1326 F (1918-19), f 2, C XXXIV, G 1919-20, RDA. Unfortunately I was not able to ascertain the outcome of the Padri sharecroppers' protest movement.
51 Upadhya, *Reply to Vidyanand*, pp. 2-3.
52 R.S. King, 'Strictly Confidential Note', 14-17 Jan. 1920, letter 1, f 14S, C XXVI, G 1919-20, RDA.
53 *Ibid.*
54 See Saraya Manager to Chief Manager, 16 June 1928, f 1a-1c, C XCIII, G 1927-28, RDA.
55 Note of 11 Aug. 1920, on the contents of a letter from Lakshmi Kant Jha, f 14H, C XXVI, G 1919-20, RDA.
56 'Conference Papers', letter 1, f 14S, C XXVI, G 1919-20, RDA.
57 *Ibid.*
58 'Special Grievances of Purnea tenants', *ibid.* See also my 'Agrarian Relations', p. 67.
59 Upadhya, *Reply to Vidyanand*.
60 Letters 21 and 22, f 14H, C XXVI, G 1919-20, RDA.
61 Comment by Gadadhar Pandit Jha, 'Notes of 15th January Conference', f 14S, C XXVI, G 1919-20, RDA.
62 Letter 22, f 14H, C XXVI, G 1919-20, RDA.
63 See the Head Office circular to managers Rohika and Rajnager, n.d., held with letter 1, f 14H, C XXVI, G 1919-20, RDA. The circular called on the Rohika and Rajnager circle managers to bring rent enhancement suits against those local leaders who had assisted Vidyanand, to initiate damages suits against ryots who had cut trees without permission, to offer jeth ryots a commission of 10 per cent of the money realised if they brought people forward to have transfers of holdings recorded on payment on the 'usual' fee of one quarter of the purchase price, to establish and keep up to date a register of 'loyal' and 'disloyal' ryots, and to investigate and take action upon any Raj legal claims against 'disloyal' tenants. In the margin of the circular the words 'Not Issued' are written. This comment probably refers to the circular in general, but may merely refer to this particular copy. I have been unable to confirm that the circular had not been sent out and

would be grateful for information on this point from any scholar who may in future work on the Darbhanga Raj records.
64 Letter 18, f 14H, C XXVI, G 1919-20, RDA; Moti Lal, Tehsildar, Nawahakhar Group to Manager, Naredigar, 28 March 1920, held with letter 29A, f 14H, C XXVI, G 1919-20, RDA.
65 'Report on Samiah case', f 14H, C XXV, G 1919-20, RDA.
66 D. Sunder, Manager Naredigar to His Highness the Maharaja, 1 Sept. 1920, f 14H, C XXVI, G 1919-20, RDA.
67 D. Sunder, 'Confidential Note', 22 Jan. 1920, f 14Z24, C XXV, G 1919-20, RDA.
68 Swami Vidyanand to the Lieutenant-Governor, Bihar and Orissa, 17 Nov. 1919, quoted in Upadhya, *Reply to Vidyanand*, pp.31-6.
69 *Ibid.*, p.35.
70 *Ibid.*, p.36. For another instance in which the police failed to protect Vidyanand from intimidation by representatives of the landed interest see GOI HPf 50, Sept. 1920, NAI; GBO PS f 333, 1920, BSA.
71 Guise, Note, GBO PS f 333, 1920, BSA.
72 GBO FR(2), March 1920, PS f 8, 1920, BSA.
73 Subsequently Vidyanand assumed a more radical stance, and in 1922 began calling for the abolition of the zamindari system. But by this time conditions were much less favourable for the mounting of mass protest. *Searchlight*, 29 Dec. 1922.
74 Petition from Raghunandan Sahu and others, f 5C, C X, G 1921-22. The Telis' offer to pay a cash fee for the right to produce oil perhaps indicates that they were vexed more by the arbitrary behaviour of the *amlas* than by the exaction of the perquisite itself. However the offer to pay cash may also have been a ploy. Once money changed hands, then receipts could be demanded; and the Telis could use these receipts as evidence in court to show that the practice continued, in the hope of being awarded a court decision declaring it illegal.
75 Pandoul Manager to Chief Manager, 15 Dec. 1921 and 7 Apr. 1922, f 5C, C X, G 1921-22, RDA.
76 Head Office notes, 3 May 1922, f 5C, C X, G 1921-22, RDA.
77 Chief Manager to Manager Pandoul, 5 May 1922, f 5C, C X, G 1921-22, RDA.

78 Comment by Gadadhar Jha, 'Notes of 15th January Conference', f 14S, C XXVI, G 11 1919-20, RDA.
79 G. McDonald, 'Unity on Trial: Congress in Bihar, 1919-39', in D.A. Low (ed.), *Congress and the Raj: Facets of the Indian Struggle, 1917-1947*, (London, New Delhi, 1977), pp.292-5.

Chapter 4

1 Brown, *Gandhi's Rise*, pp.307-8.
2 *Ibid.*, p.322.
3 *Behar Times*, 5 Jan. 1900.
4 Yang, 'Riots in Saran', p.13.
5 Anil Seal, 'Imperialism and Nationalism in India', in Gallagher, Johnson & Seal, (eds), *Locality, Province and Nation, Essays on Indian Politics 1870-1940* (London 1973).
6 *Ibid.*, p.8.
7 This account of the rise of nationalist activity in Bihar is based on McDonald, 'Unity on Trial'. See also Mrinal Kumar Basu, 'Regional Patriotism: A Study in Bihar Politics (1907-1912)', *Indian Historical Review*, III, 2 Jan. 1977.
8 See F. Tomasson Jannuzi, *Agrarian Crisis in India. The Case of Bihar*, (New Delhi 1974), pp.107-116.
9 McDonald, 'Unity on Trial', pp.292-3; J.H. Broomfield, 'The Regional Elites: A Theory of Modern Indian History', in T.R. Metcalf, *Modern India, An Interpretive Anthology*, (London 1971), p.69; Vijay Chandra Prasad Chaudhury, *The Creation of Modern Bihar*, (Darbhanga 1964) pp.200-205.
10 Gait to Vincent, 6 Aug. 1917, HP f 47, Oct. 1917, NAI. See also Prasad, *Mahatma Gandhi*, p.46.
11 See Brown, *Gandhi's Rise*, pp.78, 267-8.
12 McDonald, 'Unity on Trial', pp.293-4; Prasad, *Mahatma Gandhi*, p.75.
13 K.K. Datta, *Rajendra Prasad*, (New Delhi 1970).
14 Owen, *Bihar 1921*, p.12; GGB, *Statutory Commission*, XII, p.20.
15 H.F. Owen, 'Towards Nationwide Agitation and Organisation: The Home Rule Leagues, 1915-18', in D.A. Low (ed.), *Soundings in Modern South Asian History*, (London 1968) and 'Organizing for the Rowlatt

Satyagraha of 1919', in Ravindar Kumar (ed.), *Essays on Gandhian Politics. The Rowlatt Satyagraha of 1919*, (London 1971).
16 Prasad, *Mahatma Gandhi*, pp.38-42; Brown, *Gandhi's Rise*, pp.269-70.
17 *Ibid.*, Chap.6; Francis Robinson, *Separatism among Indian Muslims. The politics of the United Province's Muslims, 1860-1923*, (Cambridge 1974); A.C. Niemeijer, *The Khilafat Movement in India, 1919-24*, (The Hague 1972).
18 Brown, *Gandhi's Rise*, pp.253, 260, 261; Richard Gordon, 'Non-cooperation and Council Entry 1919 to 1920', in Gallagher, Johnson & Seal (eds), *Locality, Province and Nation*, p.146.
19 Brown, *Gandhi's Rise*, p.287.
20 Prasad, *Mahatma Gandhi*, p.40.
21 GBO FR(1), Dec. 1920, PS f 8, 1920, BSA; Brown, *Gandhi's Rise*, p.288.
22 The legislature elected in November 1920 consisted predominantly of great zamindars and of non-congress lawyers, but also included Swami Vidyanand and three of his colleagues, representing electorates in the north of Bhagalpur and Darbhanga. Owen, *Bihar 1921*, p.13.
23 GBO FR(1), Dec. 1920, PS f 8, 1920, BSA; GBO, *Synopsis of History of NCO movement*, PS f 286, 1924, BSA; Prasad, *Mahatma Gandhi*, pp.42, 43.
24 Brown, *Gandhi's Rise*, pp.297-300; Gopal Krishna, 'The Development of the Indian National Congress as a Mass Organization, 1918-23', in T.R. Metcalf, *Modern India, An Interpretive Anthology* (London 1971), pp.257-72; Prasad, *Mahatma Gandhi*, pp.44-45.
25 Brown, *Gandhi's Rise*, pp.309-12.
26 W. Swain, Confidential Report, 25 Apr. 1921, GBO PS f 37, 1921.
27 Brown, *Gandhi's Rise*, pp.315-16; GGB, *Statutory Commission*, XII, pp.273, 274, 374.
28 Forrest to GBO Chief Secretary, 2 July 1921, PS f 37, 1921, BSA.
29 Lakshmi Mishra, 'An Account of the non-cooperation movement', PS f 434, 1923, BSA.
30 'Reports of Hat looting', PS f 21, 1921; Forrest, Tirhut Commissioner, to Rainey, CBO Chief Secretary, 20 Jan. 1921, PS f 12, 1921; R.S.F. Macrae, Deputy Inspector General Police to GBO Chief Secretary, 20 Jan. 1921, PS f 21, 1921; Purnea Special Report Case 11, Report II,

19 Feb. 1921, PS f 21, 1921; all in the BSA. See also Report by Toplis, 12 Feb. 1921, pp.33-4, PS f 93, 1921, BSA.
31 Macrae, Deputy Inspector General Police to GBO Chief Secretary, 20 Jan. 1921, PS f 21, 1921, BSA.
32 Forrest to Rainey, GBO Chief Secretary, 20 Jan. 1921, PS f 12, 1921, BSA.
33 Rajendra Prasad denied that Congress had responsibility for the incidents. *Autobiography*, pp.133-4.
34 The phenomenon of market looting requires further research. Disturbances at markets were always likely to occur, quite independently of the impact of political movements. Villagers were hostile towards merchants, since they knew from harsh experience that merchants might short-change them or give them short measure. Thieves and hoodlums and the poor and mendicant gathered in the market place, and could easily, for their own advantage, be drawn into and help magnify any disturbance that might get under way. An adverse price/supply situation was the essential pre-condition of market looting. In 1918 and in the first months of 1942 scarcity and high prices coincided with the occurrence of market looting during periods when no mass political agitation was under way. GBO FR(2), May 1918, PS f 8, 1918, BSA; GBO FR(2), Jan. 1942, Freedom Movement Papers, (hereafter FMP) f 76, 1942, BSA.
35 Extract from diary of Gopalganj Police Inspector, 13 Feb. 1921, PS f 58, 1921, BSA.
36 In some instances the 'Lat Saheb', i.e. the Governor of the Province had featured in the story in the place of the Englishman. F.S. McNamara, 'Report on the gathering of mobs in the Dhanaha thana', 1/2 April 1921, and Basti (United Provinces) Police Superintendent's diary, extract dated 2 April 1921, both in PS f 148, 1921, BSA.
37 Forrest, Tirhut Commissioner to Rainey, Chief Secretary GBO, 2 July 1921, PS f 37, 1921, BSA, italics in original.
38 Saran Special Report Case 10, Report I, 20 Feb. 1921 and Saran Special Report Case 10, Report II, 28 Feb. 1921, both in PS f 58, 1921, BSA.
39 Champaran Police Superintendent to Deputy Inspector General Police, 21 June 1921, PS f 287, 1921, BSA.
40 Bhagalpur Commissioner to Chief Secretary, 1 June 1921, PS f 184, 1921, BSA.

Notes to pages 101-107

41 Champaran Police Superintendent, report, 23 April 1921, PS f 37, 1921, BSA.
42 Brown, *Gandhi's Rise*, p.313; GGB, *Statutory Commission*, XII, p.15; Niemeijer, *Khilafat Movement*, pp.128-9, 132.
43 GGB, *Statutory Commission*, XII, pp.14-16; Prasad, *Mahatma Gandhi*, p.49; D.A. Low, 'The Government of India and the first non-cooperation movement, 1920-2', in Kumar, *Rowlatt Satyagraha*, pp.306, 308; Niemeijer, *Khilafat Movement*, pp.131, 137-8.
44 GGB, *Statutory Commission*, p.15.
45 *Synopsis of history of NCO movement*, PS f 286, 1924, BSA.
46 Diary of Muzaffarpur Police Superintendent, 29 Dec. 1921, PS f 3, 1922, BSA.
47 Telegram from Muzaffarpur Police Superintendent, 30 Dec. 1921, PS f 3, 1922, BSA.
48 Confidential diary, 16 Jan. 1922, PS f 146, 1922, BSA.
49 Purnea Police Superintendent, confidential diary, 8 Feb.1922, report of 18 Feb. 1922, PS f 146, 1922, BSA.
50 GOI HP files 563 and 677, 1922, NAI.
51 W.F. Crawley, 'Kisan Sabhas and Agrarian Revolt in the United Provinces 1920 to 1921', *Modern Asian Studies*, 5, 2, 1971, pp.108-9; Majid Hayat Siddiqi, 'The Peasant Movement in Pratapgarh', *Indian Economic and Social History Review*, 9, 1972, p.306; Brown, *Gandhi's Rise*, p.327.
52 Owen, *Bihar 1921*, Chap.1.
53 Diary of Muzaffarpur Police Superintendent, 11 April 1922, PS f 335, 1922, BSA.
54 *Autobiography*, p.324.
55 W.H. Vincent's note of an interview with Mr. Atkins, 12 May 1921, HP f 49, 1921, NAI; GBO PS f 37, 1921.
56 GBO Chief Secretary to GOI Army Department Secretary, 10/11 March 1922, HP f 49, 1921, NAI.
57 Memorandum *ibid*.
58 Statements by Mr. Craik, *ibid*. pp.33ff, p.41.
59 GBO Chief Secretary to GOI Army Department Secretary 10/11 March 1922, *ibid*.
60 GGB, *Statutory Commission*, XII, p.16. GBO Chief Secretary to GOI Home Secretary, 10 Dec. 1921, HP f 441, 1921, NAI.
61 For an example of police oppression and corruption in

relation to a market looting incident see E.H. Johnston, Monghyr District Magistrate to Drake-Brockman, 17 March 1921; E.H. Johnston to Bhagalpur Commissioner, 21 Feb. 1921; and Monghyr Special Report Case 22, Report II, 4 March 1921; all in PS f 66, 1921, BSA.
62 GBO Chief Secretary to GOI Army Department Secretary, 10/11 March 1922, HP f 49, 1921, NAI.
63 PS f 1, 1921, BSA. The administration responded with a small wage increase.
64 GBO Chief Secretary to GOI Army Department Secretary, 29 May 1921, HP f 49, 1921, NAI.

Chapter 5

1 Datta, *Freedom Movement*, I, p.467; Prasad, *Mahatma Gandhi*, pp.74-7; GGB *Statutory Commission*, XII, pp.19-21.
2 McDonald, 'Unity on Trial', p.294; Punyanand Jha, 'Split in Purnea District Congress Committee. Its Causes and Effects', Feb. 1929, AICCP f G2 (Kwi) 1931 NML; Prasad, *Mahatma Gandhi*, p.75.
3 See G. Pandey, 'Mobilization in a Mass Movement: Congress 'Propaganda' in the United Provinces (India), 1930-34', *Modern Asian Studies*, 9, 2, 1975.
4 Judith M. Brown, *Gandhi and Civil Disobedience, The Mahatma in Indian Politics, 1928-1934*, (London 1977) p.116.
5 For economic conditions see GBO, *Land Revenue Administration Reports* for 1929-30 to 1933-34, (Patna, 1930-1935).
6 *Ibid.*, 1930-31 *Report*, p.18; P.T. Mansfield, *Bihar and Orissa in 1930-31*, (Patna 1932).
7 See Tanika Sarkar, 'The First Phase of Civil Disobedience in Bengal, 1930-31', *Indian Historical Review*, IV, 1, July 1977, p.83.
8 For discussion of the tactical options available, see Jaleshwar Prasad, 'Non-Payment of Taxes in Bihar', *Searchlight*, 12 Feb. 1930, reprinted as Appendix II, Datta, *Freedom Movement*, II, pp.419-21. Because of the difficulty of manufacturing salt in Bihar, Rajendra Prasad was at first lukewarm about the salt campaign but bowed to Gandhi's wishes. See the report of his speech of 23 Feb. 1930 in *Searchlight*, 26 Feb. 1930.

See also Datta, *Freedom Movement*, II, p.53; Brown, *Gandhi and Civil Disobedience*, p.115; Prasad, *Mahatma Gandhi*, pp.81-83.
9 *Searchlight*, 19 Apr. 1930. See also 'Nonias join hands with Satyagrahis', *Searchlight*, 28 Apr. 1930.
10 Whitty, Tirhut Commissioner to Briscoe, Chief Secretary, 16 Apr. 1930, PS f 139, 1930; MacKensie, Saran Police Superintendent to McDowell, 9 Apr. 1930, PS f 139, 1930; Hamid, Champaran Police Superintendent to District Officer, 17 Apr. 1930, PS f 138A 1930; all in BSA. See also Datta, *Freedom Movement*, II, pp.61, 85, 86.
11 Brown, *Gandhi and Civil Disobedience*, p.115; Sumit Sarkar, 'The Logic of Gandhian Nationalism: Civil Disobedience and the Gandhi-Irwin Pact (1930-1931), *Indian Historical Review*, III, 1, July 1976, p.128.
12 MacKensie to McDowell, 9 Apr. 1930, PS f 139, 1930, BSA.
13 Champaran Police Superintendent, 'Report on working of Satyagraha Movement', 10 May 1930, PS f 138B, BSA. Moreover the arrival of the monsoon in late June made the collection of suitable earth impossible. Datta, *Freedom Movement*, II, p.91.
14 Brown, *Gandhi and Civil Disobedience*, p.117 and note 67, pp.117-18; Prasad, *Mahatma Gandhi*, pp.84-5.
15 Brown, *Gandhi and Civil Disobedience*, note 41, p.144.
16 Case 66, 1930, Report I, 11 Sept. 1930, and 'Commitment Order in Case of Emperor versus Ram Chandra Sah and 5 Others', 19 July 1930, both in PS f 139B, BSA.
17 Swanzy, Champaran District Officer to Horsefield, Commissioner Excise and Salt, 5 Dec. 1930 and Chief Secretary to Home Political Department, 9 Dec. 1930, both in PS f 138B, 1930, BSA.
18 Special Report Case 117, Report dated 1 Nov. 1930, PS f 158, 1930, BSA. See also 'Extract Confidential Diary Police Superintendent Champaran', 14 July 1930 and Special Report Case 80, Report dated 10 Aug. 1930, both in PS f 138B, 1930, BSA; Sec., AICC to Sec., Bihar PCC, 28 July 1930, AICCP f G80, 1930.
19 Brown, *Gandhi and Civil Disobedience*, p.127; Bondurant, *Conquest of Violence*, pp.23-26, 39-40, 42-3.
20 Sinha to Horsefield, Commissioner Excise and Salt, 22 May 1930, FMP f 84, 1920-42, BSA.
21 Commissioner of Excise to Collectors of Shahabad,

Patna and Bhagalpur, 3 June 1930, FMP f 84, 1920-42, BSA; Champaran Police Superintendent, 'Report on the working of the Satyagraha movement', 20 May 1930, PS f 138B, 1930, BSA.
22 'Note by Mr McPherson', p.7, PS f 411, 1921, BSA.
23 Hallet to Home Secretary, 14 Apr. 1931, HP f 33/V/1931, NAI.
24 Saran Police Superintendent, extract from confidential diary for period ending 8 June, PS f 139B, 1930, BSA; Saran Police Superintendent, memorandum to Inspector General Police, 6 Aug. 1930, PS f 379, 1930, BSA [hereafter Saran memorandum].
25 Champaran Police Superintendent, 'Report on the working of the Satyagraha movement', 20 May 1930; Khan to Middleton, Tirhut Commissioner, 9 June 1930; Excise Superintendent's Report, 2 June 1930; all in PS f 138B, 1930, BSA; Datta, *Freedom Movement*, II, pp.121-2.
26 Brown, *Gandhi and Civil Disobedience*, pp.145, 300; GGB, *Statutory Commission*, XII, p.374.
27 Jaleshwar Prasad, 'Non-Payment of Taxes'.
28 Darzia Bazaar public meeting, 27 Dec. 1930, resolutions, PS f 49, 1931, BSA [hereafter Darzia resolutions].
29 Jaleshwar Prasad, 'Non-Payment of Taxes'.
30 Extract Confidential Diary, Champaran Police Superintendent, 23 Oct. 1930, PS f 138B, 1930, BSA.
31 Special Report Case 28, 1930, Report I, 30 May 1930, and Special Report Case 36, 1930, Report I, 2 June 1930, both in PS f 138B, 1930; Bhagalpur Commissioner to Chief Secretary, 9 June 1930, PS f 172, 1930; all in BSA.
32 Ayyar, Beguserai Subdivisional Officer to Zaman, Monghyr District Magistrate, 14 Aug. 1930, PS f 166, 1930, BSA.
33 Brett to Tirhut Commissioner, 10 Aug. 1930, PS f 379, 1930, BSA; Weekly Confidential Reports from Saran Police Superintendent, 2 Sept. and 2 Oct. 1930, PS f 139B, 1930, BSA.
34 Tirhut Confidential Reports, Saran, 16 Aug. 1930, PS f KW23, BSA.
35 Ayyar, Beguserai Subdivisional Officer, to Zaman, Monghyr District Magistrate, 14 Aug. 1930, PS f 166, 1930, BSA.
36 Champaran Police Superintendent, 'Report on the working of Satyagraha movement', 20 Aug. 1930, PS f 138B, 1930, BSA; Bihar Provincial Congress Committee Reports, 5 and 12 Sept. 1930, AICCP f 11, 1930, NML.
37 Saran memorandum; Rajendra Prasad to General

Secretary, 7 Oct. 1931, AICCP f 75, 1931, NML; Prasad, *Mahatma Gandhi*, p.96; Darzia resolutions; Bihar Provincial Congress Committee, 'A Note on Government excesses in Bihar', HP f 5/80/1930 NAI; 'Happenings in Champaran', *Searchlight*, 1 Feb. 1931.
38 Yang, 'Riots in Saran', p.20.
39 Saran memorandum, p.11.
40 *Ibid.*, p.10.
41 Report by MacKensie, 4 Oct. 1930, PS f 172, 1930, BSA.
42 Deputy Inspector General Police, Northern Range, 'Report on the situation in Bihpur and Kissenganj police stations in the District of Bhagalpur', Sept. 1930, PS f 172, 1930, BSA [hereafter Report on Bihpur]; Hallett, Chief Secretary to Home Secretary, 28 June 1930, PS f 172, 1930, BSA. See also Prasad, *Mahatma Gandhi*, pp.90-94.
43 Report on Bihpur, paras 10, 18. Unfortunately further details on the rival markets are not available. In this instance agrarian tension combined with nationalist agitation.
44 *Ibid.*, para 18. See also C.R. Murray, *Bihar and Orissa in 1929-30*, (Patna 1931); Hallett to Home Secretary, 28 June 1930, PS f 172, 1930, BSA.
45 Report on Bihpur, para 18.
46 *Ibid.*
47 R.D.K. Ninnis, Bhagalpur Police Superintendent, 'Bihpur Affairs', 11 June 1930, PS f 172, 1930, BSA [hereafter Bihpur Affairs].
48 *Ibid.*
49 *Ibid.*
50 Anant Prasad to the private secretary to His Excellency the Governor of Bihar and Orissa, 11 June 1930, PS f 172, 1930, pp.60-5. For Rajendra Prasad's account see his *Autobiography*, pp.315-18.
51 Datta, *Freedom Movement*, II, pp.94-9; *Young India*, 19 June 1930, extract reproduced in FMP f 60, 1930-33, BSA *Searchlight*, June and July 1930.
52 Bihpur Affairs; Report on Bihpur, para 9.
53 Prasad, *Autobiography*, p.317.
54 Bihpur Affairs, p.14.
55 Ninnis, 'Bihpur Affairs' 21 July, PS f 172, 1930, BSA; 'Bihpur Satyagraha', *Searchlight*, 31 Oct. 1930; Bihar Provincial Congress Committee, 'Weekly Reports from Bihar', 20 and 24 Oct. 1930, AICCP f 11, 1930, NML; Bihpur Affairs; Report on Bihpur, paras 12, 14 and 15.

56 Report on Bihpur, paras 13, 14, 16, 18, 19.
57 D.A. Low, 'Civil Martial Law: The Government of India and the Civil Disobedience Movements, 1930-34', in D.A. Low, (ed.) *Congress and the Raj: facets of the Indian struggle 1917-1947*, (London 1977), pp.165-70.
58 Speech to the annual police parade, *Searchlight*, 26 Feb. 1930.
59 Johnston, 'Brief advance report on Riot at Bhorey on 16/12/1930'; Johnston, Additional report on Bhorey riot, dated 17 Dec.; Saran Special Report Case 108, 1930, Report I, 17 Dec. 1930, and Report II, 30 Dec. 1930; all in PS f 139B, 1930, BSA; GBO Communique, 18 Dec. 1930, PS f 148, 1931, BSA; Darzia Resolutions.
60 Dixon to Hallett, 30 Jan. 1930; and Darbhanga Special Report Case 4, 1931, Report III; both in PS f 72, 1931, BSA.
61 Dixon to Hallett, 30 Jan. 1930; Darbhanga Special Report Case 3, 1931, Reports III and IV; Chief Secretary to Dixon, 14 Feb. 1931; Scott, Tirhut Commissioner to Hallett, 9 Feb. 1931; all in PS f 72, 1931, BSA.
62 Saran Special Report Case 15, 1931, Reports II, XI and XII; Chandrika Singh, 'First Information Report', 26 Jan. 1931; Rameshwar Singh, Subdivisional Officer to S.A. Khan, District Magistrate, 28 Jan. 1931; all in PS f 23, 1931, BSA.
63 Government of Bihar and Orissa, Communique on the Beguserai Riot, PS f 32, 1931, BSA [hereafter Beguserai Report]. This communique presents the findings of an inquest by the Monghyr District Magistrate. See also Anugrah Narayan Sinha, 'Tragic Episode at Beguserai', *Searchlight*, 1 Feb. 1931 and Datta, *Freedom Movement*, II, p.150. The number of wounded is unclear. It was rumoured that to avoid police harassment some of the wounded hid in the villages and did not attend dispensaries for treatment.
64 Monghyr Special Report Case 4, 1931, Report II, 30 Jan. 1931 [hereafter Monghyr Report II]; Dain to Hallett, 29 Jan. 1931, PS f 32, 1931, BSA.
65 Monghyr Police Superintendent, confidential diary, 2 Jan. 1931 and Beguserai Subdivisional Officer, 'Demi-official letter', 6 Feb. 1931, PS f 32, 1931, BSA; Monghyr Police Superintendent, 'Intermediate confidential diary', 19 Sept. 1930, and confidential diary, 16 Nov. 1930, PS f 166, 1930, BSA.
66 Monghyr Report II; Dain to Hallett, 29 Jan. 1931, PS f 32, 1932, BSA.

67 Whitty, 'Visit to Beguserai in connection with the rioting of the 26th January', 17 Feb. 1931, PS f 32, 1931, BSA.
68 'Babu Bishundeva Narayan Singh's Report', *Searchlight*, 10 Feb. 1931.
69 10 Feb. 1931.
70 Brown, *Gandhi and Civil Disobedience*, p.21.
71 Sarkar, 'Logic of Gandhian Nationalism', pp.136-41.
72 Brown, *Gandhi and Civil Disobedience*, p.288; Braj Kishore Prasad to Vallabhai Patel, 21 July 1930, f G80, 1930, AICCP, NML; Prasad, *Mahatma Gandhi*, pp.45, 75.
73 Quoted in Sarkar, 'Logic of Gandhian Nationalism', p.127.
74 Brown, *Gandhi and Civil Disobedience*, pp.293, 299-300.
75 Low, 'Civil Martial Law', p.170; Datta, *Freedom Movement*, II, p.153. For a perceptive analysis of the context within which Gandhi agreed to the pact see Sarkar, 'Logic of Gandhian Nationalism'.
76 McDowell, Deputy-Inspector General Police, 'Report for the week ending 21 March 1931', HP f 33/V/1931, NAI; Tirhut Commissioner, 'Confidential Report', 13 Jan. 1931, PS f 20, 1931, BSA; Muzaffarpur Police Superintendent, Confidential Diary, 2 April 1931, PS f 40, 1931, BSA. Meanwhile the Bihar Provincial Congress Committee criticised the Bihar and Orissa Government for being lackadaisical and obstructive in its implementation of the provisions of the pact. Datta, *Freedom Movement*, II, pp.154, 163-4.
77 Muzaffarpur Police Superintendent, Confidential Diary, 2 Jan. 1931, PS f 40, 1931, BSA.
78 Confidential Diary, 7 April 1931, PS f 40, 1931, BSA.
79 McDowell, Deputy-Inspector General Police, 'Report for the week ending 21 March 1931', HP f 33/V/1931, NAI.
80 *Ibid.*; Excise Sub-Inspector, Siwan Circle, 'Tour Diary', 15, 25 April 1931, HP f 33/V/1931, NAI; Monghyr Police Superintendent to Dain, 10 Sept. 1931, PS f 166, 1931, BSA.
81 'The Bihar I Knew', *Indian Nation*, 26 Oct. 1964. See also Sarkar, 'Logic of Gandhian Nationalism', pp.143-5.
82 Rajendra Prasad, 'Statement' No.2, 24 April 1941; M.K. Gandhi to H.W. Emerson, Home Secretary, 31 May 1931; Hallett, Chief Secretary to Home Secretary, 14 April 1931; all in HP f 33/V/1931, NAI.

83 'Notes of discussion with Babu Rajendra Prasad', 16 July 1931, HP f 33/V/1931, NAI.
84 GBO, Report to GOI, 2 Dec. 1931, PS f 20, 1931, BSA.
85 Low, 'Civil Martial Law', p.173.
86 *Ibid.*, pp.165-72.
87 *Ibid.*, pp.173-4; Brown, *Gandhi and Civil Disobedience*, pp.298-300; R.J. Moore, *The Crisis of Indian Unity 1917-1940*, (London 1974), pp.246-9, 292-3.
88 J.E. Scott, Commissioner Tirhut, 'Note on collision in Motihari town on 26th January 1932', and GBO Chief Secretary to GOI Home Secretary, incorporating report by Muzaffarpur District Magistrate, 1 March 1932, HP f 5/80/1932, NAI; Datta, *Freedom Movement*, II, pp.184-7.
89 M.N. Roy, 'The Bihar I Knew', *Indian Nation*, 23 Nov. 1964.
90 Telegrams, Viceroy to Secretary of State, 19 Mar., 18 Apr., 20 May 1932, HP f 36/1/1932, NAI; GBO FR(2), Jan. 1933, HP f 18/1/1933, NAI.
91 Brown, *Gandhi and Civil Disobedience*, pp.141, 209-10; Gyanendra Pandey, 'A Rural Base for Congress: the United Provinces 1920-40', in D.A. Low, (ed.) *Congress and the Raj: facets of the Indian struggle, 1917-1947*, (London 1977).
92 Brown, *Gandhi and Civil Disobedience*, pp.144, 212.
93 See the GBO, *Land Revenue Administration Reports*, 1930-34.
94 M.G. Hallett to G. Scoones, 22 June 1945, Hallett Papers, MSS EUR f E251/43, IOL; Lectures to Eastern Command, 3 June 1940 and 6 June 1941, Hallett Papers, IOR MSS EUR f E251/36 and f 251/37, IOL.
95 See for example the editorial in the *Searchlight*, 28 April 1930. See also Bihar Provincial Congress Committee, 'A Short Note on Repression in the Congress Province of Bihar', AICCP f P4, 1932, NML; C.F. Andrews to H.G. Haig, Home Member, 4 April 1932, HP f 40/2/1932, NAI; Datta, *Freedom Movement*, II, pp.137-41.
96 Anil Seal, 'Imperialsim and Nationalism in India', in Gallagher, et. al., *Locality, Province and Nation*, p.8.
97 McDowell, Deputy-Inspector General Police, 'Report for the week ending 21 March 1931', HP f 33/V/1931, NAI.
98 Rajendra Prasad, 'Report of some incidents regarding picketting', 17 April 1931, AICCP f G56, 1931, NML. See also Prasad, *Mahatma Gandhi*, p.78.
99 The comments made here owe much to discussion with D.A. Low and Roger Stuart.

100 'Note of further discussion with Rajendra Prasad on 16 July', HP f 33/V/1931, NAI.

Chapter 6

1 GBO, *Land Revenue Administration Reports*, for 1930-31, 1931-32, (Patna 1931, 1932); Purnea FR(1) March 1931, PS f 44, 1931, BSA.
2 GB Revenue Department, Land Revenue Branch, B proceedings, May 1937, f VIA-8/1937, BSA; Geof Wood, 'The Legacy of the Past: The Agrarian Structure', in J.L. Joy and Elizabeth Everitt (eds), *The Kosi Symposium. The Rural Problem in North-East Bihar: Analysis, Policy and Planning in the Kosi Area*, (University of Sussex 1976) pp.93-112, p.98.
3 GBO, *Land Revenue Administration Report, 1932-33*, (Patna 1934), p.20.
4 Hauser, 'Bihar Kisan Sabha', pp.11, 26-30.
5 GBO, *Land Revenue Administration Report, 1932-33*, p.19.
6 Dain, *ibid.*, pp.19-20.
7 'Chief Manager's note on the Retrenchment Committee Report', f 10G, C Head Office, G 1937-38 RDA [hereafter Chief Manager's note].
8 'Report of the Bihar Kisan Enquiry Committee', PP f VII, 1937, microfilm 6, ch.3, pp.1-2, NML [hereafter Kisan Report].
9 Registrar, Co-operative Societies to Member, Board of Revenue, 9 Feb. 1934, GB Revenue Department, Land Revenue Branch, B proceedings, May 1937, f VIA-8/1937 BSA.
10 'Retrenchment Committee Report', pp.9, 17 and marginal note p.13; Chief Manager's note, pp.5, 8-10; Manager Alapur to Chief Manager, 22 Dec. 1937, all in file 10G, C Head Office, G 1937-38; Inspection Report, f 6H2, C Padri G 1938-39; Jhanjharpur AAR, 1348 F (1940-41) f 16D2, G 1941-42; Padri AAR, 1348 F (1940-41), f 16D1, G 1942-43; Note on discussion on administration of Purnea circles by the Chief Manager, 24 Apr. 1941, 16D37, C Head Office, G 1941-42; all in the RDA.
11 Kisan Report, ch.1, p.18.
12 The *kisan sabhas* formed by Swami Vidyanand and his

Notes to pages 143-145

followers set out to defend the interests of the tenants by militant agitation. But often also *kisan sabhas* either were infiltrated or created by conservative local notables who proclaimed the need for social harmony and who sought to use the *sabhas* to contain kisan discontent. GBO Police Abstract 1786, Special Branch 1 Nov. 1919, BSA; PS f 417, 1922 BSA; Hauser, 'Bihar Kisan Sabha', p.36.

13 Swami Sahajanand was born in approximately 1889. He became a *sanyasi* in 1907 and was drawn into Congress politics in the early 1920s. He became interested in *kisan* problems while engaged in social work on behalf of the Bhumihar Brahman Sabha at Bihta in Patna district in the late 1920s. Hauser, 'Bihar Kisan Sabha', pp. 82-5.

14 A Bihar Provincial Kisan Sabha had a brief existence in the early 1920s before disappearing into obscurity. In 1929, under Sahajanand's leadership, a new Bihar Provincial Kisan Sabha was created, only to be suspended soon afterwards so as not to distract attention from Congress activity during the civil disobedience movement. The organisation was re-established in 1933. Hauser, 'Bihar Kisan Sabha', pp. 35-6; *Searchlight*, 29 Dec. 1922.

15 Hauser, 'Bihar Kisan Sabha', p.15.

16 *Ibid.*, p.16; preamble to 'The Manifesto of the Bihar Provincial Kisan Sabha', July 1936, Agriculturalists' Unions, f 149, 1936, JPNP, NML [hereafter Kisan Manifesto, 1936].

17 Hauser, 'Bihar Kisan Sabha', pp. 66-73, 79-80, and McDonald, 'Unity on Trial', pp. 299-305.

18 McDonald, 'Unity on Trial', p.304.

19 In 1922 Swami Vidyanand called for zamindari abolition, but did not elicit a substantial response, in part because of the negative reaction of the Bihar Congress. The Congress had agreed that a meeting of the All India Kisan Sabha would be held in conjunction with the annual session of the Indian National Congress, scheduled to be held at Gaya town in December 1922. But when it became known that Vidyanand intended to put a resolution calling for zamindari abolition, the Bihar Congress leaders refused to accommodate an All India Kisan Sabha meeting and denied recognition to the Bihar Provincial Kisan Sabha. *Searchlight*, 29 Dec. 1922. Hauser, 'Bihar Kisan Sabha', pp. 100-7.

20 Kisan Manifesto, 1936; Hauser, 'Bihar Kisan Sabha', pp.102-7.
21 B.R. Tomlinson, *The Indian National Congress and the Raj, 1929-1942. The Penultimate Phase*, (London 1976), p.77; R. Prasad to J. Nehru, 18 Dec. 1937 and Secretary, Bihar Provincial Congress Committee to General Secretary, All India Congress Committee, 30 Dec. 1937, f G98, AICCP, NML.
22 D.N. Dhanagare, 'Congress and Agrarian Agitation in Oudh, 1920-22 and 1930-32', *South Asia*, 5, Dec. 1975, pp.67-77; Gyanendra Pandey, 'A Rural Base for Congress'.
23 Tomlinson, *National Congress and Raj*, ch.3; McDonald, 'Unity on Trial' pp.305-6; Hauser, 'Bihar Kisan Sabha', pp.34, 55-6.
24 GB FR(1) Feb. 1937, HP f 18/2/1937, NAI.
25 Prasad, *Autobiography*, pp.427-30; 'Report of the Violence Enquiry Committee', f P6, 1939-40, AICCP, NML [hereafter Violence Report]; Ramanand Singh to J. Nehru, 10 Nov. 1936, P5, 1936, AICCP, NML; GB FR(2) Nov. 1936, FR(2) Dec. 1936, FR(1) Feb. 1937, HP Files 18/11/1936, 18/12/1936, 18/2/1937, NAI; Tomlinson, *National Congress and Raj*, pp.79, 83.
26 GB FR(1) Feb. 1937, HP f 18/2/1937, NAI; Tomlinson, *National Congress and Raj*, pp.78-80.
27 GB Fortnightly Reports for April-July, HP files 18/4/1937, 18/5/1937, 18/6/1937, 18/7/1937, NAI.
28 For conditions in the 1930s see 'A Plea for Justice', HP f 51/5/1936, NAI.
29 Tomlinson, *National Congress and Raj*, ch.3. Tomlinson's account of developments in Bihar attempts unsuccessfully to explain Congress political activity almost exclusively in terms of factional conflicts within the party organisation over material interests. He admits (p.77) the importance of ideology and policy but fails to integrate them into his analysis.
30 McDonald, 'Unity on Trial', pp.307-311; 'Sahajanand's Statement of September 1937', f G98, 1937-38, AICCP, NML; GB FR(1) Sept. 1937 to GOI, HP f 18/9/1937, NAI.
31 Hauser, 'Bihar Kisan Sabha', pp.118-22; McDonald, 'Unity on Trial', pp.307-9. See also M.V. Harcourt, 'Kisan Populism and Revolution in Rural India: The 1942 Disturbances in Bihar and East United Provinces', in D.A. Low, (ed.) *Congress and the Raj: facets of the Indian struggle, 1917-1947*, (London 1977), pp.331-2.

32 GBO FR(2) March 1936, HP f 18/3/1936; GB FR(1) July 1936, HP f 18/7/1936; GB FR(1) Dec. 1937, HP f 18/12/1937; all in the NAI; *Indian Nation*, 10 April and 5 Aug. 1938; GB 'Fortnightly Reports on Agrarian Troubles (Patna Division), 1938', f 62, FMP, BSA; 'A short history of the agrarian trouble in the Barihiya Tal area', Land Reform files, f 226, 1938, JPNP, NML; GB, *Land Revenue Administration Reports*, 1935-36, p.14, 1936-37, p.13, 1937-38, pp.11-12.

33 GB FR(2) Nov. 1937, HP f 18/11/1937, NAI. Ramnandan Misra was the son of Rajendra Prasad Misra, a middle-range Bhumihar zamindar of Raghunathpur village in Darbhanga. Rajendra Prasad Misra had an annual income of 20,000 to 25,000 rupees, of which about one-tenth went to the government in land revenue payments. Ramnandan Misra was born in 1906, and became involved in politics while studying for his matriculation. In 1922 he joined the Congress and left school to take part in non-cooperation. He studied briefly at the National College at Benares and then became a full-time political worker. He also became involved in social uplift work, and was active in anti-purdah activity. His increasing interest in socialism led to conflict with his family, with whom he eventually broke all ties. (This breaking of ties is one striking point of contrast between his career and that of mainstream nationalist leaders.) Interview, Laheriaserai town, 31 Oct. 1976.

34 GB FR(1) and (2) Dec. 1937, HP f 18/12/37, NAI; letters cited in note 21 above. For the all-India context of this ban see Tomlinson, *National Congress and Raj*, pp.113-18.

35 Dhanraj Sharma and fifteen others to the President, Bihar Provincial Congress Committee, 7 Jan. 1938, f P6, 1936, AICCP, NML; Assistant Secretary, BPCC to General Secretary AICC 13 Sept. 1937, f P6, part II, AICCP, NML; Violence Report, pp.4-5. For details on intra-Congress struggles in Darbhanga in the period preceding the 1937 Legislative Assembly elections, see Tomlinson, *National Congress and Raj*, pp.78-9.

36 Violence Report. McDonald's 'Unity of Trial' is an excellent introduction to the disturbances at the time of the Haripura delegate elections. But McDonald generalises too far on the basis of events within the single district of Darbhanga and exaggerates the extent of Congress disunity and the strength of the left-wing challenge to the orthodox Congressmen.

37 Krishna Chandra Mukerji, General Secretary, Bihar CSP, Darbhanga Branch to J.P. Narayan, 5 Aug. 1938, CSP f 23, 1937-38, JPNP, NML; GB FR(2) June 1938, FR(1) Aug. 1938, FR(1) Sept. 1938, HP files 18/6/1938, 18/8/1938, 18/9/1938, NAI.
38 Ramnandan Misra to Dear Comrade (presumably J.P. Narayan), Laheriaserai, 17 Aug. 1938, Agriculturalists' Unions, f 149, 1936, JPNP, NML.
39 S.M. Wasi, *Bihar in 1938-39*, (Patna 1942) p.7.
40 Under the tenancy law produce rent had an equivalent status to cash rent. In actuality, however, payers of cash rents could more easily demand receipts and were more able to secure and advance their rights than sharecroppers. Note by R.N. Prasad on 'Agrarian trouble in...the district of Purnea', PS f 120(I), 1940, p.19, BSA.
41 Kisan report, ch.2, p.56; Murari Prasada to Chief Manager, 29 June 1938, f 34f, C Pandoul, L 1938-39, RDA.
42 See for example the Village Note for Kubaul, February 1901, village 407, Bahera thana, Collectorate Record Room, Laheriaserai town, Darbhanga.
43 See the documents cited in note 10 above and particularly the Padri 'Inspection report' of 7 May 1938.
44 GB FR(1) Aug. 1937, HP f 18/8/1937.
45 For conflicting evidence concerning one area in south Bihar see 'A short history of the agrarian trouble in the Barahiya Tal area', Land Reform f 226, 1938, JPNP, NML; Rajendra Prasad to Jawaharlal Nehru, 10 Mar. 1937, f P6(i), 1937, AICCP, NML; GB FR(1) March 1937, HP f 18/3/1937; Hauser, 'Bihar Kisan Sabha', pp.11, 26, 30, 111.
46 For information on the *bakast* campaign and on agrarian relations and political developments in north Bihar I am grateful to Ramnandan Misra. His information was particularly helpful because many of the official files relating to bakast protest have been lost or destroyed, Walter Hauser of the University of Virginia has undertaken important research into the *bakast* movement in Bihar as a whole. Hauser has isolated five centres of peasant discontent, and has visited them to make an extensive series of interviews. In addition he has located many non-official documents and has delved into previously unused district level records.
47 Bihar Landholders' Association Papers, S.N. Sinha

Library, Patna; *Indian Nation*, 2 April, 27 July, 31 July 1938; Hauser, 'Bihar Kisan Sabha', pp.127-30; Note by M.G. Hallet dated 26 Sept. 1938 enclosed with Hallett to Brabourne, 27 Sept. 1938, MSS EUR F 125/45, IOL.

48 *Indian Nation*, 2 April 1938; Swami Sahajanand Saraswati, 'Tenancy Measures in Bihar', in R.G. Ranga (ed.), *Peasants and Congress*, (Madras 1938?); Note by Halett cited in note 47 above.

49 H.K. Prasad to Rajendra Prasad, 30 June 1938, f IA 1938 (microfilm 8), PP, NML. See also Hauser, 'Bihar Kisan Sabha', pp.129-30.

50 *Indian Nation*, 1 July 1938; Note by Hallett cited in note 47 above.

51 Wasi, *Bihar 1938-39*, p.7. Failure to give receipts was a breach of the tenancy law but no effective enforcement machinery existed. Hauser, 'Bihar Kisan Sabha' pp.127, 131.

52 The letter concludes: 'So my labour is daily increasing and almost the whole day I have to remain in these cases. You were pleased to send word...that special remuneration would be paid for this heavy work'. Anup Lall Thakyr, Raj Muktear, Madhubani to Pandoul circle manager, 8 June 1939, f 56A. C Pandoul L 1938-39 RDA.

53 Padri AAR 1347 F(1939-40) f 16D1, C Padri, G 1941-42, RDA.

54 Ramnandan Misra, 'A short note on the conditions of tenants of Raj Darbhanga of parri elaka', Land Reform file 226, 1938, JPNP, NML. See also the circular of 6 July 1939 accompanying this document.

55 *Ibid.*; Padri AAR 1344 F (1936-37) f 10H3, C Padri G 1937-38, RDA.

56 Ramnandan Misra, 'Conditions of Tenants'.

57 'Inspection report', 7 May 1938, f 6H2, C Padri, G 1938-39, RDA; Padri AAR 1344 F (1936-37) f 10H3, C Padri, G 1937-38, RDA.

58 GBO FR(1) June 1936, HP f 18/6/1936 NAI; Ramnandan Misra, 'Conditions of Tenants'; AICC Foreign Department Newsletter 2, 18 June 1936, f XI, 1936 (microfilm 4), JPNP, NML.

59 'Inspection report', 7 May 1938, f 6H2, C Padri, G 1938-39, RDA.

60 *Ibid.*; Special Officer to Chief Manager, 31 Oct. 1938, f 6H2, C Padri, G 1938-39, RDA.

61 During the 1930s the Darbhanga Raj senior management

made continuing efforts to reorganise and rationalise the administration of the Raj estates. See the Conference Proceedings, 13 May 1937 and 10 Jan. 1938, f 10F G 1937-38; Conference Minutes 4, 5 May 1938, f 10D3, G 1938-39, RDA.
62 Padri AAR, 1347 F. (1939-40), f 16D1, G 1941-42, RDA.
63 *Ibid.*
64 Misra, 'Conditions of tenants'. For Danby's response to Misra's charges, see *Indian Nation*, 16 July 1939.
65 H.R. Krishnan, 'Report on enquiry', 29 Aug. 1939 and Note dated 13 July 1939, PS f 79(X), 1939, BSA.
66 Hauser, 'Bihar Kisan Sabha', pp.33-4 and Harcourt, 'Kisan Populism', pp.323-35.
67 Roy, 'North Bihar Village', pp.304-6. See also K.P. Sinha, Collector's Office, Darbhanga to R. Russell, Chief Secretary to Government of Bihar, 13 March 1939, PS f 79, 1939, BSA.
68 Swami Sahajanand and his supporters contended that, though they hoped that kisan protest would be non-violent, the kisans had every right to use violence in self-defence. See the 'All India Kisan Bulletin', 14 Jan. 1938, and Ramnandan Misra to Rajendra Prasad, 17 Jan. 1938, f G98, 1937-38, AICCP, NML. See also Ranga, *Peasants and Congress*, pp.67-8.
69 Roy, 'North Bihar Village', p.306.
70 See Martin Hoskins, 'Land-Holding and Development in the Kosi area', and Wood, 'Agrarian Structure', both in J.L. Joy and Elizabeth Everitt (eds), *The Kosi Symposium, The Rural Problem in Northeast Bihar: Analysis, Policy and Planning in the Kosi Area*, (University of Sussex 1976) pp.82, 107.
71 GB FR(1) July 1939, HP f 18/7/1938 NAI; *Indian Nation*, 11 July 1939.
72 Hauser, 'Bihar Kisan Sabha', p.132; GB FR(1) Feb. 1939, HP f 18/2/1939, NAI; GB FR(1) May 1939, HP f 18/5/1939, NAI.
73 GB FR(1) March 1939, HP f 18/3/1938, NAI.
74 GB FR(2) April 1939, HP f 18/4/1939; GB FR(1) May 1939, HP f 18/5/1939; GB FRS (1) and (2) June 1939, HP f 18/6/1939, NAI.
75 GB FRS (1) and (2) June 1939, HP f 18/6/1939, NAI; *Indian Nation*, 21 July 1939. Another prominent kisan leader, Dhanraj Sharma, was arrested and sentenced to six months rigorous imprisonment and a 200 rupees fine. *Indian Nation*, 26 July 1939.

Notes to pages 161-164

76 GB FR(1) July 1939, HP f 18/7/1939, NAI; see also *Indian Nation*, 6, 16 July.
77 R. Russell, note dated 13 July 1939 in PS f 79(X), 1939, BSA.
78 GB FR(1) July 1939, HP f 18/7/1939, NAI.
79 'Account of the Bakast struggle', by the publicity officer, Darbhanga District Kisan Sabha, no date, but internal evidence indicates second half of July 1939, Land Reforms file 226, 1938, JPNP, NML.
80 GB FR(2) July 1939, HP f 18/7/1939, NAI; 'Account of the Bakast struggle'; H.R. Krishnan, 'Report on Enquiry', 29 Aug. 1939, PS f 79(X), 1939, BSA.
81 GB FR(2) July 1939, HP f 18/7/1939, NAI. See also GB FR(2) Dec. 1937, HP f 18/12/1937, NAI.
82 Hauser, 'Bihar Kisan Sabha', p.27, footnote 1; 'Babu Rajendra Prasad's Comprehensive Statement addressed to the tenantry', 27 Dec. 1937, Bihar Landholders' Association Papers, Sinha Library, Patna; Padri AAR, 1347 F. (1939-40) f 16D1, G 1941-42, RDA.
83 GB FRS(1) and (2) Aug. 1939, HP f 18/8/1938, NAI.
84 GB FR(1) Sept. 1939, HP f 18/8/1939, NAI.
85 Interview, Ramnandan Misra, Laheriaserai town, 4 Nov. 1976.
86 McDonald, 'Unity on Trial', p.312, note 20.
87 GB, *Land Revenue Administration Report for 1939-40*, pp.12-13, and for *1940-41*, pp.11-12.
88 GB FR(2) Sept. 1939, HP f 18/9/1939; GB FRS(1) and (2) Oct. 1939, HP f 18/10/1939, NAI.
89 Congress was to remain out of office for six years. Because of the length of this period it is tempting to regard the withdrawal from office as the epitome of idealistic self-sacrifice over a matter of principle. But as B.R. Tomlinson points out, in 1939 no one could predict the length of the period during which Congress would remain in the political wilderness, and hence the resignation can be seen as in part a bargaining ploy designed to pressure Britain into the making of further constitutional concessions. Tomlinson, *National Congress and Raj*, p.111.
90 *Ibid.*, Chap.3 and p.111.
91 Harcourt, 'Kisan Populism', p.333; McDonald, 'Unity on Trial', p.306. For developments in the Bihar Provincial Kisan Sabha in the early years of the war, and their relationship to nationalist politics see Hauser, 'Bihar Kisan Sabha', pp.143-8.

92 GB FRs (1) and (2), Nov. 1939, HP f 18/11/1939, NAI. See also Stewart to Linlithgow, 15 Nov. 1939, MSS EUR F 125/46, IOL.
93 GB FR(1) Dec. 1939, HP f 18/12/1939, NAI; Stewart to Linlithgow, 8 Dec. 1939, MSS EUR F 125/46, IOL; Hauser, 'Bihar Kisan Sabha', p.136.
94 GB FR(1) Dec. 1939, HP f 18/12/1939; GB FR(1) Jan. 1940, HP f 18/1/1940, NAI. In the ensuing months there were some minor disturbances, but in late May the administration reported that 'Purely agrarian agitation has almost ceased'. See GB Fortnightly Reports for February, March, and May 1940, HP files 18/2/1940, 18/4/1940 and 18/5/1940, NAI.
95 *Amrita Bazar Patrika*, 20 Dec. 1937, clipping held in f G98, 1937-38, AICCP, NML. See also Tomlinson, *National Congress and Raj*, pp.69-70.
96 For criticism of the Congress in government see Rajendra Prasad to Sri Krishna Sinha, Chief Minister of the Bihar Government, 4 Mar. 1938, Bihar Ministry Affairs, f 3B 1938, PP, NML; Confidential notes on the Ministers enclosed with Mainwaring to Puckle, 31 Aug. 1938, MSS EUR 125/45, IOL.
97 In Bihar in the 1930s Communist activists paid attention to railway and industrial workers in the towns of south Bihar, but did not involve themselves in agrarian agitation.
98 Hauser, 'Bihar Kisan Sabha', pp.75-8; Harcourt, 'Kisan Populism', p.331.
99 The main centre of dissidence was the Dhamdaha thana in Purnea. PS f 120(1), 1940, BSA; GB Fortnightly Reports for 1939, 1940; Hoskins, 'Land-Holding and Development', pp.79-80, and Wood, 'Agrarian structure', pp.106-8. For information about *Adivasi* discontent in Champaran where conditions broadly similar to those in Purnea prevailed, see GB Fortnightly Reports for June, July and August of 1938, HP files 18/6/1938, 18/7/1938, and 18/8/1938, NAI.
100 Preamble to 'The Manifesto of the Bihar Provincial Kisan Sabha', Agriculturalists' Unions f 149, 1936, JPNP, NML.
101 Hauser, 'Bihar Kisan Sabha', p.20.
102 GB Fortnightly Reports for April, June, July and August 1936, July and September 1937 and June 1938, HP files NAI; Muzaffarpur Collector to Tirhut Commissioner, 1 Sept. 1938 and R.S.L. Norsering, 'Enquiry into Allegations', Police file 51, 9, 1940 (includes 51,

Notes to pages 167-170

15, 1938 and 51, 21, 1937), Commissioner's Record Room, Muzaffarpur town; *Indian Nation*, 9, 22 July, 4 Aug. 1938; Hallett to Linlithgow, 11, 27 Nov. 1937, IOR L/P and J/5/169.
103 Quoted from Sahajanand's presidential address to the annual session of the All-India Kisan Sabha, 14, 15 March, 1944 in Hauser, 'Bihar Kisan Sabha', p.19.
104 GB, *Land Revenue Administration Report, 1939-40*, p.11; Jhanjharpur Manager to Chief Manager, 25 April 1938, f 10F, G 1937-38, and marginal note on the Chief Manager's note on the Rohika AAR 1348 F (1940-41) f 26D2, C Rohika, G 1941-42, RDA. See also Roy, 'North Bihar Village', pp.306-7.
105 Jannuzi, *Agrarian Crisis in India*; Geof Wood, 'From Raiyat to Rich Peasant', *South Asian Review*, 7 (1) 1973.
106 GB FR(2) Nov. 1939, HP f 18/11/1939, NAI. For comments on the effective co-operation which developed between the Congress and the police and administration see Hallett to Linlithgow, 19 Aug., 11 and 25 Nov. 1937, IOR L/P and J/5/169, and Hallett to Linlithgow, 20 Jan. 1938, MSS EUR 125/44, IOL.
107 'D.I.B.'s report of the political situation in Bihar', 15 Jan. 1941, HP f 31/1/41; Stewart to Linlithgow, Tlg 29 July 1942, document 360 in Nicholas Mansergh (ed.), *Constitutional Relations Between Britain and India. The Transfer of Power, 1942-47*, (London, 8 volumes, 1970-), II; GB FR(2) Oct. 1942, NAI. Hallett to Linlithgow, 14 April and 8 May 1939; Brett to Hallett, 26 March 1939; Note by R.E. Russel, 30 March 1939; Hallett's summary dealing with police administration dated 28 May 1939 and enclosed with Hallett to Linlithgow, 29 May 1939; Stewart to Linlithgow, 15 Nov. 1939; all in MSS EUR 125/146, IOL.

Chapter 7

1 Datta, *Freedom Movement*, III, pp.21-5, 27-30; Francis G. Hutchins, *India's Revolution. Gandhi and the Quit India Movement*, (Cambridge, Massachusetts 1973), pp.217-20; M.V. Harcourt, The 'Quit India' Movement, August 1942: A Case Study of Militant Indian Nationalism, University of Western Australia, M.A. thesis, 1967;

Linlithgow to Churchill, Tlg 31 Aug. 1942, document 662 in Mansergh, *Transfer of Power*, II, pp.853-4.
2. GB FR(1) April 1941, HP f 18/4/1941, NAI.
3. For a general account of conditions see the annual *Land Revenue Administration Reports*.
4. GB FR(2) Jan. 1942, FMP f 76, 1942, BSA; GB FR(1) Dec. 1940, HP f 18/12/1940, NAI; GB FR(1) May 1941, HP f 18/5/1941, NAI.
5. GB FR(2) July 1942, HP f 18/7/1942, NAI; GB FR(2) June 1942, HP f 18/6/1942, NAI.
6. Stewart to Linlithgow, 22 Dec. 1939, MSS EUR F 125/46, IOL; GB FR(1) July 1942, HP f 18/7/1941, NAI; Stewart to Linlithgow, 15 July 1942, MSS EUR F 125/49, IOL; A.W. Flack, H.B. Martin, R.F. Mudie, Reminiscences, District Officers' Collection, MSS EUR F 180/17, 21 and 78, IOL.
7. Johannes H. Voigt, 'Co-operation or Confrontation? War and Congress Politics, 1939-42', in D.A. Low, (ed.) *Congress and the Raj, facets of the Indian struggle 1917-1947*, (London 1977), pp.352-4, 362; Tomlinson, *National Congress and Raj*, pp.141-2.
8. Voigt, 'Co-operation or Confrontation?', pp.360-1; Datta, *Freedom Movement*, III, p.382; Harcourt, 'Kisan Populism', p.335; Tomlinson, *National Congress and Raj*, pp.151-2.
9. Harcourt, 'Kisan Populism', p.335.
10. 'Extract from provincial report', 19 Mar. 1941, HP f 3/19/1941, NAI; GB FR(2) Dec. 1940, HP f 18/12/1940, NAI; GB FR(1) Jan. 1941, HP f 18/1/1941, NAI; GB FR(2) March 1941, HP f 18/3/1941, NAI; GB FR(1) Apr. 1941, HP f 18/4/1941, NAI; Members of the Congress Party in Shahabad District Board to Rajendra Prasad, 7 Aug. 1941, AICCP f P6, 1940, NML.
11. Voigt, 'Co-operation or Confrontation?', p.361.
12. 'History of the Civil Disobedience Movement, 1940-41', HP f 3/6/1942, NAI.
13. Datta, *Freedom Movement*, III, pp.1-3.
14. D.A. Low, 'The Indian Schism', *Journal of Commonwealth Political Studies*, IX, 2, July 1971, pp.165, 167; Tomlinson, *National Congress and Raj*, pp.154-7; Voigt, 'Co-operation or Confrontation?', pp.361-5; R.J. Moore, 'The Problem of Freedom with Unity: London's India Policy, 1917-47', in D.A. Low, (ed.) *Congress and the Raj; facets of the Indian struggle, 1917-1947*, (London 1977).

15 Voigt, 'Co-operation or Confrontation?', pp.366-8.
16 Datta, *Freedom Movement*, III, p.3.
17 GB FR(2) May 1942, HP f 18/5/1942, NAI; Stewart to Linlithgow, 25 May 1942, MSS EUR F 125/49, IOL; Datta, *Freedom Movement*, III, pp.14-15.
18 GB FR(1) Feb. 1942, HP f 18/2/1942, NAI.
19 Datta, *Freedom Movement*, III, p.3.
20 GB FR(1) July 1942, HP f 18/7/1942, NAI.
21 GB FR(2) May 1942, HP f 18/5/1942, NAI. See also FR(1) for the same month.
22 'D.I.B.'s report of the political situation in Bihar', 15 Jan. 1941, HP f 31/1/1941, NAI. See also Stewart to Linlithgow, 27 Feb. and 25 May 1942, MSS EUR F 125/49 IOL and see Stewart to Linlithgow, Tlg, 29 July 1942, document 360 in Mansergh, *Transfer of Power*, II.
23 Appendix II to 'D.I.B.'s report'.
24 'D.I.B.'s report'. See also D. Pilditch, 'Memorandum on the Bihar Police', MSS EUR F 125/49, IOL. [hereafter Pilditch Memorandum].
25 'D.I.B.'s report'.
26 Datta, *Freedom Movement*, III, p.16; GB FRs (1) and (2), July 1942, HP f 18/7/1942, NAI.
27 'Note by R.F. Mudie', 19 Sept. 1944, HP f 3/15/1943, NAI.
28 R.N. Lines, District Magistrate Darbhanga to Chief Sec., 22 Dec. 1942, FMP f 84, 1920-42, BSA; Philip Woodruff, *The Men Who Ruled India*, (London, 2 vols, 1953, 54), vol.II, *The Guardians*, p.308; Stewart to Linlithgow, 16 Sept. 1942, para 12, MSS EUR F 125/49, IOL; Pilditch Memorandum, para 10.
29 Datta, *Freedom Movement*, III, pp.28-30, 41.
30 Chief Sec. GB to Home Sec. GOI, 17 Sept. 1942, HP f 3/33/1942, NAI.
31 Datta, *Freedom Movement*,III, p.51; R.N. Lines, District Magistrate Darbhanga to Chief Sec. GB, 22 Dec. 1942, FMP f 84, 1920-42, BSA.
32 Woodruff, *The Men Who Ruled India*, II, p.308. See also 'Report of damage to Telegraph and Telephone apparatus, north Bihar division', FMP f 65, 1940-42, BSA.
33 Chief Sec. GB to Home Sec. GOI, 17 Sept. 1942, HP f 3/33/1942, NAI; Datta, *Freedom Movement*, III, pp.63, 65.
34 *[Secret] Report on the Civil Disturbances in Bihar, 1942*, (Patna 1944), pp.13, 14 and Appendix 'C',

pp. 32-6; GOI, 'Verbatim record of the proceedings of the Conference of Provincial Representatives convened in connection with the Congress disturbances, 1942-43', HP f 3/89/1942, NAI [hereafter Provincial Conference Proceedings], p.56; B. Sivaram, Purnea District Officer to Chief Sec., 27 Aug. 1942, FMP f 93, 1942-44, BSA; Monghyr District Magistrate, 'Situation in the Beguserai Subdivision', FMP f 47, 1942, BSA.

35 Monghyr Magistrate, 'Situation in Beguserai', cited in ibid., p.26.
36 Jay Prakash Narayan, 'To All Fighters for Freedom', reprinted as Appendix J to Datta, *Freedom Movement*, III. See also Arun Chandra Bhuyan, *The Quit India Movement. The Second World War and Indian Nationalism*, (Delhi 1975), p.89. And see P.N. Chopra (ed.), *Quit India Movement. British Secret Report*, (Faridabad 1976, a reprint of 'Wickenden's Report on the Disturbances of 1942/43', with appended documents), pp.74, 75, 90, 91, 104.
37 Judgement in High Court, Patna on case of Jubba Mallah vs. King Emperor, HP f 3/31/1944.
38 Bihar Congress Committee, 'Circular No.1', quoted in Datta, *Freedom Movement*, III, pp.37-40; R.N. Lines, Darbhanga District Magistrate to Chief Sec., 22 Dec. 1942, FMP f 84, 1920-42, BSA.
39 GB FR(2) Feb. 1939, HP f 18/2/1939, NAI.
40 According to Datta, a Congress meeting held in Patna on the evening of 12 August passed resolutions in favour of sabotage. Apparently this was the first occasion in the Quit India campaign on which the Bihar Congress sanctioned the use of sabotage. But before the meeting was held, sabotage already had begun with an attack, in the afternoon of 12 August, on the records held in the Kadamkuan post office. Datta, *Freedom Movement*, III, p.45. For pamphlets urging the employment of sabotage, see the appendices to ibid. See also Bhuyan, *Quit India Movement*, pp.88, 89.
41 Hauser, 'Bihar Kisan Sabha', pp.148-51; Stewart to Linlithgow, 24 March 1942, MSS EUR F 125/49, IOL; Surindra Gopal, 'Peasant Movement in Bihar During the Second World War', A.N. Sinha Institute, *Behavioural Scientist. Essays in Honour of Professor Sachchidananda*, (Patna 1978).
42 Jay Prakash Narayan had been arrested in early 1941 for anti-war propaganda. At the start of the revolt

Ramnandan Misra was in Bombay and Madras, and was arrested in Cuttack, Orissa, in late August 1942. Ajit Bhattacharjea, *Jay Prakash. A Political Biography*, (Delhi 1975), pp.77-80; Chopra, *British Secret Report*, pp.262, 273-4; Datta, *Freedom Movement*, III, Appendix H.

43 Official claims were based on a circular distributed by the Andhra Provincial Congress Committee in July 1942 which advocated the cutting of telegraph and telephone wires during the forthcoming campaign. Bhuyan, *Quit India*, pp.53, 90. See also Prasad, *Autobiography*, pp.535-6, 538, 549-50.

44 See for example Champaran Police Superintendent, 'Situation in Champaran up to 9 November 1921', PS f 539, 1921, BSA; United Provinces Government Press Communique, 6 Feb. 1922, HP f 563, 1922, NAI.

45 FR(2) Dec. 1920, PS f 7, 1920, BSA; Memorandum from Saran Police Superintendent to Inspector General Police, 6 Aug. 1930, BSA; HP f 5/80/1932, NAI.

46 However some of the local Congress leaders who had not been considered important enough to arrest used their influence to deter groups of demonstrators from violent activity. Monghyr District Magistrate 'Report on the Civil Disobedience movement', FMP f 45, 1942, p.5, BSA; R.N. Lines, Darbhanga District Magistrate to Chief Sec. GB 22 Dec. 1922, FMP f 84, 1920-42, BSA.

47 By 26 August south Bihar was generally under control, and the government reported that 'The position north of the river is expected to improve now that the forces of law have been reinforced'. Bihar Government Communique, 26 Aug. HP f 3/22/1942, NAI. For details of the deployment of troops see GB, *Civil Disturbances*, p.12.

48 Harcourt, 'Kisan Populism', pp.322-3, 346-8.

49 See for example R.N. Lines, Darbhanga District Magistrate to Chief Sec., GB, FMP f 84, 1920-42, BSA.

50 'List of Killed', FMP f 69, 1942, BSA.

51 See Rutherford to Linlithgow, 4 April 1943, MSS EUR F 125/50, IOL.

52 Madhubani Subdivisional Officer to Darbhanga District Magistrate, 16 Dec. 1942, FMP f 84, 1942, BSA. The Darbhanga District Magistrate reported that '...the movement has first entirely been led by the upper castes, principally Babhans, Rajputs, Brahmins and Khatris, and the masses did nothing. As the feelings

of the masses were, however, inflamed and promises of loot were held out, they also came in...' R.N. Lines, Darbhanga District Magistrate to Chief Sec., GB, 22 Dec. 1942, FMP f 84, 1920-42, BSA.

53 Beguserai Subdivisional Officer, 'Report on Civil Disobedience Movement', 22 Dec. 1942, FMP f 45, 1942, BSA. See also B. Sivaram, Purnea District Magistrate to Chief Sec., 24 Aug. 1942, FMP f 93, 1942-44, para 14, BSA, and Sivaram to Chief Sec., 3 Sept. 1942, FMP f 84, BSA.

54 GB FR(2) Sept. 1942, HP f 18/9/1942, NAI; GB FR(2) Nov. 1942, HP f 18/11/1942, NAI.

55 Possible exceptions to this general absence consisted, in south Bihar, of the burning of three kutcherries of the Banaili Raj, and in north Bihar, of the burning of one of the kutcherries of the Grant estate in the Sonbarsa area. But the attack on the Grant estate kutcherry probably resulted from a combination of anti-British and anti-zamindar feeling. GB FRs (1) Oct. and (2) Nov. 1942, FMP f 76, 1942, BSA.

56 Harcourt, 'Kisan Populism', p.335; Hauser, 'Bihar Kisan Sabha', pp.141-51; Swami Sahajanand and Yadunandan Sharma, press statement, 25 August 1942, quoted in M.A. Rasul, *History of the All India Kisan Sabha*, (Calcutta 1974), pp.86-7; Jay Prakash Narayan, 'Within the Congress', in B.N. Ajuha (ed.), *'J.P.' India's Revolutionary Number One*, (Lahore 1947), p.41.

57 Datta, *Freedom Movement*, III, Appendices A and H. Some local Communist Party workers defied the party's anti-Congress policy and took a leading part in the August revolt. GB FR(1) Sept. 1942, HP f 18/9/1942, NAI; Beguserai Subdivisional Officer, 'Report on Civil Disobedience Movement', 22 Dec. 1942, FMP f 45, 1942, BSA.

58 For examples of zamindars who supported the revolt see GB, FR(1) June 1943, HP f 18/6/1943, NAI; Chandrika Prasad, 'Statement', 30 May 1952, FMP f 84, 1920-42, BSA. For comments on the inaction of the zamindars see Governor of Bihar to Viceroy, Tlg XX, 2 Sept. 1942; Stewart to Linlithgow, 19 Sept. and 12 Oct. 1942, all in EUR F 125/49, IOL. However some zamindars did eventually support the authorities. The Madhubani Subdivisional Officer reported that when looting had become widespread '...the zamindars and mahants began to be afraid and came forward to help

Notes to pages 183-187

the authorities for their own safety'. Madhubani Subdivisional Officer to Darbhanga District Magistrate, 16 Dec. 1942, FMP f 84, BSA.
59 Umarpathi Tewari, Interview, Dumeri village, Darbhanga, 17 Oct. 1976.
60 Parihar AAR 1349F (1941-42) f 16D2, C Parihar, G 1942-43, RDA.
61 Padri AAR 1349 F (1941-42), f 16D3, C Padri G 1942-43, RDA. See also Nishankpur AAR 1349 F (1941-42) f 16D1, C Nishankpur, G 1942-43, RDA and Bhawanipur AAR 1349 F (1941-42) 16D2, C Bhawaninpur, G 1942-43, RDA.
62 See for example H.P. Sinha, Saran District Officer to Chief Secretary, GB, 29 Jan. 1943, FMP f 84, 1942, BSA.
63 Voigt, 'Co-operation or Confrontation?', p.368; Woodruff, *Men Who Ruled India*, II, pp.307-8.
64 Harcourt, 'Kisan Populism', pp.320, 343.
65 See R.N. Lines to the Chief Sec., 22 Dec. 1942, FMP f 84, 1920-42, BSA. For details of the attack, led by Jaglal Chaudhury, on the Garkha thana in Saran, which culminated five days of meetings and propaganda, see Judgement in Special Cases 4 and 5, King Emperor vs. Jaglal Choudhury and others, 4 Nov. 1942, and Justice C.M. Agarwala, 'Criminal Review 2, 1942', 8 Dec. 1942, HP f 3/80/1942, NAI. For a graphic account of an attack on a United Provinces thana see R.H. Niblett quoted in Harcourt 'Kisan Populism', pp.318-20.
66 In the attacks on police stations in Darbhanga the rebels captured four muskets, three shotguns and one revolver. Deputy Inspector General Police, Muzaffarpur, Memorandum 635C, 1 Oct. 1942, FMP f 49, 1910-23, 1942, BSA. Throughout Bihar the insurgents captured a submachine gun, 4 rifles, 20 shot guns, 12 muskets, 20 revolvers and pistols, and 4 bayonets. Chief Sec., GB to Home Sec., GOI, 17 Sept. 1942, HP f 3/33/1942, NAI.
67 In Bihar during the period when the rising was at its height groups of demonstrators carried fire-arms on only six occasions and used them on five. Chief Sec., to Home Sec., GOI, 17 Sept. 1942, HP f 3/33/1942, NAI.
68 Deputy Inspector General Police, Muzaffarpur, Memorandum 635C, 1 Oct. 1942, FMP f 49, 1910-23, 1942 BSA. See also Datta, *Freedom Movement*, III, p.65.
69 F.T. Parsons, Champaran Police Superintendent to

Deputy Inspector General Police, Muzaffarpur, 1 Sept. 1942, FMP f 84, BSA.
70 Summary of incidents in Saran, Special Abstract 31, 24 Aug. 1942, FMP f 84, 1942, BSA; Datta, *Freedom Movement*, III, p.60.
71 GB, *Civil Disturbances*, p.31.
72 R.N. Lines, Darbhanga District Magistrate to Chief Sec., GB, 22 Dec. 1942, p.9, FMP f 84, 1920-42, BSA.
73 *Ibid.*, p.6; Monghyr District Magistrate, Report on Civil Disobedience Movement 1942, pp.53, 54, FMP f 47, 1942, BSA; GB, *Civil Disturbances*, p.31, Appendix 'G'.
74 One Bihar official noted that 'We have 495 thanas and there is not a single one of those that could be called a defensible building'. Provincial Conference Proceedings, pp.46, 56.
75 B. Sivaram, Purnea District Officer to Chief Secretary, GB, 27 Aug. 1942, paras 13, 14, FMP f 93, 1942-44, BSA.
76 *Ibid.*, para 13; F.J. Parsons, Champaran Police Superintendent to Deputy Inspector General Police, Muzaffarpur, 7 Sept. 1942, FMP f 84, 1942, BSA; Monghyr District Magistrate, 'Report on Civil Disobedience Movement 1942', section entitled 'Difficulties caused by the burning of houses and summary reprisals by certain military units without the knowledge of the district civil authorities', FMP f 47, 1942, BSA.
77 H.P. Sinha, Saran District Officer to Chief Sec., GB, 29 Jan. 1943, FMP f 84, 1942, BSA; GB FR(1) Dec. 1942, HP f 18/12/1942, NAI.
78 For example see the documents dealing with Jaglal Choudhary cited in note 65 above.
79 M.K. Sinha, Purnea Police Superintendent, Report VI, 4 Sept. 1942, FMP f 93, 1942-44, BSA.
80 Stewart to Linlithgow, 12 Oct. 1942, MSS EUR F 125/49, IOL; Stewart to Linlithgow, letters 1-GB and 2-GB, both 4 Jan. 1943, and Rutherford to Linlithgow, 13 March 1943, all in MSS EUR F 125/50, IOL.
81 Bhagalpur Commissioner to Chief Sec., GB, 9 June 1944, FMP f 95, 1943-45, BSA; GB FR(2) March 1943, HP f 18/3/1943, NAI; GB FR(2) April 1943, HP f 28/4/1943, NAI; Purnea District Magistrate to Chief Sec., GB FMP f 94, 1942, BSA; Datta, *Freedom Movement*, III, pp.275-88.
82 GB FR(2) Oct. 1943, FMP f 79, 1943, BSA; GB FR(2) Aug. 1943, HP f 18/8/1943, NAI; GB FR(1) Sept. 1943, HP f 18/9/1943, NAI; J.W. Houlton, Bhagalpur Com-

Notes to pages 190-192

missioner to Y.A. Godbole, Chief Sec., 1 Sept. 1943, FMP f 91, 1942-43, BSA.
83 Telegram, Foreign Office, New Delhi, to Minister, Kathmandu, 26 Nov. 1942; Extract from Demi-Official Letter 20388, 29 Dec. 1942; Note on Conference at Muzaffarpur, 27 Sept. 1942; all in HP f 3/39/1942, NAI.
84 Datta, *Freedom Movement*, III, pp.268-9.
85 *Ibid.*, pp.272-4.
86 *Ibid.*, p.274; GB FR(2) May 1943, HP f 18/5/1943, NAI; GB FR(1) Oct. 1943, HP f 18/10/1943, NAI.
87 Harcourt, '"Quit India" Movement', p.64.
88 See GB FRs for March to December 1943, HP f 18/3/1943, 18/4/1943, 18/5/1943, 18/6/1943, 18/7/1943, 18/8/1943, 18/9/1943, 18/10/1943, 18/11/1943, 18/12/1943, NAI. The second December report notes that 'The monthly number of dacoities has been halved since last July and is now not far from the Triennial average'.
89 GB FR(2) Sept. 1942, HP f 18/9/1942, NAI; GB FR(1) Jan. 1943, HP f 18/1/1943, NAI; Provincial Conference Proceedings, pp.19-20, 56; 'Supplementary report for the second half of April for the Bhagalpur Division', enclosed with GB FR(1) May 1943, HP f 18/5/1943, NAI; GB FR(2) June 1944, FMP f 80, 1944, BSA.
90 Pilditch, Memorandum, 9 Nov. 1942 and Stewart to Linlithgow, 16 Sept. 1942, both in MSS EUR 125/49; IOL; Linlithgow to Rutherford, 27 Jan. 1943, and enclosures; Rutherford to Linlithgow, 13 and 14 Feb. 1942 and enclosure with letter of 13 Feb.; all in MSS EUR F 125/50, IOL.
91 J.W. Houlton to Godbole, Chief Sec., GB, 18 July 1943; District Magistrate Purnea to Chief Sec., GB, 24 June 1944; both in FMP f 94, 1942, BSA; 'Provincial Conference Proceedings', pp.19-29; GB FR(1), April 1943, HP f 18/4/1943, NAI; GB FR(1) Oct. 1945, FMP f 81, 1945-47, BSA; Appendix to HP f 3/46/1944, NAI; Rutherford to Linlithgow, 5 March 1943, MSS EUR F 125/50, IOL.
92 Harcourt, '"Quit India" Movement', Ch.7.
93 See for example Datta, *Freedom Movement*, III.
94 Bhuyan, *Quit India.* Hutchins, *India's Revolution.*
95 Harcourt, 'Kisan Populism', pp.323-5.
96 Harcourt's analysis of kisan turbulence in the 1930s takes insufficient account of the pivotal part played by rich peasants and exaggerates the intensity and extent of kisan protest. See 'Kisan Populism', pp.328-33 and Ch.6 above.

97 Unable to establish that most small-holders suffered from the scarcity in the months leading up to the revolt, Harcourt suggests that the psychological effect of the threat of increasing scarcity created anxiety and encouraged small-holders to launch themselves into protest. 'Kisan Populism', p. 339. This intriguing suggestion requires further research.
98 GB FR(2) June 1943, HP f 18/6/1943; GB FR(1) July 1943, HP f 18/7/1943, NAI.
99 Harcourt, 'Kisan Populism', pp. 340, 342-3.
100 M.V. Harcourt comments:
> Probably the CSP agitators were quite sincere in their belief that a nationalist revolution would have to precede a social one and that they therefore should not antagonize rightist nationalists by measures exacerbating class hostility. Nevertheless if there is a moral in the story of the Gangetic valley rebellion it is this: revolutions are not made by half measures.

'"Quit India" Movement', p. 67. On the weakness of the left see, Tomlinson, *National Congress and Raj*, pp. 145-6.

BIBLIOGRAPHY

Arrangement

1. Government archives
2. Darbhanga Raj archives
3. Private papers
4. Newspapers
5. Collections of documents
6. Official publications
7. Articles, books, papers and theses
8. Interviews

1. GOVERNMENT ARCHIVES

Bihar State Archives

"Police Abstracts", 1912-1920.
"Reports on Native Newspapers", 1916-1922.
Political Special Department files, 1914-1945.
Freedom Movement Papers, 1912-1952.
Land Revenue Department files, 1912-1945.

Bihar State Archives and West Bengal Archives

Bengal Revenue Department, Land Revenue Branch, files and proceedings, 1875-1911.

Collectorate Record Room, Laheriaserai

"Village notes" for Darbhanga c. 1900.

Commissioner's Record Room, Muzaffarpur town

Police and Political files, 1916-1946.

India Office Library, London

Confidential correspondence between the Bihar Governor and the Viceroy, 1937-1943.
"Wickenden's Report on the Disturbances of 1942-43", with appended documents, by Justice Wickenden. (Consulted in reprint edited by P.N. Chopra entitled *Quit India Movement. British Secret Report* (Faridabad, 1976).)

National Archives of India

Fortnightly Reports to the Government of India from the Government of Bihar (and Orissa) 1918- 946.
Home Political Department files, 1910-1946.

2. DARBHANGA RAJ ARCHIVES

General Department, 1910-1946

Annual Administrative Reports.
Conference Papers.
Darkasht [i.e. 'Petition'] files.
Head Office files.
Management files.
Miscellaneous files.

Law Department, 1910-1946

Civil Cases files.
Criminal Cases files.

3. PRIVATE PAPERS

Nehru Memorial Museum and Library

All India Congress Committee Papers.
Jay Prakash Narayan Papers.
Rajendra Prasad Papers.
Swami Sahajanand Saraswati Papers.

S.L. Sinha Library

Bihar Landholders' Association Papers.

India Office Library
    District Officers' Collection.
    Hallett Papers.

4. NEWSPAPERS

Indian Nation, 1932-1946.

Searchlight, 1919-1946.

5. COLLECTIONS OF DOCUMENTS

    K.K. Datta (ed.) *Writings and Speeches of Mahatma Gandhi Relating to Bihar 1917-1942* (Patna 1960).
    Mansergh, N. (ed.) *Constitutional Relations Between Britain and India. The Transfer of Power, 1942-47* (London, 8 volumes, 1970-).
    Misra, B.B. (ed.) *Select Documents on Mahatma Gandhi's Movement in Champaran, 1917-18* (Patna 1963).

6. OFFICIAL PUBLICATIONS

Government of Bengal

Bengal District Gazetteers (Various districts, Calcutta, 1907+).

Government of Bihar (and Orissa)

(a) Annual publications. (Patna, various dates)

Bihar (and Orissa) in..., and particularly:

    G.E. Owen, *Bihar and Orissa in 1921* (Patna 1922)
    H.C. Prior, *Bihar and Orissa in 1922* (Patna 1923)
    G.E. Owen, *Bihar and Orissa in 1928-29* (Patna 1930)
    C.R. Murray, *Bihar and Orissa in 1929-30* (Patna 1931)
    P.T. Mansfield, *Bihar and Orissa in 1930-31* (Patna 1932)
    S.M. Wasi, *Bihar in 1938-39* (Patna 1942)

Reports on:

Administration of Civil Justice in the Province of Bihar (and Orissa).
Administration of the Police in the Province of Bihar (and Orissa).
Land Revenue Administration of the Province of Bihar (and Orissa).

(b) Other publications.

Report of the Committee on the Agrarian Conditions in Champaran (2 vols, Patna, 1917).
[Secret] Report on the Civil Disturbances in Bihar, 1942 (Patna, 1944). Held in the India Office Library.
Synopsis of History of NCO Movement (Patna, 1924).

Government of Great Britain

India Office and Burma Office List (London, annual)
Indian Statutory Commission (12 vols, London, 1930)

Government of India

Census of India, 1880-1961

7. ARTICLES, BOOKS, PAPERS AND THESES

Ahmad, M. Razi, "Indigo Unrest in Champaran and Mahatma Gandhi", Patna University Ph.D. thesis, 1966.

Ahmed, Qeyamuddin, "Origin and growth of the Darbhanga Raj (1574-1666), based on some contemporary and unpublished documents", *Indian Historical Records Commission Proceedings,* XXXVI, Part II, 1961.

Ajuha, B.N. (ed.), *'J.P. India's Revolutionary Number One,* (Lahore 1947).

Alavi, Hamza, "Peasants and Revolution", in Gough and Sharma, *Imperialism and Revolution.*

———, "Rural Bases of Political Power in South Asia", *Journal of Contemporary Asia,* 4, No. 4, 1974.

"An Ex-Civilian", *Life in the Mofussil; or The Civilian in Lower Bengal* (2 vols, London 1878), I.

Arnold, David, "The Police and Colonial Control: An Introduction" and "The Indian Policeman", in his *"Law and Order". Essays on the Policing of Colonial Madras, 1858-1947,* forthcoming.

———, "The Armed Police and Colonial Rule in South India, 1914-1947", *Modern Asian Studies,* II, 1, 1977.

Baden-Powell, B.H. *The Land-Systems of British India* (3 vols, London, 1892), I.

Bagchi, Amiya, "Foreign Capital and Economic Development in India: A Schematic View", in Gough and Sharma, *Imperialism and Revolution.*
——, "Reflections on Patterns of Regional Growth in India during the Period of British Rule", *Bengal Past and Present,* XLV, 1, No.180, Jan.-June 1976.
Basu, Mrinal Kumar, "Regional Patriotism: A Study in Bihar Politics (1907-1912)", *Indian Historical Review,* III, 2, January 1977.
Beames, J. *Memoirs of a Bengal Civilian* (London, 1961).
Bhattacharjea, Ajit, *Jay Prakash. A Political Biography* (Delhi, 1975).
Bhuyan, Arun Chandra. *The Quit India Movement. The Second World War and Indian Nationalism* (Delhi, 1975).
Bihar Research Society, "Maharajadhiraj Dr Kameshwara Singh Memorial Volume", *Journal of the Bihar Research Society,* XLVIII, 1962.
Blair, Harry W. "Caste, Politics and Democracy in Bihar State, India: The Elections of 1967", Duke University Ph.D. thesis 1969.
Bondurant, Joan. *Conquest of Violence, The Gandhian Philosophy of Conflict* (Princeton, 1958).
Brass, Paul R. *Language, Religion and Politics in North India* (London, 1974).
Broomfield, J.H. "The Regional Elites: A Theory of Modern Indian History", in T. Metcalf, (ed.) *Modern India, an Interpretive Anthology,* (London, 1971). First Pub.*Indian Economic and Social History Review,* III, 3, Sept. 1966.
Brown, Judith M. *Gandhi's Rise to Power: Indian Politics 1915-1922* (London, 1972).
——, "The Role of a National Leader: Gandhi, Congress and Civil Disobedience, 1929-34", in Low, *Congress and the Raj.*
——, *Gandhi and Civil Disobedience. The Mahatma in Indian Politics, 1928-34* (London, 1977).
——, "Gandhi and India's Peasants, 1917-22", *Journal of Peasant Studies,* 1, 4, July 1974.
Carter, A.T. "Political Stratification and Unstable Alliances in Rural Western Maharashtra", *Modern Asian Studies,* 6, 4, 1972.
Chaudhuri, Binay Bhushan, "Agrarian Movements in

Bihar and Bengal, 1919-1939", in B.R. Nanda (ed.), *Socialism in India* (Delhi, London, 1972).

Chaudhury, Vijay Chandra Prasad, *The Creation of Modern Bihar* (Darbhanga, 1964).

Chopra, P.N. (ed.) *Quit India Movement. British Secret Report*, (Faridabad, 1976), a reprint of "Widkenden's Report on the Disturbances of 1942-43", with appended documents, (New Delhi, 1944). Original held in India Office Library.

Crawley, W.F. "Kisan Sabhas and Agrarian Revolt in the United Provinces 1920 to 1921", *Modern Asian Studies*, 5, 2, 1971.

Datta, K.K. *History of the Freedom Movement in Bihar*, (3 vols, Patna, 1957).

―――, *Rajendra Prasad* (New Delhi, 1970).

Desai, A.R. (ed.) *Peasant Struggles in India* (Delhi, 1979).

Dewey, Clive. "The History of Mithila and the Records of the Darbhanga Raj", *Modern Asian Studies*, 10, 1976.

Dewey, Clive, and A.G. Hopkins (eds), *The Imperial Impact. Studies in the Economic History of Africa and India.* (London, 1978).

Dhanagare, D.N. *Agrarian Movements and Gandhian Politics* (Agra, 1975).

―――, "Congress and Agrarian Agitation in Oudh, 1920-22 and 1930-32", *South Asia*, 5, Dec. 1975.

―――, "Peasant Movements in India c. 1920-1950", Sussex D.Phil. thesis, 1973.

―――, "Social origins of the peasant insurrection in Telengana (1946-51)", *Contributions to Indian Sociology*, New Series, 8, 1974.

―――, "Peasant Protest and Politics - The Tebhaga movement in Bengal (India), 1946-47", *Journal of Peasant Studies*, 3, 3, 1976.

Filgate, T.R. "The Behar Planters' Association, Ltd", in Wright, *Bengal and Assam, Behar and Orissa* (London, 1917).

Fisher, C.M. "Indigo Plantations and agrarian society in North Bihar in the nineteenth and early twentieth centuries", Cambridge University D.Phil. thesis, 1976.

―――, "Planters and Peasants: The Ecological Context of Agrarian Unrest on the Indigo Plantations of North Bihar", in Clive Dewey and A.G.

Hopkins (eds), *The Imperial Impact. Studies in the Economic History of Africa and India* (London, 1978).

Gallagher, John and Gordon Johnson and Anil Seal (eds), *Locality, Province and Nation: Essays on Indian Politics, 1870-1940* (London, 1973).

Gandhi, M.K. *An Autobiography. The Story of My Experiments With Truth* (London, 1966).

Gopal, Surindra, "Peasant Movement in Bihar during the Second World War", in A.N. Sinha Institute, *Behavioural Scientist. Essays in Honour of Professor Sachchidananda* (Patna, 1978).

Gordon, Richard. "The Hindu Mahasabha and the Indian National Congress, 1915 to 1926", *Modern Asian Studies*, 9, 2, 1975.

———, "Non-cooperation and Council Entry 1919 to 1920", in Gallagher, Johnson and Seal, *Locality, Province and Nation: Essays on Indian Politics, 1870-1940* (London, 1973).

Gough, Kathleen and Hari P. Sharma, *Imperialism and Revolution in South Asia* (New York, London, 1973).

Grierson, George A. *Bihar Peasant Life*, (London, 1885).

Guha, Ranajit, *A Rule of Property for Bengal. An Essay on the Idea of Permanent Settlement* (Paris, 1963).

———, "Neel-Darpan: The Image of a Peasant Revolt in a Liberal Mirror", *The Journal of Peasant Studies*, 2, 1, Oct. 1974.

Hagen, James R. and Anand A. Yang, "Local Sources for the Study of Rural India: The 'Village Notes' of Bihar", *The Indian Economic and Social History Review*, XIII, 1, 1976.

Harcourt, M.V. "The 'Quit India' Movement, August 1942: A Case Study in Militant Indian Nationalism", University of Western Australia, M.A. thesis, 1967.

———, "Kisan Populism and Revolution in Rural India: The 1942 Disturbances in Bihar and East United Provinces", in Low, *Congress and the Raj*.

Harrison, F.C. "The Behar Ryot at Home", *Calcutta Review*, Oct. 1890.

Hauser, Walter. "The Bihar Provincial Kisan Sabha, 1929-1942. A Study of an Indian Peasant Movement", University of Chicago Ph.D. thesis, 1961.

Hauser, Walter, "The Indian National Congress and Land Policy in the Twentieth Century", *Indian Economic and Social History Review*, 1963-4, No.1.

Henningham, Stephen, "The Social Setting of the Champaran Satyagraha: The Challenge to an Alien Elite", *Indian Economic and Social History Review*, XIII, 1, 1976.

―――, "Elite Adjustment and Social Control in Bihar: The Darbhanga Raj, 1879 to 1962", Australian National University, South Asian History Section seminar paper, July 1976.

―――, "Agrarian Relations in North Bihar: Peasant Protest and the Darbhanga Raj, 1919-20", with appendix on the Darbhanga Raj General Department Records, *Indian Economic and Social History Review*, XVI, 1, 1979.

―――, "The Contribution of 'Limited Violence' to the Bihar Civil Disobedience Movement", *South Asia*, March 1979.

Herring, Ronald J., 'Radical Politics and Revolution in South Asia, *Journal of Peasant Studies*, 7, 1, 1978.

Hoskins, Martin. "Land-Holding and Development in the Kosi area", in J.L. Joy and Elizabeth Everitt, (eds) *The Kosi Symposium. The Rural Problem in North-east Bihar: Analysis, Policy and Planning in the Kosi Area*, (University of Sussex, 1976).

Houlton, Sir John Wardle. *Bihar: The Heart of India* (London, Calcutta, 1953).

Hunter, Sir William Wilson. *Bengal MS Records* (2 vols, London, 1894) I.

Hutchins, Francis G. *India's Revolution. Gandhi and the Quit India Movement* (Cambridge Massachusetts, 1973).

Huttenback, R.A., *Gandhi in South Africa, British Imperialism and the Indian Question, 1860-1914*, (London, 1971).

Inglis, James [under the pseudonym 'Maori'] *Sport and Work on the Nepaul Frontier* (London, 1878).

Jannuzi, F. Tomasson. *Agrarian Crisis in India. The Case of Bihar*, (New Delhi, 1974).

Jha, Hetukar. "Nation Building in a north Indian region. The Case of Mithila", unpublished manuscript (Sociology Dept. Patna University).

Jha, Hetukar. "Lower-Caste Peasants and Upper-Caste Zamindars in Bihar, (1921-1925): An Analysis of Sanskritization and Contradiction between the Two Groups", *Indian Economic and Social History Review*, XIV, 4, 1977.

Jha, Jata Shankar. "A Peep into the Darbhanga Raj Records Office", *Indian Archives*, XII, 1958.

———, *A History of Darbhanga Raj* (Patna, 1968).

———, *Biography of an Indian Patriot, Maharaja Lakmishwar Singh of Darbhanga* (Patna, 1972).

———, *Beginnings of Modern Education in Mithila, Selections from Educational Records of the Darbhanga Raj, 1860-1930* (Patna, 1972).

Joy, J.L. and Everitt, Elizabeth (eds), *The Kosi Symposium. The Rural Problem in North-East Bihar: Analysis, Policy and Planning in the Kosi Area* (University of Sussex, 1976).

Karna, M.N. "Health, Culture and Community in a North Bihar village", Patna University Ph.D. thesis, 1970.

Klein, Ira. "Population and Agriculture in Northern India, 1872-1921", *Modern Asian Studies*, 8, 2, 1974.

Kling, B.B. *The Blue Mutiny. The Indigo Disturbances in Bengal 1859-1862* (London, 1966).

Krishna, Gopal. "The Development of the Indian National Congress as a Mass Organization, 1918-23", in Metcalf, *Modern India*. Originally published in *Journal of Asian Studies*, XXV, 3.

Kumar, Ravinder. "The Political Process in India", *South Asia*, 1, 1971.

———, (ed.), *Essays on Gandhian Politics – The Rowlatt Satyagraha of 1919* (London, 1971).

Low, D.A. (ed.) *Congress and the Raj: Facets of the Indian Struggle 1917-1947* (London, New Delhi, 1977).

———, "'Civil Martial Law': The Government of India and the Civil Disobedience Movements, 1920-34", in his *Congress and the Raj*.

———, "The Indian Schism", *Journal of Commonwealth Political Studies*, IX, 2, 1971.

———, "The Government of India and the first non-cooperation movement, 1920-2", in R. Kumar, *Essays on Gandhian Politics – The Rowlatt Satyagraha of 1919*, (Oxford, 1971).

Low, D.A. (ed.), *Soundings in Modern South Asian History* (London, 1968).

Maori [pseudonym for James Inglis] *Sport and Work on the Nepaul Frontier*, (London, 1878).

McDonald, G. "Unity on Trial: Congress in Bihar, 1919-39", in D.A. Low, (ed.) *Congress and the Raj; facets of the Indian Struggle 1917-1947*, (London, New Delhi, 1977).

Metcalf, Thomas R. (ed.) *Modern India. An interpretive Anthology*, (London, 1971).

Mishra, G. *Agrarian Problems of Permanent Settlement. A Case Study of Champaran* (New Delhi, 1978).

―――, "Indigo Plantation and the Agrarian Relations in Champaran during the Nineteenth Century", *The Indian Economic and Social History Review*, III, 4 Dec. 1966.

―――, "Socio-Economic Background of Gandhi's Champaran Movement", *The Indian Economic and Social History Review*, V, 3 Sept. 1968.

Moore, Jr, Barrington. *Social Origins of Dictatorship and Democracy. Lord and Peasant in the Making of the Modern World* (London, 1967).

Moore, R.J. *The Crisis of Indian Unity 1917-1940* (London, 1974).

―――, "The Problem of Freedom with Unity: London's India Policy, 1917-47", in D.A. Low, (ed.) *Congress and the Raj; facets of the Indian Struggle 1917-1947*, (London, New Delhi, 1977).

Musgrave, P.J. "Landlords and Lords of the Land: Estate Management and Social Control in Uttar Pradesh, 1860-1920", *Modern Asian Studies*, 6, 3, 1972.

Narayan, Jay Prakash. "Within the Congress", in B.N. Ajuha (ed.) *"J.P." India's Revolutionary Number One* (Lahore, 1947).

Neale, Walter C. *Economic Change in Rural India. Land Tenure and Reform in Uttar Pradesh 1800-1955* (London, 1962).

―――, "Land is to Rule", in Robert Eric Frykenberg (ed.) *Land Control and Social Structure in Indian History* (London, 1969).

Niemeijer, A.C. *The Khilafat Movement in India, 1919-24* (The Hague, 1972).

O'Donnell, C.J. *The Ruin of an Indian Province: An Indian Famine Explained* (London, 1880).

Owen, H.F. "Towards Nationwide Agitation and Organisation: the Home Rule Leagues, 1915-18", in D.A. Low, (ed.) *Soundings in Modern South Asian History*, (London, 1968).

———, "Organizing for the Rowlatt Satyagraha of 1919", in Ravinder Kumar, (ed.) *Essays on Gandhian Politics. The Rowlatt Satyagraha of 1919*, (London, 1971).

Pandey, Gyanendra. "A Rural Base for Congress: the United Provinces 1920-40", in D.A. Low, (ed.) *Congress and the Raj; facets of the Indian Struggle 1917-1947*, (London, 1977).

———, "Mobilization in a Mass Movement: Congress 'Propaganda' in the United Provinces (India), 1930-34", *Modern Asian Studies*, 9, 2, 1975.

———, *The Ascendency of the Congress in Uttar Pradesh, 1926-34. A Study in Imperfect Mobilization*, (Oxford, 1979).

Pouchepadass, Jacques. "Local leaders and the intelligentsia in the Champaran satyagraha (1917): a study in peasant mobilization", *Contributions to Indian Society*, New Series, 8, 1974.

Prasad, Rajendra, *Autobiography* (Bombay, 1957).

———, *Satyagraha in Champaran* (Madras, 1928).

———, *Mahatma Gandhi and Bihar. Some Reminiscences*, (Bombay, 1949).

Raj Darbhanga. *Raj Darbhanga Directory 1941* (Darbhanga, 1941).

Ranga, R.G. (ed.) *Peasants and Congress*, (Madras, 1938?).

Ray, Rajat, K. "The Crisis of Bengal Agriculture, 1870-1927 – The Dynamics of Immobility", *Indian Economic and Social History Review*, X, 3, 1973.

Reeves, P.D. "The Landlords' Response to Political Change in the United Provinces of Agra and Oudh, India, 1921-1937", Australian National University Ph.D. thesis, 1963.

———, "The Politics of Order. 'Anti-non-co-operation' in the United Provinces, 1921", *Journal of Asian Studies*, XXV, 2, Feb. 1966.

———, "Landlords and Party Politics in the United

Provinces, 1934-7", in Low, *Soundings in Modern South Asian History*.

Reid, D.J. "Indigo in Behar", in A. Wright (ed.) *Bengal and Assam, Behar and Orissa*, (London, 1917).

Robb, Peter. "Hierarchy and Resources: Peasant Stratification in late Nineteenth Century Bihar", *Modern Asian Studies*, 13, 1, Feb. 1979.

Rasul, M.A. *History of the All-India Kisan Sabha*, (Calcutta, 1974).

Robinson, Francis, *Separatism among Indian Muslims. The politics of the United Province's Muslims, 1860-1923*, (Cambridge, 1974).

Rothermund, Dietmar. "Government, Landlord and Tenant in India, 1875-1900", *Indian Economic and Social History Review*, VI, 4, Dec. 1969.

———, "A Survey of Rural Migration and Land Reclamation in India, 1885", *Journal of Peasant Studies*, 4, 3, April 1977.

Roy, Ramashray. "Conflict and Co-operation in a north Bihar village", *Journal of the Bihar Research Society*, XLIX, 1963.

———, "A Study of the Bihar Pradesh Congress Committee, Bihar, India", University of California, Berkeley, Ph.D. thesis, 1966.

Sahajanand, Swami. "Tenancy Measures in Bihar", in R.G. Ranga (ed.), *Peasants and Congress*, (Madras, 1938?).

Sarkar, Sumit. "The Logic of Gandhian Nationalism: Civil Disobedience and the Gandhi-Irwin Pact (1930-1931)", *Indian Historical Review*, III, 1, July 1976.

Sarkar, Tanika. "The First Phase of Civil Disobedience in Bengal, 1930-31", *Indian Historical Review*, July 1977, IV, 1.

Seal, Anil. "Imperialism and Nationalism in India", in Gallagher, Johnson and Seal (eds), *Locality, Province and Nation. Essays on Indian Politics, 1870-194* , (London, 1973).

Sen, Gertrude Emerson. *Voiceless India* (Benares, rev. edn, 1946).

Siddiqi, Majid Hayat, *Agrarian Unrest in North India. The United Provinces, 1918-22*, (Delhi, 1978).

———, "The Peasant Movement in Pratapgarh", *Indian Economic and Social History Review*, 9, 1972.

Singh, Shyam Narayan, *History of Tirhut from the earliest times to the end of the Nineteenth Century*, (Calcutta, 1922).

Sinha, Sachchidananda. *Some Eminent Behar Contemporaries*, (Patna, 1944).

Spate, O.H.K., A.T.A. Learmonth and B.H. Farmer. *India, Pakistan and Ceylon: The Regions*, (London, 3rd edn, 1967).

Tendulkar, D.G. *Gandhi in Champaran* (Calcutta, 1957).

Thorner, Daniel and Alice. *Land and Labour in India*, (London, 1962).

Tomlinson, B.R. "India and the British Empire, 1880-1935", *Indian Economic and Social History Review*, XI, 2-3, 1974.

────, *The Indian National Congress and the Raj, 1929-1942. The Penultimate Phase*, (London, 1976).

Tuchman, Barbara W., *The Proud Tower: a portrait of the world before the war, 1890-1914*, (New York, 1970).

Upadhya, Badrinath. *Reply to 'The Open Letter' Printed in the Searchlight Steam Press with a foreword from an alleged Sanyasi calling himself Swami Vidyanand*, (Bankipore, n.d.).

Voigt, Johannes H. "Co-operation or Confrontation? War and Congress Politics, 1939-42", in D.A. Low, (ed.) *Congress and the Raj; facets of the Indian Struggle, 1917-1947*, (London, 1977).

Whitcombe, Elizabeth. *Agrarian Conditions in Northern India. Volume One: The United Provinces under British Rule, 1860-1900* (Los Angeles, London, 1972).

Wilson, Minden. *History of Behar Indigo Factories, Reminiscences of Behar, Tirhoot and its inhabitants of the past, History of Behar Light Horse Volunteers*, (Calcutta, 1908, first published 1885).

Wolf, Eric R. *Peasant Wars of the Twentieth Century*, (New York, 1969).

Wood, Geof. "From Raiyat to Rich Peasant", *South Asian Review*, 7(1), 1973.

────, "The Legacy of the Past: The Agrarian Structure", in J.L. Joy and Elizabeth Everitt, (eds) *The Kosi Symposium. The Rural Problem* in *North-East Bihar: Analysis Policy and Planning in the Kosi Area*, (University of Sussex, 1976).

Woodruff, Philip. *The Men Who Ruled India* (London, 2 vols, 1953, 54), vol.II, *The Guardians*.

Wright, Arnold (ed.), *Bengal and Assam, Behar and Orissa*, (London, 1917).

Yang, Anand A. "An Institutional Shelter: The Court of Wards in late Nineteenth Century Bihar", *Modern Asian Studies*, XIII, 2, 1979.

―――, "The Agrarian Origins of Crime: A Study of Riots in Saran District, India, 1866-1920", *Journal of Social History*, XIII, 2 (Winter 1979).

―――, "Peasants on the Move: A Study of Internal Migration in India", *Journal of Interdisciplinary History*, X, 1, Summer 1979.

8. INTERVIEWS

The following formal interviews yielded valuable insights and information. Numerous informal discussions also were of great assistance.

R.L. Chandapuri (former President, All India Backward Castes Association), Patna, 10 and 17 April 1976.

E.C. Danby (former indigo planter), Falmouth, 11 January 1980.

Buddhikar Jha (senior officer in the Darbhanga Raj administration), Darbhanga town, 20, 25, 27 September 1976.

Jageshwar Mishra (officer in the Darbhanga Raj administration),Darbhanga town, 15, 23 September, 12 October 1976.

Ramnandan Misra (former Congress Socialist and Kisan Sabha activist), Laheriaserai town, 30, 31 October, 1 November 1976.

Umarpathi Tewari (former officer in the Darbhanga Raj administration and former Bihar government revenue officer), Dumeri village, Darbhanga, 17 October 1976.

GLOSSARY

anna	one-sixteenth of a rupee
abwab	illegal cess
adivasi	member of a 'tribal' semi-Hinduised group
amin	accountant; landlord's agent specialising in financial matters
amla	agent, retainer of a landlord
bakast (*bakasht*)	land held under direct control by a landlord, but over which a tenant can accrue occupancy rights
begari	labour service exacted from a socially subordinate person for which no wage or a below-market wage is paid
benami	holding of land under false name or in the name of a client or relative
bigha (*beegha*)	a unit of area which varied from locality to locality; in north Bihar roughly equivalent to one acre
chaukidar (*chowkidar*)	village watchman, locally appointed member of auxiliary police force
dacoit	member of a robber band
dafadar	senior village watchman, supervisor of a group of watchmen
dahnal	land which has had its productivity lowered by flooding
darkasht	petition
diara	land subject to flooding; fertile land on river bank, or forming an island in a river
dehat	landlord's sphere of influence, a rural area, the countryside generally
elaka	local area, unit of a landlord's estate
jamadar	supervisor; head assistant of landlord or indigo planter
jethryot	head tenant; rich peasant responsible for collecting a landlord's rents from his tenants
kutcherry (*cutcherry*)	landlord's store-house and/or office building

kisan	cultivator, farmer, peasant
harijan	Gandhi's term for a member of an 'untouchable' group
lakh	100,000 (usually of rupees)
lathi	quarter-staff carried by peasants as weapon, standard weapon of Bihar constabulary
mahant (mahanth)	priest in charge of a temple who controls areas of temple-owned land nearby
mauza	'revenue village'; an area of land, which may or may not cover the same area as a residential village and its lands, owned by a landlord or a group of landlords
mofassal (mofussil)	the countryside, the interior
mukhtiar (mukhtear)	lower court lawyer
nilami	tenancy holding recently purchased at an auction sale from a tenant unable to meet his rent payments
patwari (patwary)	village accountant responsible to landlord for keeping land and rent records
ryot (raiyat)	a tenant with permanent or 'occupancy' rights to his land; more generally, a cultivator or peasant
ryoti (raiyati)	land in which an occupancy tenant has permanent rights
salami	fee paid for settlement of holding
satyagraha	non-violent civil disobedience
sharabeshi	arrangement whereby a tenant pays a higher rent in return for no longer being expected by his landlord to grow a particular crop on a portion of his holdings
swaraj	self-rule; independence from Britain
swami	religious leader; title assumed by a religious mendicant
tamasha	festival; public function
tawan	lump sum paid by a tenant in return for being released from the obligation to grow a particular crop for his landlord
thana	police station building; area under jurisdiction of the staff of a police station

thikadar	lessee from a landlord of proprietary rights
tinkathia	system under which a tenant grows a particular crop on 3/20th of his holding
tehsil	unit within a landlord's holdings
tehsildar	collector of rents on behalf of landlord in a tehsil
vakil	higher court lawyer, agent, emissary
zamindar	landowner; landlord with rights guaranteed by the Permanent Settlement of 1793
zirat (seerat, zeerat)	land held by a landlord in which no other rights can accrue

INDEX

Abwabs, in Darbhanga Raj, 75, 82, 86; increase rental demand, 134; in indigo industry, 44, 50; *kisan sabha* movement and, 168; landlords and, 19, 20; in Shillingford indigo concern, 58; survey and settlement and, 72

Adivasis, 8, 166, 167, 188

Agrarian relations, 196, 197-8, 199-200; in Darbhanga Raj, 70, 74-6, 79, 86-8, 141-3, 155-8, 161-2, 183-5; in early twentieth century, 4-6, 7, 11-15, 17-19, 30-3, 70-3; Great Depression and, 139-43; and indigo, 40, 43-68 *passim;* and *kisan sabha* movement, 140-4, 148-9, 150-63, 165, 167-8; and non-cooperation, 101, 103; and Quit India revolt, 183-5; *see also* Economic conditions, *Kisan sabha* movement, Landlords, Peasants

Agriculture, commercial, 31, 40; *see also* Agrarian relations, Economic conditions, Cash crops

Ahimsa, 113, 115, 130, 173

Ali brothers (Muhammad and Saukat), 102

All-India Congress Committee, and individual satyagraha, 165; and *kisan sabha* movement, 150, 160; and non-cooperation, 101-2, 103, 104; and Quit India revolt, 170, 176, 179; and resignation Congress Ministry, 163-4; *see also* Bihar Congress, Indian National Congress, Nationalism

Amlas, in Darbhanga Raj, 70, 73-86 *passim,* 155, 156, 161, 162; in indigo industry, 39, 41, 43-4; oppression by, 72-3, 79, 156

Amritsar Massacre, 107, 129

Anti-indigo planter protest, in Bhagalpur, 50-5, 76; Bihar Congress and, 47-8, 68-9; British administration and 37, 41, 55, 58, 63, 67-8, 98; in Champaran, 36, 41, 44-50, 55, 58-9, 60-3, 66; in Darbhanga Raj, 56-7, 64-5; Gandhi and, 46-9, 50, 66; in Muzaffarpur, 59-60, 63-4, 78; in nineteenth century, 37, 41, 42; police and, 45, 54, 55, 60, 61, 62, 63, 67-8; in Purnea, 56-8, 64-5; village elite and, 46, 66; *see also* Indigo industry, Indigo planters

Bakast, lands, 150, 151-3; legislation, 153-5; protest, 156-68

Beguserai, area, large Bhumihar population in, 11; town,

and civil disobedience movement, 127-30
Bengal, Blue Mutiny in, 37; famine of 1943, 173; Presidency, 17, 19-20
Bettiah, Maharani, 6; Raj, 41
Behar Planters' Association, 41
Bhagalpur, division and town, 16
Bhagalpur district, 6, 10, 16, 22, 30; anti-indigo planter protest in, 50-5, 76; civil disobedience movement in, 109, 120-4, 135; *kisan sabha* movement in, 148, 154; non-cooperation movement in, 98, 101; Quit India revolt in, 177, 186, 189, 190, 191, 194; Vidyanand's movement in, 53-4, 76, 78, 79, 83, 84
Bhorey *thana* (Saran), 119, 126, 133
Bhumihars, 9, 11, 46, 49, 51-5, 120, 127-8, 130, 148, 149, 159, 182, 189, 190
Bihar Congress, and *ahimsa*, 113, 115; and anti-indigo planter protest, 47-8, 68-9, 198; and civil disobedience movement, 109-38 *passim;* early history, 91-4; factionalism in, 146-50; finances, 130-1, 132; and *kisan sabha* movement, 144, 146-7, 148-51, 160-9 *passim;* and left-wing, 198; and non-cooperation movement, 90, 94-106 *passim;* and mass turbulence,
196-7; and Quit India revolt, 170, 176, 178-85 *passim,* 191, 194-5; support for, 92-4, 105, 130, 132, 137, 196-7; and Vidyanand's movement, 70, 77, 88-9, 197-8; *see also* All-India Congress Committee, Bihar Congress Ministry, Indian National Congress, Nationalism
Bihar Congress Ministry (1937-39), 139, 148, 153, 163-4, 165, 168, 169
Bihar Provincial Khet Mazdoor Sabha, 167
Bihar Provincial Kisan Council, 144
Bihar Provincial *Kisan Sabha,* 139, 143, 144-5, 151, 166; *see also kisan sabha* movement
Bihar Legislative Assembly, 82, 96, 147
Bihpur, 120-4, 132
Boycott, of foreign cloth, 97; of indigo factory, 64; of Legislative Assembly elections, 96; of markets, 58, 60-1; social, 115, 159
Brahmans, 5, 6, 11, 80, 81, 101, 126, 130, 158
British administration, and anti-planter protest, 37, 41, 55, 58, 63, 67-8; in Bihar and United Provinces, 17, 176; and civil disobedience movement, 118-38 *passim;* and Congress, 2, 92, 102-3, 106, 199; constitutional initiatives, 91, 146; and economic conditions, 196; finances, 17, 18, 19, 21, 108, 116; and indigo planters, 23, 37, 38, 41,

55, 57, 58, 63, 67, 107; and *kisan sabha* movement, 151, 159, 164, 166, 168, 169; and landlords, 17-19, 30-2, 85, 88, 107, 108, 197; and non-cooperation movement, 98, 106-7; and Quit India revolt, 170, 175, 176-7, 179, 185, 187, 190-1, 194; and Vidyanand's movement, 78, 85, 88
Broucke, J. (indigo planter), 61, 62

Cash crops, 31, 43, 65
Caste, and anti-planter protest, 46, 49, 51-5, 62, 63; and civil disobedience movement, 115, 118, 119, 120, 121-30 *passim;* and *kisan sabha* movement, 148, 156, 158, 159-60, 162, 166; and non-cooperation movement, 97, 101, 103, 105; and Quit India revolt, 178, 180-2, 189-90; rivalries in Congress, 148; and selection election candidates, 147; system and important castes, 7-12; and Vidyanand's movement, 78, 80, 81, 83, 86; and village elite, 5; and village factionalism, 5, 14
Chamars, 12, 97
Champaran district, 6, 16, 30, 173; anti-indigo planter protest in, 36, 41, 44-50, 58-9, 60-3, 66; civil disobedience movement in, 133; indigo in, 37; *kisan sabha* movement in, 146; non-cooperation movement in, 99-100, 101; Quit India revolt in, 186, 187; *satyagraha* in (1917), 47-9

Chaukidars, 20; and civil disobedience movement, 116-19, 120-4; and non-cooperation, 100; organisation, 20-3; and Quit India revolt, 178, 189, 191; and Vidyanand, 84; vulnerability, 125
Chauri Chaura Massacre, 104
Chauterwa indigo factory, 61-2
Civil Disobedience Movement, and anti-*chaukidari* campaign, 116-19; at Bihpur, 120-4; and British administration, 137-8; compared with non-cooperation, 110, 111, 130, 135; compared with Quit India revolt, 113; decline of, 130-1; economic conditions and, 111, 126; and Gandhi/Irwin Pact, 131-2; initiation, 109; limited violence and, 112-14, 115, 124, 135, 136, 138; in 1932-1934, 133-4; organisation, 110-11; and police, 119-30, 131, 135-6, 138; and prohibition campaign, 115-16; and salt campaign, 114; in Saran, 119-20; support for, 134-5
Collective fines, 62, 185-6, 189
Communal conflict, 15
Communist Party of India, 179
Congress, see All-India Congress Committee, Bihar Congress, Indian National Congress, Nationalism
Congress Socialist Party, 139; and Bihar Congress, 114-17, 148-50, 164-6; organisation, 144-5; and Quit India revolt, 179; *see also kisan sabha* movement

Crime, 20, 53, 119; economic pressures and, 32, 172-3, 174, 181, 182; police and, 175-6; and Quit India revolt, 181, 182, 183, 189
Cripps, Sir Stafford, 174

Danby brothers, E.C. Danby (indigo planter), 78; G.P. Danby (Darbhanga Raj Chief Manager), 157
Darbhanga district, 5, 6, 23-4, 25, 28, 30; civil disobedience movement in, 114, 126-7; *kisan sabha* movement in, 146, 149-50, 151, 155, 156-65 *passim*; non-cooperation movement in, 98, 104; Quit India revolt in, 177, 179, 181, 184, 186, 187, 194; Vidyanand's movement in, 75-6, 78, 79, 80, 81
Darbhanga, Maharajas of, 5; Kameshwar Singh, 183-4, 197; Lakmeshwar Singh, 202; Rameshwar Singh, 6, 73, 77
Darbhanga Raj, 36; administration of, 73-4, 81-2; archives, 201-7; and *bakast* protest, 156-8; and Great Depression, 141-2; history of, 202; indigo in, 42, 64-5; and legal system, 155; and Quit India revolt, 183-5; and rent suits, 142-3; size and wealth, 6; and Vidyanand's movement, 70, 74-89
Dhanuks, 12
Dusadhs, 12, 23, 117

Earthquake, (1934), 140
Economic conditions, British policy and, 18-19, 30-3, 199-200; during Champaran *satyagraha*, 47; and civil disobedience movement, 111, 112, 134; and dissidence, 196; in early twentieth century, 3-7, 18-19, 30-3; Great Depression and, 112, 139-41; and indigo cultivation, 40; and *kisan sabha* movement, 139-42, 165; and non-cooperation movement, 98, 101; population growth and, 30-3, 71, 79; post-World War One, 70-1, 85; and Quit India revolt, 171-3, 181-3, 185, 192-3, 194
Education, 13

Factionalism, in Bihar Congress, 146-50, 164, 173; in villages, 14
Fisher, C.M. 40, 200

Gandak (river), 3, 61
Ganges, 3, 7, 189
Gandhi, M.K., and *ahimsa*, 113, 189; and anti-indigo planter protest, 36, 46-9, 50, 61, 63, 66; and civil disobedience movement, 131; and individual *satyagraha*, 173; and Marwari support for Congress, 93; and non-cooperation movement, 90, 93, 96-105 *passim*; and Quit India revolt, 189; and Vidyanand, 74-5, 77, 80
Gandhi/Irwin Pact, 131-2, 133, 144
Government of India, 20; *see also* British administration

Grain, dealing in, 7, 19, 171, 185, 193; prices of, 139, 171-3, 193
Grazing, and anti-indigo planter protest, 49, 52, 58-9, 62; population pressure and, 71; and Vidyanand's movement, 75, 76, 79
Great Depression, 112, 139-41
Gurkhas, military police, 24, 133; watchmen, 54, 55

Harcourt, M.V., on *bakast* campaign, 158; on office resignation, 164; on Quit India revolt, 180, 190, 192-4
Harijans, 4, 8, 12, 61-2, 97, 166, 167
Haripura delegate elections, 149-50
Hathwa Raj, and indigo, 42, and Saran district, 6
Hauser, Walter, 158, 162
Home Rule movement, 94

Indian Nation, 159
Indian National Congress, and civil disobedience movement, 109, 110, 111; and Khilafat movement, 94; and *kisan sabha* movement, 144, 149; and non-cooperation movement, 90, 101-2; reorganisation to facilitate mass politics, 96-7; Vidyanand and, 76; *see also* All-India Congress Committee, Bihar Congress, Nationalism
Indigo industry, decline of, 42, 65; labour in, 13, 39, 41; in nineteenth century, 37, 42; organisation of, 38-9, 42; and subsistence agriculture, 40; wartime revival, 50; *see also* Anti-indigo planter protest, Indigo planters
Indigo planters, 8, 13; administration and, 23, 37, 38, 41, 55, 57, 58, 63, 67, 107; character of, 40-1; discontent with, 39-41; as landlords, 6, 14, 37-41 *passim*, 44-52 *passim*, 56, 58, 67; markets boycotted, 58, 60-1; as money-lenders, 41, 46, 78; in nineteenth century, 37; *see also* Anti-indigo planter protest, Indigo industry

Karjee, Jamuna, 160
Kateya *thana* (Saran), 100-1, 119
Kayasths, 9, 10-11, 12
Khilafat movement, 90, 94-5, 102
Kisan Enquiry Committee, 143
Kisan sabha activists, and Quit India revolt, 193-4
Kisan Sabha movement, aims, 145; and *bakast*, 151, 166-68; and administration, 159, 164, 168, 169; compared civil disobedience, 163; and Congress 146-51, 160-9 *passim*; Congress Socialist Party and, 144-5; in Darbhanga, 151, 156-63, 165; and Darbhanga Raj, 156-8; economic conditions and, 139-42, 165; and 1937 elections, 146, 147; organisation of, 143; and peasant

campaigns, 148, 149, 150-1, 156-63, 165-8; and police, 159, 161, 163, 166, 167; rent suits and, 142-3, 156, 157; support for, 144, 168; Swami Sahajanand Saraswati and, 139, 143, 144, 145, 148-9, 167-8; and zamindari abolition, 145
Kisan sabhas, established by Congress, 95
Koeris, 12, 80, 101, 156
Kosi (river), 3, 189
Kumar, Nathuni, 53
Kurmis, 9, 12

Labour, conflict over, 15; control of, 7; and civil disobedience movement, 111; and the Darbhanga Raj, 75, 80, 81; and Great Depression, 140-3; health of, 13; in indigo industry, 13, 39, 41, 64; and *kisan sabha* movement, 167-8; over-supply of, 19; and Quit India revolt, 181, 182; Second World War and, 171-3; in social structure, 4, 12
Landed interest, 14, 66
Landlords, and British administration, 30-2, 85, 88, 107, 108, 197; and caste, 11; and civil disobedience movement, 112, 113, 130, 131; and Congress, 68, 93-4, 112, 113, 131, 183, 196-7; and economic conditions, 18-19, 30-2; and Great Depression, 141-3; great landlords, 6; indigo planters as landlords, 68; and *kisan sabha* movement, 151-5; and non-cooperation movement, 105; Permanent Settlement and, 17-19; and population growth, 32-3, 70, 72; and Quit India revolt, 183-5, 193, 195; and revenue demand, 20; and social conflict, 14; in social structure, 8; and village elite, 3, 5; *see also* Agrarian relations
Latipur estate, 51
Law (and legal system), and anti-indigo planter protest, 53; *bakast* lands, 152-5; boycott of courts, 97; injustice of, 20, 22, 71; planters as arbitrators, 41; rent suits, 142-3; supports British rule, 22; survey and settlement and, 72; *see also* Lawyers, Legislation
Lawyers, 8, 22, 47
Left-wing, and Quit India revolt, 179, 183, 185, 193-4
Legislation, Act of Indemnity (Quit India revolt), 189; Act X of 1859, 71; Bakast Restoration Act, 153-6; Bengal Tenancy Act of 1885, 51, 52, 71, 79, 153; Emergency Powers ordinance, 1932, 133; Government of India Act, 1935, 146; Montagu-Chelmsford reforms, 70, 78, 94, 96, 107, 108; rent reduction (1930s), 162; *see also* Law and Legal system
Limited Raj, 27, 199
Limited violence, and the British administration, 136, 137; and the civil disobedience

movement, 109, 111, 114, 115, 124, 135, 136, 138, 198-9; defined, 112-13; Rajendra Prasad and, 136-7
Local government, 37, 94, 110

McDonald, G., 164
Madhuban, Zamindar of, 6
Magahiya Doms, 62, 97
Mahants, 59-60, 132
Maithil Brahman, 6, 158
Malaviya, Madan Mohan, 74
Markets, boycott of, 58, 60-1; looting of, 98-9, 172-3
'Martyrs' of 1942, 180
Marwaris, 7, 93, 126-7, 130
Messianism, 99, 100
Military, 24, 106; and Quit India revolt, 170, 174, 180, 181, 184, 185-9, 190
Misra, Ramnandan, and *kisan sabha* movement, 149, 150, 156, 157; and Quit India revolt, 190
Money-lending, 7, 19, 157, 185
Monghyr district, 6, 10, 11, 16; civil disobedience movement in, 118, 127-30, 132; *kisan sabha* movement in, 146, 148, 161; non-cooperation movement in, 98; Quit India revolt in, 177, 181-2, 186, 189, 191; Vidyanand's movement in, 78
Moore, Jr., Barrington, 11
Musahars, 61, 62
Muslims, and anti-indigo planter protest, 45; and civil disobedience movement, 111, 126, 127, 130; communal conflict, 15; and Khilafat movement, 94-5; and non-cooperation, 101; and prohibition, 97; in social structure, 4-9 *passim*; and Vidyanand, 80
Muslim League, 174
Muzaffarpur district, 5, 6, 16, 28; anti-indigo planter protest in, 59-60, 63-4, 78; civil disobedience movement in, 132, 133; indigo in, 37; *kisan sabha* movement in, 146, 161; non-cooperation movement in, 98, 103, 104, 105; Quit India revolt in, 1, 177, 179, 184, 186, 187, 189; Vidyanand's movement in, 78

Narar village, 75, 81
Narayan, Jay Prakash, 165; and *kisan sabha* movement, 145, 162, 165; and Quit India revolt, 179, 183, 190
Narayanpur estate, 51
Nationalism, 77, 91, 94, 113, 191-2; *see also* All-India Congress Committee, Bihar Congress, Indian National Congress
Nepal, 3, 71, 173; and Quit India revolt, 187, 190
1937 elections, 146, 147
Ninnis, R.D.K., 121-2, 123, 124
Non-cooperation movement, and anti-indigo planter protest, 98; British administration and, 106-7; compared with civil disobedience

movement, 110-11, 130, 135; compared with Quit India revolt, 113; Congress and, 90, 94-105, 106; decision to participate in, 94-5; economic conditions and, 98, 101; Gandhi and, 90, 93; high point of, 102-3; and Khilafat movement, 94-5; and Legislative Assembly elections, 96; and market-looting, 98-9; mass support for, 97, 105; and messianic expectations, 99-100; and police, 100-1, 103-5, 108; programme of, 90; prohibition campaign and, 97-8; suspension of, 104; and swadeshi, 102; Vidyanand and, 77, 95; village elite and, 105

Nonias, 62

North Bihar, administrative history, 3; agrarian relations, 4-6, 7, 11-15, 17-19, 30-3; British administration of, 15-20, 21, 27; caste system, 7-12; *chaukidars*, 22-3; collaborators in British rule, 27; communications, 13; distribution of power and wealth, 7-12; economic conditions, 3-7, 18-19, 30-3; education, 13; health, 12-13, 28, 30; landlords, 3-20 *passim*; law and legal system, 20, 22; limitations of sources on, 35; Limited Raj in, 27; limits on expression of tension, 12-13; military, 24; Muslims, 4, 5, 7, 8, 9; peasants, 4-5, 33-4; Permanent Settlement in, 17-19, 30-3; physical features, 3; police, 24-7; population growth in, 4, 19, 28-33 *passim*; social conflict, 14-15; social structure, 4-7, 8; towns and townsfolk, 7; village elite, 5, 7, 14, 15, 34

Padri circle, *bakast* protest in, 156-8, 163; and Quit India revolt, 184; and Vidyanand's movement, 80, 81

Panchayats, *chaukidari*, 23, 37, 64, 74, 116, 118; and civil disobedience movement, 114, 116, 118; and non-cooperation movement, 100

Patna, 7; and civil disobedience movement, 132, 136; nationalist centre, 92; and Quit India revolt, 177; Vidyanand and, 76

Patwaris, 12, 74, 86, 155

Peasants, 1-2; and anti-indigo planter protest, 44-66; and civil disobedience movement, 112-13, 114-34 *passim*; and Congress, 95, 198; economic conditions and, 30-2, 40, 98, 99, 101, 111, 139-43, 171-3; and *kisan sabha* movement, 139-69 *passim*; and non-cooperation movement, 95, 97-105; non-radicalism of, 196-200; in north Bihar society, 4-5, 7-8, 11-12; population growth and, 28-32, 33-4; and Quit India revolt, 170, 183-5, 192-3, 194; unrest among, 1917-23, 33-4; and Vidyanand's movement, 70-89

Permanent Settlement of 1793, 17-19, 30-3, 67, 71, 76
Planters, see Anti-indigo planter protest, Indigo industry, Indigo planters
Police, and anti-indigo planter protest, 45, 54, 55, 60-8 *passim*; *chaukidars*, 22-3; and civil disobedience movement, 115, 116-30, 131, 135-6, 138; corruption among, 24-5, 27; and *kisan sabha* movement, 159, 161, 163, 166, 167; and non-cooperation movement, 100-1, 103-5, 108; organisation and strength, 22-7, 107-8, 125, 138, 175-6, 191; and Quit India revolt, 170, 175-6, 177-8, 180, 181, 184-9 *passim*, 191; support landlords, 71; and Vidyanand's movement, 84-5
Population growth, 4, 19, 28-9; and agrarian relations, 70-3; economic effects, 30, 32-3; and Vidyanand's movement, 70-3, 79, 87
Prasad, Braj Kishore, 47-8
Prasad, Rajendra, background and education, 94; on Bhagalpur Congress, 95; at Bihpur, 122, 123; in Champaran, 47-8; criticises Vidyanand, 77; friendship with Maharaja Kameshwar Singh, 197; and limited violence, 136-7; on non-cooperation in Muzaffarpur, 105; on selection election candidates, 147

Prohibition campaign, and civil disobedience movement, 115-16; and non-cooperation movement, 97-8, 103-4
Purnea district, 6, 14, 16, 27, 30; anti-indigo planter protest in, 56-8, 64-5; civil disobedience movement in, 115; non-cooperation movement in, 98, 103; Quit India revolt in, 1, 177, 186, 188, 194; Vidyanand's movement in, 76, 82, 83

Quit India revolt, absence of radicalism, 183-5, 194-5; armament of rebels, 186-7; compared with civil disobedience movement, 178, 180; compared with non-cooperation movement, 180; compared with revolt of 1857, 170; economic and political context, 171-6, 181-3, 192-3; first stage, 176-7; guerilla activity in aftermath, 189-90; Harcourt on, 180, 192-4; initiation and extent, 170; *kisan sabhas* and, 194; left-wing and, 179, 180; middle peasants and, 193; organisation, 178-9, 186; police and, 170, 187-9, 191; re-establishment of British rule, 185-9; scholarly discussion of, 192; support for, 180-3; tactics of rebels, 189

Radhanager village, 158-9
Rajputs, 11, 101
Ram, Jagjivan, 167

Ramnager, Maharaja of, 6
Rebellion of desperation, 181-2; *see also* Quit India revolt
Rents, 19, 20, 60, 101; legislation, 71, 162; raised in lieu of indigo cultivation, 44, 45, 49, 52; refusal to accept, 83, 86; rent strikes, 53, 117, 134, 148; rent suits, 142-3, 156, 157
Revenue, 135; excise, 97-8, 116; land, 6, 17, 18, 19-20; strike, 117
Revolt, nationalist, 181-2; *see also* Quit India revolt
Rowlatt Satyagraha, 94
Roy, M.N., 132-3
Roy, Ramashray, 11, 158
Ryots, see Peasants

Sabotage, as Congress weapon, 180
Sahai, Baldeo, 122
Sahajanand Saraswati, Swami: background, 143; and *kisan sabha* movement, 139, 143, 144, 145, 148-9, 167-8; and Quit India revolt, 179, 183
Sahay, Shyamnandan, opposes non-cooperation movement, 64; supports civil disobedience movement, 132
Saran district, 6, 11, 16, 28, 33; civil disobedience movement in, 114, 116, 119-20, 126, 127, 132; *kisan sabha* movement in, 150, 160; non-cooperation movement in, 99, 100-1, 105; Quit India revolt in, 177-8, 186, 187

Satyagraha, *bakast*, 151, 160; Champaran, 1917, 47-9; individual, 165, 173-4; Rowlatt, 94; salt, 114
Searchlight, 114, 129
Sharecroppers, 72; and Great Depression, 141, 142; and *kisan sabha* movement, 151-5, 158, 167; post-World War One, 34; in social structure, 4, 8; and Vidyanand's movement, 80-1
Sharma, Jadunandan, 159
Shillingford brothers (Alec and Charles), 57-8
Shukul, Raj Kumar, 46
Singh, Satya Narain, 162
Singh, Siaram, 189-90, 191
Singh, Thakur Nawab, 105
Sinha, Sri Krishna, and *ahimsa*, 113; and *bakast* protest, 157, 169
Social structure, 4-7, 8
Sonbarsa, Bhagalpur, 50-5, 120, 190
Students, and civil disobedience movement, 114, 131; and non-cooperation movement, 96; and Quit India revolt, 177, 179, 182
Survey and Settlement operations, 50, 72, 79
Swadeshi campaign, 102, 114

Tehsildars, 73, 74, 83
Telis, 10, 78, 81, 86-7
Thikadars, 6, 14
Tinkathia, 38, 49, 59
Tirhut division, 16; centre of non-cooperation, 102
Tomlinson, B.R., 164
Trees, 49, 53, 58; and Vidyanand's movement, 70, 71, 75, 76, 78, 82

United Provinces, 3; agrarian unrest in, 104, 134, 197; compared with Bihar, 17, 176, 197; Congress in, 88, 197; non-cooperation and, 100, 104

Upadhya, Badrinath, 82

Vidyanand's movement, *see* Vidyanand, Swami

Vidyanand, Swami (Bishu Bharan Prasad), 35; and anti-indigo planter protest, 36, 53-4, 56, 66, 76, 78; background, 74; coercion against, 84-5; and Congress, 70, 76, 77, 88-9, 95, 197, 198; elected to Legislative Assembly, 70, 78; leads movement against Darbhanga Raj, 70, 74-85, 87, 88; and non-cooperation movement, 77, 95, 98; repercussions of movement, 85-7; support for, 78, 81

Village Defence Organisation, 176

Village elite, and *ahimsa*, 113; and anti-*chaukidari* campaign, 117; and anti-indigo planter protest, 66; and Congress, 93-4; controls village society, 7; and civil disobedience movement, 110, 112, 134; defined, pivotal role of, 5; and Great Depression, 141, 143; high prices beneficial to, 34; and *kisan sabha* movement, 158; leads protest, 34; and limited violence, 199; and 1937 elections, 146-7; and non-cooperation movement, 105; and Quit India revolt, 181; and social conflict, 14-15; and Vidyanand, 81, 82-3, 87

Women, and anti-indigo planter protest, 44; and Quit India revolt, 187

World War, First, 50, 70, 71; Second, 163, 171, 174-5

Yadavs, 11, 12, 80, 81, 83, 101, 126, 130, 156, 158, 162

Yang, Anand, A., 27, 199

Zamindari system, abolition, 145, 168; British administration and, 17-18, 31-2, 85, 91, 183; and Congress, 77, 197; and economic conditions, 17-19, 30-2; *see also* Landlords, Permanent Settlement

Zamindars, *see* landlords